Trevor Rees-Jones was born in 1968. A former soldier, he then joined the security staff of Mohamed Al Fayed, the controversial Egyptian multi-millionaire business-man and owner of Harrods, and worked as personal bodyguard to Fayed's son Dodi. In the summer of 1997, as a friendship developed between Dodi and Diana, Princess of Wales, Trevor found himself a first-hand wit-ness to the events leading up to the crash that would kill them both on 31 August in Paris.

Following his discharge from hospital Trevor returned to the UK in October 1997, and was an inside party to the French investigation that followed. He resigned from his job with Fayed the following April, and now lives in Oswestry, Shropshire.

THE
BODYGUARD'S
STORY

Diana, the Crash,
and the Sole Survivor

TREVOR REES-JONES

with Moira Johnston

WARNER BOOKS

A *Warner* Book

First published in Great Britain in 2000
by Little, Brown & Company
This edition published in 2001 by Warner Books

Copyright © 2000 by Trevor Rees-Jones

The moral right of the author has been asserted.

A CIP catalogue record for this book
is available from the British Library.

ISBN: 0 7515 3126 X

Typeset in Bodoni by M Rules
Printed and bound in Great Britain
by Clays Ltd, St Ives plc

Warner Books
A Division of
Little, Brown & Company (UK)
Brettenham House
Lancaster Place
London WC2E 7EN

*To the friends and families of those
who died in the crash*

Contents

Trevor's Statement

Telling my story in a book is the last thing I ever dreamed I'd be doing. If anyone had suggested it to me in the year after the crash, I'd have said, 'Bollocks!' From the very beginning, from the days when I was still unconscious in hospital, my family tried to lie low and stay out of the limelight. When I woke up, I shared the feeling completely. We'd lived a plain and quiet sort of life in Oswestry, a town in Shropshire. You never value it until it's lost, do you? And that's what happened on the day of the crash.

The media were all over us – me, my mum and step-dad, even my grandmother in Wales. Most of the stories were wrong, some were just made up. We decided right off we'd give no interviews. In the two and a half years since the crash, I've given only one, because I felt badly for my employer, Mohamed Al Fayed, who'd lost his son.

But I regretted it straight away and still do. Even after I'd resigned my job, and might have felt freer to speak out, I still wouldn't. I just needed to put my life on hold until the French investigation of the crash was over, and until I could get my mind sorted out about the whole thing. All I aimed for was to get fit again, and get back to the normal life I loved – a job, my mates, rugby.

But that's not realistic, is it? I began to see that my life could never go back to what it was. I wasn't the same person I was before the crash. I wouldn't want to be. How could you be part of such a tragedy, with the three other people in the car killed – one of them the Princess of Wales – and not be changed?

It wasn't guilt I felt. They'd died on my shift, and I'll live with that for the rest of my life. But I look in the mirror every day and know that I did the best I could. I can't remember the crash itself, or the three minutes before it. My memory's gone for everything that happened after the car pulled away from the Ritz until I woke up in hospital ten days later. There is no one living who can know exactly what happened in that car in the last seconds, with a driver who turned out to be drunk. But I know I'd have done as good a job as anyone could have done to prevent the crash and keep my principals safe.

It's the attacks on my professionalism that began shortly after the crash that always riled me – so-called experts second-guessing what I should have done, when they weren't there. At first it was former Fayed security men trying to get in on the act. But then, the summer after the crash, Fayed himself began to attack me, accusing me of betraying him by resigning and, far worse, charging that my actions, or lack of them, had caused the crash. I was angry and I was hurt, I'd been ignoring everything those close to me had been warning me about. I'd tried to stay loyal. I still felt sympathetic to the man, and I'd loved the job.

But when he attacked me in *Time* magazine, on CNN, in newspapers – and included my fellow bodyguard, Kez, in his attacks – I knew I had to respond. Both for my self-respect and to get the truth out there. There was so much more about what happened than the media knew. I've learned that if you leave a silence, others will fill it. The press never stopped. I couldn't let lies and made-up stories be what people believed. Above all, I couldn't lose the respect I think I have here in Oswestry. I could have lost that, I think, if I'd not set the record straight. I had to answer Fayed.

Mr Fayed's attacks weren't the only reason why I finally thought about doing a book. The doctors can't tell me how well my health will hold up over time, or if I'll have a normal span of working years. I've had no compensation of any kind, and my lawyers and family have urged me all along to try to get some recompense for what's happened, to set a little aside for the future in case things turn out badly. Even after Mr Fayed's attacks, I never took money to answer him back in the tabloids, on television or in magazines. I've been offered more for half a day's interview than I'll personally make from all the months of work on this book. But I began to see that a book was an honourable way to let me pay my large legal bills – every penny due to my lawyers well deserved, in my view – and put a little away.

The only other route to getting any compensation was through the courts. I'm a good bloke in a fight, but to be truthful, I was never too happy about being part of the French investigation. I feel, as I think everyone involved feels – except maybe Mr Fayed – that I want nothing more to do with court battles and sensational headlines which could go on for ever. I want more than anything to put this behind me.

That's what finally persuaded me I wanted to write the book. After it's out and published and I've talked about it, I should never have to deal with the whole thing again. If anyone wants to know what actually happened or what I think, it's in here. Finish. My life can move on.

When I put all these things together, I decided to go ahead and write the book as fast as I could. In September Mr Fayed appealed against the judge's decision in France but I didn't want any part of it. The legal process could go on for ever, but I wasn't going to. Yet I was still reluctant. My parents and myself would have to re-live the last two years, with all the pain and the emotion. I try not to show my feelings, but I knew my mum would reveal personal things. I know she loves me for being the one who was always standing up for the underdog, even though, all my life, it made me the son who was always getting into trouble. But all this made me feel a bit exposed.

Still, I've done it and this book is my story, and the truth, as best I know it, of what happened in the run-up to the crash and then to me and to my family. The problem, at first, was how to tell the story when I was unconscious for a pretty crucial part of it, and still have a slightly Swiss-cheese memory, full of holes, for the rest. The doctors tell me that's normal but it doesn't help. There were also parts of the story I didn't know – how my family managed, what the lawyers found out – that are important if I'm going to tell the whole story. The truth as I see it. So I and my co-writer, Moira Johnston, decided to write the book in the third person and I asked my mother and step-dad, Ernie, my three lawyers and my mate Kez, who was with me up to the last three minutes before the crash, to add their memories.

Everything in the pages ahead is what I, and they, believe to be true, to the very best of our knowledge. And as I've found out other people's stories, I've often had quite a shock; I kept being surprised at the things I hadn't known. Without my mother's and Ernie's support I could never have attempted this book. Their courage got me through at the beginning and they've never stopped, for a day, doing everything they could to help. Their story lies at its heart.

It was only after we started work on it that I began to see what a story there was to tell. How we all survived it – the crash, Fayed, the media, the investigation, the changes in our lives – was an amazing bit of life for a bloke like me and his family to have been through, looking back. Now, I'm satisfied with what's said here. But the truth turns out to be hard on some people whose roles in the cause of the crash aren't fully understood, and on others who created myths afterwards – rubbish about the engagement ring, the assassination conspiracies and so on. They won't like it. But it is as full and honest a story as I can tell.

I need and want to thank those who helped with the book. I'd never known how books happen, but, as I saw the complexity, I gained great respect for my agent, Michael Carlisle, and my publisher, Philippa Harrison, whose passion for the story throughout has kept us all cheered on. I've learned how a good writer can listen to all the voices, then weave the many parts together into a story, and still let each voice speak out, totally believably. For that, I thank Moira Johnston. My mother and stepfather, Jill and Ernie Rees-Jones, are the least public people but they gave their story because they thought it was important – for the record, for me, and as a means of putting the crash behind us at last. I can never thank them enough. My lawyers, Ian Lucas and David Crawford in Oswestry, and Christian Curtil in Paris, put incredible effort and commitment into the book, telling key parts of the story that only they could know. Without their tenacity and courage, many of the hidden facts would never have come to light and I would have faced unbelievable pressures from the press, from Fayed, and from the international legal side, ill-equipped to protect myself. Finally, Kez has proven himself to be a true mate, sharing his memory of events and keeping me straight on some things, always with a great sense of humour.

Though I'm not given to showing sentiment, there are others I very much want to thank as well: my three brothers, Gareth, John and Chris, who have been stalwarts throughout, in Paris and since I came home. Dr Luc Chikhani, my brilliant surgeon, and the staff at La Pitié-Salpêtrière hospital, for all the hard work and the miracles they worked on me. I hope I wasn't too bad a patient. Sue's family, the Joneses, for their strong support. Lara, who cheered me up in Paris and continues to be a great friend. The Oswestry Rugby Club, for all the piss-taking so I could never get above myself. And, finally, the people of Oswestry, for closing ranks and looking after one of their own. I will never forget.

I stand by my actions, and by what I've said here. I want people to know what happened. And, since I'm the last to speak, I hope this book can be the last word on the crash. It's time to get on with life.

THE
BODYGUARD'S
STORY

Introduction

The phone ringing in the night had always been Jill
Rees-Jones's greatest dread when Trevor was in the
army in Northern Ireland. She always thought it meant a
sniper's bullet had found her son. On Sunday, 31 August
1997, when she was at home in Oswestry in bed with her
husband Ernie, at 2:45 in the morning, the phone did
ring. Jill snapped awake, panicked. It was their daughter-
in-law, Sue, calling from her mobile phone in a taxi. 'I've
just heard it on the radio. There's been a crash involving
Dodi and Diana. I'm sure everything's all right, but I
thought you ought to know.' Jill and Ernie grabbed their
dressing-gowns and ran to the television. It was being
reported that Dodi and the driver were dead. Diana and
the bodyguard seriously injured. No name. No details. No
one in Oswestry beyond the three of them knew that Jill's
strapping 29-year-old son was Dodi Fayed's bodyguard.

Not even his brothers or best friends at the rugby club knew that. As Diana and Dodi's romance became the global sensation of the summer, and as the paparazzi hunted Diana down, Trevor had been at her side. He would have to be in the car.

Sitting on the settee on that hot summer night Jill was shaking and cold, and Ernie lit the fire as they watched both television sets, switching between Sky News, BBC and ITV, taping some so they wouldn't miss a word. Their hopes plummeted with the first images of the mangled car – no one could have survived that. Yet witnesses' first chaotic fragments suggested some tenuous life, at least. '. . . Fourth passenger gravely injured . . . half his face ripped away . . .' Then Ernie heard the news Jill had dreaded all those years, and called to her in the bedroom as she was distractedly trying to think what to take to Paris to go to her son. 'They say Trevor is dead.'

Frantic for confirmation, Ernie called the contact number at Fayed's London headquarters, their lifeline. 'No, no, don't believe it. He's still alive,' he was told by the Operations desk in Park Lane. But how could they know? Ernie put on the suit that he only ever wore for funerals. He believed they would be bringing Trevor back from Paris in a box.

Lying near death in La Pitié-Salpêtrière hospital in Paris, it would be ten days before Trevor Rees-Jones would even know about the crash, or the deaths. Unconscious, his face smashed so terribly that when his mother first saw him she could recognize him only by his legs, he would be one of the last in the Western world to learn that he was the sole survivor of the most famous automobile crash in history.

Until now, Trevor has never told the story that only he can tell – the story of a very human Princess on her final odyssey, of the near-miraculous reconstruction of his face and return to the rugby pitch, and of his privileged insider's view of the French criminal investigation into the cause of the crash. Here, Trevor tells the simple truth. He speaks, for the first time, of the struggle of an ordinary man to resist the pressure heaped upon him by one of Europe's richest and most manipulative men, Mohamed Al Fayed – and responds, at last, to Fayed's accusations, in the world's press, of responsibility for the crash that killed Diana. In this book, Trevor must defend his actions and integrity and tell the truth. He speaks of an ordinary family faced with uninvited catastrophe and unimaginable pressures who found the strength to survive and prevail, their lives and souls intact.

The tragedy that took the life of one of the most enduring faces of the last century may be tucked away into the history books as simply another mystery only partially explained and with no one called to account. Trevor's story, then, becomes history's conscience, and its definitive report.

Nothing can return his life to normality; it has been changed for ever. He has been fiercely reluctant to re-open wounds for Diana's sons. But as Fayed continues the legal process, his conspiracy theories still rampant, attacking even Prince Philip, the Princes' grandfather, Trevor's story may, he believes, bring a sense of closure for William and Harry, for the millions who still mourn and for himself.

PART I

PRELUDE TO TRAGEDY

1

Dodi's Man

The presence of the Princess on Fayed's yacht, *Jonikal*, turned Trevor's job upside-down.

Trevor was Dodi's man, one-on-one close protection for the son of Mohamed Al Fayed, the Egyptian tycoon whose acquisition of Harrods had only heightened his obsession with winning a British passport and respect from royalty and the Establishment. 'The Boss' was high-profile and controversial – he'd played a part in the downfall of John Major's government, Trevor reckoned, and if he wanted to parade through Harrods with a formation of eight men plus uniformed security, and move out in two-car convoys of armoured Mercedes, fine. It reminded Trevor a bit of a rock star's entourage. And if it made the Boss happy . . .

Fayed himself may have had enemies, but the threat to Dodi was deemed so low that Trevor drove him alone through the streets of London. At the very worst, there could be a kidnap attempt, though a car crash was actually a far greater risk in a city. 'Dodi was anonymous – who'd recognize him on the street? There are lots of rich people nobody recognizes. The Sultan of Brunei could walk down the street in Oswestry and no one would know who he was,' Trevor thought. All that, however, was about to change.

Sitting in the Ops Room of Fayed's Park Lane office on the morning of 14 July 1997, with the Fayeds in the south of France with Diana and the Princes, and Dodi in Paris, Trevor was anticipating an incredibly boring two weeks. Then he checked the update and discovered that Dodi was en route to London, due back in a few hours, and would then hurry south to join the special guests. Trevor would be leaving with him as soon as the Harrods helicopter delivered Dodi back from Paris. The bodyguard was delighted. 'I'd spotted the Princess's name when I'd checked the updated list at the Ops desk a few days before. The royal group had gone out with the family three days earlier. I was a bit astonished, to be honest. I hadn't realized there was that close a relationship between the family and the Princess.

'I thought it would be a hell of an interesting trip to be on. Some lads don't enjoy the longer trips because the pressure builds up – stress levels are always higher because the family is expecting perfection on their holiday.' No one was actually sacked, Trevor had observed. 'They are just asked to resign, then given a payout after signing another confidentiality agreement. With the Princess aboard, the family would be so uptight that everything would have to be spot-on.' That was fine with Trevor.

But it had the lads on the ground in St-Tropez worried. 'Since they'd heard that the Boss had bought a massive yacht, the lads had been thinking, "Fantastic! We'll be going to sea a bit this summer,"' says Trevor's mate Alexander Wingfield, known as 'Kez', who was based at Fayed's villa in France. 'But when it came through on a memo that HRH and her sons were going to be on the trip, what they all thought was, "Bloody hell, it'll end in tears . . ." With such a high-profile person, the family would be hyper, tempers would be fraying. There're bound to be a few sackings.' After all the anticipation, 'the teams on the ground weren't looking forward to this summer trip at all'. But the lads had a saying that let them live with the hazards of working for Fayed: 'It's paying the mortgage.' Trevor had a mortgage, too, on a charming old half-timbered house on the square at Whittington, a few miles from Oswestry in Shropshire.

Yet it was Sue, not him, who was living in the house, while he rented a place from a friend back home in Oswestry. Sue had left him in May, less than two months earlier, after just two years of marriage. Trevor still hoped for a reconciliation. She was a smashing girl, a graduate of Leeds University, very independent. Trevor had helped her set up her own housewares and gift shop in Oswestry. 'You had to be besotted for a bloke like me to go down

and sell teacups and crystal, didn't you – or change your
name from Rees to Rees-Jones, just to please her.' Sue
Jones had wanted to keep her own name when they got
married and add it to his, and Trevor 'was prepared to do
anything'. By coincidence his mother Jill had joined the
same two family names when she'd married Ernie Jones
seven years earlier.

As well as his mum and stepdad there was the rugby
club to draw him back on his weeks off. There were also
visits to 'Nain', his grandmother, in the Welsh village
where his dad had been raised and buried and where
Trevor's strong Welsh roots lay too. But without Sue to go
home to, trips abroad like this were even more appealing.

'Frankly, I'd felt a bit jealous of the lads in St-Tropez:
that was where the fun and the action would be.' Working
the Ops desk in London was more routine. Calls would
come in from every home, yacht, car or aeroplane where
a family member might be. You had to be on your toes,
co-ordinating, tracking all movements. But now Trevor
was going to be in on the action.

He had quickly organized the special gear and
Harrods food the family wanted, and picked up his radios
and mobile phones. He'd strapped on his radio harness,
personal and telephone pagers and small baton. But, not
surprisingly, no gun. Carrying was illegal in England, a
ban Trevor admired. There was nothing more dangerous,
he thought, than a half-trained security guard wielding a
gun. On the training courses, they learned unarmed
combat strikes. 'But again, they're only any good if you

keep fit. Most blokes like to keep fit. The Park Lane office had a gym in the basement. Weights, punching-bag – I quite enjoyed it. But the goal is to prevent dangerous situations from happening.'

Trevor dressed and behaved to blend in. He was wearing chinos and a loose shirt that hid the beltful of gear he had to carry. He didn't want his principal to stand out either. 'In London, I'd call Dodi "Sir" when I met him in the morning, but, if we were with a group of people in a club, I'd be in a suit, like him, calling him "Dodi".'

He and Dodi rendezvoused at the Battersea heliport and flew by Harrods helicopter to Stansted airport, north-east of London. That morning Dodi had been watching the Bastille Day parade from the balcony of his Champs-Élysées apartment with his girlfriend, Kelly Fisher, the American model Trevor had often driven in London. 'I have no idea if they were engaged. I wasn't the least bit interested, to be truthful,' Trevor would later say. He called the Ops desk at Park Lane to report their arrival and they took off in Fayed's Gulfstream jet.

Mr Fayed, preparing to board the yacht to travel from St-Tropez to Cannes, would know his son's movements before they were airborne and expect to be told the moment he landed. 'He has ultimate control of every-thing, Al Fayed – knows everything that goes on,' Trevor knew, as he observed an obsession with control that seemed excessive even for the rich and famous. 'Be loyal to the Boss and he'll look after you,' was the first lesson you were taught. The second was that you never challenged this man's will. Even if you were right. Dodi didn't even seem to try.

At Nice, Trevor got the baggage and supplies transferred to a waiting van, drove to the nearby port of St-Laurent-du-Var and boarded Dodi's handsomely converted old torpedo boat, the *Cujo*. 'We're starting for Cannes,' he informed both the St-Tropez base and the *Jonikal* bridge as they cruised the forty minutes along the coast. The Fayeds and the Princess were on their way to meet them. The *Cujo* arrived first, moored, and waited as Trevor made radio contact with the captain. Then, moving towards them, they saw a fantastic yacht. Fifty yards long at least, Trevor figured. It looked half the length of a rugby pitch. Sleek and shiny white, *Jonikal* was impressive even in this playground full of megayachts.

'I'd seen the Princess before in Harrods, when she visited the Boss, Mr Fayed. The idea is not to be standing there looking at her, but you're human, aren't you? And I thought, what a good-looking woman she is.' But the Princess wasn't in Dodi's circle of friends, and Trevor had never met her. Now, as he rode the tender to Fayed's grand new yacht, Trevor spotted her on the rear deck. It was close to six o'clock in the evening, almost time for the Bastille Day fireworks. Even from a distance, he spotted the Princess's blonde hair. 'I have to admit I was looking for both her and the Princes, and when I saw them, it did bring home to me what a big summer this was going to be.

'It was well known that the Princess had dispensed

with her own security – drove around London with only a driver. She was there as a guest of "our family", the Fayeds, and was ours to protect.' For this ten-day holiday, they'd be based at the family's cliffside estate at St-Tropez, Castel Ste-Thérèse, a paradise compound of pools, terraces and gardens where Fayed maintained more than a dozen security personnel and snarling guard dogs. The Princes, William and Harry, would have their two Special Branch policemen with them. But Fayed never went out for dinner on these holidays, and since Dodi seemed likely to be taking over the task of escorting the Princess, it looked like Trevor would find himself minding the Princess of Wales.

He had already spotted several boats filled with paparazzi, stalking the *Jonikal* in the fading light – his first sight of the tabloid press. The threat was not the scopes of snipers' rifles – his mother's constant fear for him when he'd been in Belfast – it was the huge telescopic lenses of photographers who could make a fortune from a single intimate shot. Trevor believed the government still kept a discreet eye out for the safety of the mother of the future king of England. 'If the threat was so high that someone was going to get shot, then you wouldn't get anyone at my level doing the job. It would be someone from the police or Special Forces. The risk's to her privacy, isn't it. It's photographs. But a photograph never killed anyone.'

As Trevor made his way to the bridge to call the Ops Room in London to report their arrival, Dodi moved towards the rear deck where the family and royal guests were dining before the fireworks. The saga had begun.

No one in his private life, not even his mother, knew Trevor was on the yacht with the Princess in the south of France. Although, if she saw the papers, she'd soon guess. His mother and his wife Sue were the only people who knew the number to contact him via the Ops desk. 'Mum may have shared it with Ernie, but they're the only ones who knew who I worked for. Some of the rugby lads may have known I did close-protection work, but nothing more.' His week-on-week-off schedule gave him time to live a thoroughly normal life in Oswestry. Rugby training Thursday night, game on Saturday, and beers after both. In the military, close protection, and rugby, the topics were about the same: sports, women, drinking and training. He'd learned in the military to keep work and home life totally separate.

   Truthfully, a lot of it was not worth talking about. The hazard in civilian security work was not bullets but boredom. Trevor had loved his work in the 1st Battalion Parachute Regiment in Northern Ireland: covert surveillance with a four-man team, slipping into an observation post in the hills at night. He became a master at silence, self-reliance and reacting quickly to danger. 'We were a Close-Observation Platoon, the forward eyes of our battalion. We had a very good platoon there. If they'd formed the unit they were thinking of to do the job all the time, it would have been fantastic – I'd still be out there. But we were due to go back to Aldershot after my tour, and I just couldn't be bothered putting up with the bullshit again.' After six years in the army, Trevor had moved on.

Since he had his A-levels, he took a fitful stab at college to learn sports physiotherapy – the rebel middle son's way of following the medical careers of his father, a surgeon, and his mother, a nursing sister – but the courses weren't what he'd hoped they would be. He'd heard about close-protection work from some ex-military lads, and thought, 'It's hands-on. You're thinking as well as being active. I fancy that' – as well as the £25,000 a year. He took two civilian close-protection courses, learned the basics. En-bus. De-bus. Driving and walking drills. Smooth getaways. Unarmed combat.

He'd spotted an ad in a military employment newspaper and interviewed for the Fayed job in 1995. Paul Handley-Greaves, an impressive chap barely older than Trevor who was already head of personal security at 60 Park Lane, had hired him on the spot.

It was like being back in the army. A cracking bunch of blokes, roughly forty in all, and all ex-military. Trevor had never been far from this environment since he joined the Paras at the age of eighteen – he clicked straight away. 'You're doing the same job, you live together, you're playing together – you're all in the same boat, really. It was the same brilliant piss-taking humour that never lets you get away with anything.' A humour that dared you to put on airs, and kept your feelings from getting soft.

The difference was not just that you never challenged

the Boss, even if you thought professional procedures were being compromised, but that, unlike the army, 'you had to be a bloody diplomat. There was no ideal way to do things. Obviously, you had to keep the family safe. So you learned all kinds of subtle ways to defuse a potentially dangerous driving situation, say, so that it didn't anger your principal, or embarrass him in front of a friend.'

If bullets or fists are flying, then things have gone wrong. Trevor and the lads always laughed about the Hollywood view of bodyguards. 'You're not in a suit and dark glasses, shifting your eyes back and forth looking for assassins to jump out of a doorway. That would make me dizzy. Leaping in front of your principal to take a bullet – that's rubbish! That's Hollywood fantasy. Common sense and planning are the best weapons you've got. But if the shit hit the fan, I'd be happy to have a bloke like me there because I know I could do something.'

The Kevin Costner stereotype of a bodyguard made Kez Wingfield laugh too. Kez, Trevor's mate and the bodyguard who worked on this trip with him and then shared the fateful cruise that led to Paris, was as different from Trevor as chalk and cheese. A Royal Marines Commando who'd taken the elite RMP close-protection course at Longmoor, Kez was short and gabby with a passion for horses, while Trevor was a big, steady, husky bloke with a passion for rugby. Both had been raised in the military, but while Trevor was the son of a surgeon, Kez came from a colourful blend of rag-and-bone men, travellers and dockers from Hessle Road in Hull. 'Look up "grim" in the dictionary, and that's Hull,' says Kez, always ready with a quip. But Kez agreed with his mate on the bodyguards' role. 'You need a massive amount of discretion. You're not saving their life, like on the telly, you're just trying to make their life flow along smoothly. And you always obey the Boss. You still keep doing your job even though you're disappointed because you've missed a friend's wedding, or had to do overtime. If you don't, then you're not professional, and you're letting your colleagues down.'

Even working as Dodi's man you fetched and carried, did menial things, and there were other frustrations. Kez confirms that 'no one was ever jealous of big Johno [another bodyguard] or Trevor, the lads that worked with Dodi'. 'We were the people that worked the hardest just because of the hours we did,' says Trevor. 'You'd be up in the morning and then nearly every night of the week you'd be going out to either a restaurant, a film screening or a nightclub. And there's only you. That was the worst thing. If there were two of you, you could at least have a laugh together.'

Kelly Fisher would sometimes fly in for a week; the secretaries would call for a pick-up at the airport and Trevor would drive her and Dodi around. 'She was very attractive. Dodi always met up with attractive women. But the rumour that he was a playboy in that sense of the word, I didn't see it. Whoever he met at a nightclub, generally you'd drop Dodi off and then take them home.'

Friends or girlfriends, 'everyone I've seen on TV said he
was a hell of a good listener, which he probably was. I
think he was a good listener because he didn't seem to
have much to say for himself.'

Dodi's nightlife could be tedious for Trevor, but it was
his unpredictability that frustrated. You had your ideal
from basic training – four-man teams, time schedules,
well-recce'd routes and back-up vehicles – but with
Dodi, the ideal never happened. 'You could be out until
three o'clock in the morning, you'd get a message that
he'd be going somewhere at ten o'clock and then you'd
hang around until after midday, that sort of thing.' The
worst of Dodi came out when they were driving – just a
frustration for Trevor at the time, but a pattern of behaviour that becomes significant, in hindsight. 'He'd be
sitting in a traffic jam in the middle of the rush hour in
London, and it would be: "Why have you gone this way?"
He hated sitting in traffic, always wanted to push
through, to jump lanes, to try to get somewhere more
quickly. He'd order me to speed up where I knew a speed
camera was coming up – I could lose my licence, my
job. I wouldn't do it.'

'Dodi's complaining that you're not going quickly
enough,' Handley-Greaves had cautioned Trevor, as the
driving tussles continued. 'Okay, I'll go quicker then,'
said Trevor. Four weeks later, Trevor was on the carpet
again, with: 'Dodi says your driving's erratic – you're
either going too slow or too fast.' Kelly Fisher would later
tell a French judge under oath: 'Trevor was a perfect

employee, very strict in his work, but . . . Dodi was a real
dictator to him. He did not tell him, "Bring me to this
place," but "Bring me to this place, otherwise you are
fired." The situation . . . was always very tense and nervous.' Trevor agrees but adds, 'He was thoughtless to his
employees, but he wasn't vindictive. It may have sounded
like it but he didn't have it in him to be vindictive.' Dodi
was compulsive, though. About having everything in its
place in the vehicles, 'his scented wipes in a certain
compartment, sweets in another. You had to make sure
things were stocked up.'

Conversation between them was limited, at best. 'He
wasn't a bloke you could have a chat with. But, good
grief, I didn't want to be his pal. He spent a lot of time on
his mobile phone. He was always calling people up. And
I was quite happy to concentrate on what I was doing. If
you asked me, "Did you and Dodi get on well?", I'd say
he got on a hell of a lot better with his other man, John.
And yet John was taken off the job a week or two later
and I was left on. I don't know why he was taken off, and
to be honest, neither does he. Obviously, his shelf-life on
that job had just expired.'

One thing Dodi didn't really fuss about was seat-belts.
Neither man really wore them in the city. 'But if we got on
the M4 to Heathrow, a dual carriageway where the road
gets quick, seat-belts would go on. Generally, Dodi would
be in the front with me, in the Range Rover.' Nothing
would be said. He would follow Trevor's lead.

Dodi was quite heavily into cars. There was a bank of

cars which were considered his – a Range Rover, a couple of Aston Martins and a Ferrari – and he was into gadgets, toys, that sort of thing. He was also fascinated by the military. He had a massive collection of baseball caps from American warships, and things that would detect a radar trap; high-tech gadgets.

Trevor had gradually learned how to handle Dodi. 'You'd be driving, he'd look in a shop and say, "Find out about that," knowing full well that he wasn't really interested. As long as you answered, "Oh, yes, I'll do it," he usually forgot about it. He'd tell me to stop so that we could look at some new wheels, say, for one of the cars. Or, as we drove by the Lamborghini and Porsche showrooms right next to Fayed's headquarters in Park Lane, he'd go in and get some info. Ninety-nine times out of a hundred nothing would happen.' But if he took it the next step, and money was going to change hands for a new car, Trevor would be forced to play a part in a humiliating process. 'Dodi's purse-strings were still held by his father. If Dodi did something that was contravening what his father wanted, I had to report it to his father. I worked for his father, not for him.

'I'd inform the team leader and he'd pass it up to the Boss. I rarely went to Fayed direct, because, like in the military, you go through a chain of command. So his father would say no, and I'd have to tell Dodi, "Your father says you can't do it." Dodi would make a great fuss about it for a while, and I'd just sit there and say, "Talk to your father."'

It was sad, really, the relationship between the father and son, Trevor felt. Trevor had had no choice but to break free of his own dad. At seventeen, Trevor had found him dead of a heart attack, slumped over the wheel of his car, the horn stuck like a death wail. It is a memory that still cuts deeper than he'd ever shown.

'When the Boss went on telly after the crash saying what a wonderful son Dodi was, I was surprised. I must admit I didn't consider them that close. I felt the Boss would have liked Dodi to have been more like himself, a bit of a go-getter. He seemed to keep Dodi always off-guard. I'd take him to Harrods; his father would see him for only a couple of minutes. Once, on the shift before mine, Dodi turned up for a meeting and his father didn't want to see him at all. He closed the doors. They had to take him away.' And yet Dodi's father would often have him up for dinner in his penthouse apartment at Park Lane, and had indulged him from early childhood. When Dodi was fifteen he'd given him a chauffeured Rolls-Royce and a Mayfair apartment. Yet, at forty-two, Dodi could still have the cost of a set of wheels withheld from him. Trevor didn't understand it, 'But I now feel they were probably close in their own way. An eldest son must be special.'

Trevor was happy to work for Fayed. 'Fayed demanded loyalty and he demanded respect, and paid a reasonable wage to get it.' Trevor didn't know how long his shelf-life with the organization would be, but he felt he had the respect of the senior security staff for surviving with Dodi

as well as he had. And the job could be great – it could
be brilliant. You can put up with a lot to get seven days
off every fortnight. And to spend part of your summer in
St-Tropez.

As he walked forward to the bridge to call London and
chat with the lads, Trevor met the Princes' Special
Branch men. 'How do I address the Princess?' he asked
them.

'We call her "Ma'am",' one of them replied.

'What do you call the Princes?'

'Call them by their names, William and Harry.'

The team leader gave him a tour of the yacht, showed
him the basics you need to know – where's the fire-fight-
ing equipment, life-belts, first-aid kit, the loo, the Mess,
the galley. 'It was a smashing yacht, lavish in every way.'
Well-seasoned by round-the-world journeys, the *Jonikal*
had been feverishly refurbished to Fayed's extravagant
taste in the few months since he'd paid $20 million for
her. He had kept the Italian captain, Luigi Del Tevere,
who had skippered the *Jonikal* for years, but the previous
British crew had gone.

'My first impression was, "What a beautiful yacht, but
will I ever find my way around?" I didn't want to stumble
into a family area where I shouldn't be. Like when you
visit anywhere new, it seemed a lot bigger than it really
was,' Trevor reflects.

With radar, round-the-clock watches and limited
access, the *Jonikal* was secure. The photographers might

harass them, but they couldn't get on board. With a speed
of fifteen knots under her belt, she only had to turn and
head out to sea to outrun the paparazzi's small boats and
dinghies. But on land, where Trevor would be working . . .
there, Dodi's unpredictability, combined with the
Princess's celebrity, could be a security nightmare.
Trevor was in new territory, with challenges he'd never
faced before. He had to admit he enjoyed that.

He settled on the bridge with a soft drink as the fireworks began. Bursts of colour showered the night sky
along the coastline. He wasn't a great one for fireworks,
but he had to admit he'd never seen a display quite like
this one before. He wondered what else was going to
change; a few weeks earlier he'd never have imagined
that he, an ordinary bloke from Shropshire, would be in
the south of France, effectively minding the Princess of
Wales.

2

All at Sea

'Which one's she scoring with?' the several dozen security lads at the villa joked, as the holiday progressed and press clippings flowed in daily from London for the Fayeds and their royal guests to devour. Among the photos of the Princes and their mum diving and jet-skiing were shots of the Princess playfully dropping ice on Dodi's head, photos of Fayed with his arm around the Princess, and both father and son hovering over a pensive Diana on deck.

Trevor did not properly meet the Princess until the next morning, since by the time they'd travelled the hour back to St-Tropez after the fireworks, and taken the tenders ashore to the villa, everyone had been too tired to talk. 'Hello, Trevor, how are you?' she said, as a team leader introduced him on the beach. In bathing suit and flip-flops, she had the naturalness of someone he might run into on the street in Oswestry. 'Very well, Ma'am, thank you,' he replied. With the Princes, it was 'Trevor' from the start. 'They remember your name. They've got time for everyone. They've been very well brought up – cracking lads.' The running joke would be William and Harry teasing Trevor about his big, bright shirts.

This would be a good trip, Trevor sensed. The Boss, who normally would be flying back to London after three or four days, was beaming and exuding *bonhomie*, clearly pleased to be hosting the Côte d'Azur's catch of the season. Contrary to the lads' expectations, the Fayed children seemed well behaved. For five years in Oxted, the main family home in Surrey, Kez's job had been largely with the younger children, the two boys and two girls he'd watched grow up indulged and over-protected. Kez loved horses, both the fantastic, jet-black stallions that pull the Harrods carriages, gaitered with lots of feathers, and also the quiet riding horses that were available. There was even a wonderful riding instructor, but the children never rode. 'In five years, I saw one child ride perhaps three times, led by the instructor with a stable girl on either side of the horse. Mr Fayed is paranoid about his children's safety.' Fair enough. Kez was sure he loved them. But it stripped them of taking a few knocks and growing up with more responsibility and discipline – and it showed. It was the bodyguards who were forced to take the knocks.

Fayed had once handed him £200, a 'bung', after some

family fracas and, says Kez, 'That made me feel a lot
better. It was the biggest bung I ever got.'

Bungs were sweeteners to *maître d*'s, valets, drivers –
and to the bodyguards themselves. They were tips,
thank-yous for a job well done, not bribes. On a trip
abroad, everyone got £50 if things went smoothly; it was
bungs that oiled the wheels. That's the way it worked. As
well as bungs, you also got 'floats' to cover all your
expenses. In London, the secretaries would often give
you your bungs and floats, but, here, Fayed handed them
out in cash himself. 'On a trip like this, you might start,
say, with four hundred quid, and it would be gone in no
time, and you'd find yourself digging into your own
pocket,' says Kez.

With the security at the villa and the *Jonikal* secure,
Trevor's days were freed up to do the proper kind of
reconnaissance he rarely got the chance to do with Dodi
in London. Media presence was large, but not yet causing
a problem, he'd been told.

On the first morning Trevor walked from the estate down
to the beach, a familiar route. He'd been here on two
previous family holidays. He knew the drill. Go down to
the beach to help the lads set everything up for the
family, taking a stone and dirt trail that gave you a good
tour of the layout. He was shocked at the number of press
boats sitting offshore.

Like all French beaches, this one was public. And it
was tiny. It was the lads' job to claim it. 'We'd put

everything out, the jet-skis, inflatable toys, beach chairs, umbrellas, so that it looked like a family had settled in for the day.' The family and royals would turn up at about ten or eleven.

As the morning went on Trevor got his first real experience of paparazzi on the hunt for a superstar as photographers set up their tripods precariously on the rocks. In addition to the photographers, there were the tourists. The beach was quite a rough and stony place off the sand, but people would sit on the edge of it and just ogle the Fayed encampment, hoping for sightings of the Princess.

Fayed was upset about tourists being too close by and annoyed with a press helicopter that buzzed overhead. But you couldn't arrest French families for standing on a public beach. Diana seemed concerned, at first, with the loss of the privacy she'd so wanted for her and the boys on this holiday, and made a much-publicized trip out to a paparazzi boat to ask them to give her some peace. It would appear to the bodyguards that an unspoken pact had been struck. She and the boys accommodated the cameras during the day in return for peaceful nights. 'They weren't hiding at all. There was a small jetty at the beach and our tenders were going back and forth to the *Jonikal* all the time, so there was plenty of opportunity to take photos,' says Kez.

Debbie Gribble, the *Jonikal*'s chief stewardess, has been widely quoted as seeing the seeds of romance planted the very first night Dodi and Trevor boarded. As tall and slim as the Princess, this lively, athletic New Zealander had, in years of work in international hotels and on yachts, perfected the skills of staying close but remaining invisible, and being alert to every nuance from the shipboard guests. It was Debbie who checked discreetly to see that the Dom Pérignon flowed into spotless crystal, beds were perfect, and the daily *al fresco* lunch on the deck salon was flawless. That night, she orchestrated the serving of a feast on the aft deck prepared by four chefs, each serving up his specialities. According to the *News of the World* in a post-crash interview, it was at this meal that she saw a full-blown food fight between Dodi and Diana, and then 'destiny' as 'something passed between them'.

'I never said it,' Debbie states. 'In my mind, both families were thoroughly enjoying themselves, eating, drinking and watching the firework display. There may have been a photographers' boat around, and Dodi, I think, started hurling fruit from the elaborate fruit platters at them. This, in turn, began a free-for-all with both lots of children, and Diana and Dodi in on it. I *never* saw any canoodling that night.'

Sometimes Trevor minded the children during the day. 'I get on well with kids, and they were okay with me because I was a new face, a new plaything for them to get to know.' But the kids were basically Kez's job. Trevor's was organizing the nightlife. 'There'd usually be the royal party of three, plus Dodi, Fayed's wife, Mrs Heini, and the two elder Fayed girls, Camilla and Jasmine, plus three or four of us security lads and the Princes' police. We'd generally drive in, then walk through St-Tropez, almost filling the road. They'd be in the most casual kit, jeans, trousers and shorts, but you can't be low-profile when you're a dozen people, most of them big men.'

'Mrs Heini', as the lads called Fayed's wife, was, as Trevor saw her in linen trousers, loose shirts and little make-up, simply 'a blonde, good-looking Nordic woman'. A former Finnish beauty queen and model whom Dodi had introduced to Fayed, she had been installed at Oxted and borne him two of their four children before he married her in 1985. Jasmine, a blossoming seventeen-year-old brunette with Arab looks, and Camilla, five years younger, provided young company for the Princes on these evenings out.

Ashore, the evenings had an eerie calm. St-Tropez, one of the trendiest places on the Côte d'Azur, should have been the worst place for the world's most famous woman to try to have a private holiday: the streets were crowded with people. But only a few would turn and look at them as they went by, and usually the journalists weren't there.

'One of the policemen and I would drive out beforehand and try as best we could to plan the evening,' Trevor recalls. 'We'd recce the roads, routes, hospitals, possible venues for little adventures, walks, window-shopping. There was one road in and one road out of St-Tropez. The first restaurant we checked was about half an hour's drive out of town. We liked it and got it all booked up.'

Trevor 'bunged' the *maitre d'* – gave him £100 to assure good care for his unnamed party that night.

On the way back, Trevor spotted a fairground set up along the road. He noted it as a point of interest they might want to stop at after dinner. They worked out how to get into the grounds – checked on admission prices, and whether there was secure parking.

'We had four or five security at the restaurant that night. We sat with the Princes' two policemen on the terrace outside and kept checking on the family. There were just the two of them, not the massive entourage you'd expect to be assigned to the heirs to the throne. And what surprised me was how relaxed they were with the Princes and Princess. William and Harry came out of the restaurant, and I chatted away with them. The police did not cramp. They kept their distance and let their charges enjoy themselves. We popped into the funfair after dinner. It was a very relaxed atmosphere that night.'

With the Princess and the boys along, Trevor noticed a whole new mood. 'I always thought that their presence brought out the best in the family we worked for. There didn't seem to be any back-biting. Our family is quite demanding, you know. If you're not there at their beck and call they tend to throw their teddy-bears out of the pram. The Princess and her boys created a much lighter atmosphere. And if Fayed wasn't there, which he never was in the evenings, things were a hell of a lot easier. We trod on eggshells when he was around.'

The funfair was the best of nights. It was the night

Trevor rode the bumper cars and loop-the-loops with
William and Harry. 'The kids wanted someone to go on
the rides with them. "Come on!" they'd say. I was being
encouraged by Mrs Heini and the Princess but I was very
reluctant at first. I didn't want to dampen the kids' fun,
and I just didn't see it as my place, really. Then one of
the policemen went on, and I thought, if they think it's all
right, then it's obviously no problem. So I went. Looking
back, it was a good idea because you don't want just anybody sitting by the people you're looking after.' What
totally natural kids they were, he thought. The Princess
got noticed, but no one pestered her. There were no
paparazzi there at all. Everyone wanted to go back the
next night. It was during these evenings in town that
Trevor got to know the Princess and her sons, and got an
inkling of the impact of celebrity on their daily lives.

One night he realized just how tenuous was their hold
on privacy. The whole group had been aboard the *Sakara*,
Fayed's comfortable old schooner, which was backed up
to the dock at the doorstep of one of St-Tropez's most
popular spots, the Café de Paris. A big crowd had formed
around the gangplank, tourists and paparazzi, as the
family came off to go for a walk. 'You couldn't have a
worse place to try to protect people. All the cafés were
there, thousands of people. A wave of people moved forward to engulf the party. Tourists were jostling to get in
front, coming from everywhere, trying to stick their cameras in the Princess's face to get a photo.'

The Fayed security team, taking its lead from the

Princes' police, learned precious lessons that night as these two low-key characters went to work. 'It was dead relaxed. They could be somebody's uncle.' But when the pressure came, they were brilliant. 'So polite but very firm, explaining to people, asking them to just back off – and they backed off. It could have been a mêlée, but it wasn't even hairy. You knew, though, that you were working for a living,' Trevor reflects. The event was sobering. 'When you see that, you appreciate that this woman has got no privacy whatsoever.' The evening stroll was cancelled. 'You could see that it got to her.'

Trevor and Kez were all the more impressed with the police when they learned that they weren't even armed. The reason wasn't heroics or principles. 'There had been too much paperwork involved to get weapons across to France. Even the royal protection group was trapped in bureaucratic red tape!'

The police were relaxed, but the security team was holding its collective breath. There had been none of the forced resignations they'd expected. They could hardly believe this great spirit that had spread over the place. Some of the lads reported that the Princess wasn't always this good-natured – that she could get hacked off at times as well – and Trevor would learn from some of her drivers that she could be pretty intense and had fired people for not doing as she asked.

But you couldn't fake what Trevor saw as her 'chirpy, very bubbly, very easy-going personality' for ten consecutive days, with the make-up off, the glamour and formality stripped away, in front of bodyguards she didn't need to impress. She was chatty and Trevor was not going to just stand there and say nothing.

He glimpsed a serious side to Diana when she received word of the murder of her good friend, the fashion designer Gianni Versace, on 15 July. 'I don't remember who started talking about it, but I was walking up from the Fisherman's Hut to go to the cars to get ready to go out. I bumped into Diana and Harry and she was talking about how she had to fly to the funeral and how sad she was. She was pretty down about it. I obviously sympathized, but didn't really know how to comment. I think I said something like, "Let's hope we have a good evening again," meaning the funfair, to change the subject.'

But it was mostly an upbeat Princess Trevor and Kez remember. 'She used to take the mickey out of things I'd wear,' Kez laughs. 'I had this really big pair of shorts. She'd say, "Couldn't you get any in large?" So I'd give the mickey back: "I like them skin-tight like this."'

One morning, when Kez was standing by the tenders down at the beach, 'she took the mickey out of my sketchy yachting skills. "So you've got your boat here," she said, as if she was chatting up the owner of a super-yacht, looking for a ride. "Well, yes, that's mine alongside here," I said, gesturing grandly to the bobbing little tender. "Do you fancy coming for a spin?" She had a life-jacket on over her bathing suit in a minute, and off we went, me driving and one of the lads in the bow. The guy in the bow was taking the mickey out of me being in the Marines, calling me "codhead". "Codhead?" "Oh, just an affectionate nickname." She picked it up, laughing. "Codhead." She loved it. Wouldn't let it go.' The adventure ended with a resounding thunk when Kez put in a bit too hard as he came alongside the dock.

It is easy to fall into the *Hello!* view of celebrity families – the apparently endless holidays, dinners, functions and social engagements, the posed family photographs and the beautifully kept homes and gardens. Since the accident Fayed himself has painted a picture of family bliss, saying that Diana found real happiness on her holiday with his normal family. Indeed, there were moments when the boys behaved just like any other youngsters. Prince Harry had done his part to give Omar, Fayed's youngest, a lesson in fair play. It was the buzz of the organization. 'Omar wanted his own way and Prince Harry argued back. Omar went for him, so Harry gave him a good scutching. "Fair's fair" was the lads' view afterwards.' Kez heard it. He was in the next room. But, like Harry's personal policemen, he didn't stop it. You had to let boys be boys, even if they were Princes. 'The jungle drums spread news of the fight like wildfire. All the bodyguards said, "Yes! Prince Harry kicked his arse!" It gladdened my heart,' laughs Kez.

But this is perhaps some way from being a 'normal family'. All the Fayed children were a bit unusual in Kez's view, including the older ones. 'Here's Dodi, a bit of a waster. Mr Fayed, you can say what you like about him,

but he's highly motivated, whereas Dodi has sort of
strolled through life without a care, the way it looked to
me.'

Dodi was playing a tricky and secretive game with his
girlfriend, Kelly Fisher, whom he had abandoned on
Bastille Day in Paris. As she would later tell a French
judge, Dodi had flown her to St-Tropez two days later, on
16 July. There, he kept her hidden on the family's boats
while he spent his days with the royal guests. 'There was
a rumour going around among the lads, sort of a joke, that
Dodi's girlfriend was on the *Cujo*,' Trevor confirms. 'A
couple of the evenings when I was left with Dodi, the
Princess and Mrs Heini, they'd spend the end of the
evening on the *Sakara* having a drink, and then they'd
say, "It's time to go," and the Princess and Mrs Heini
would get into the car and we'd drive back to the villa. I
accompanied the Princess and Mrs Heini because the
main threat was to the Princess. There was no specific
threat against Dodi, the yacht was secure, and also I was
staying at the villa. At this stage Dodi was still "an
unknown" and I was not giving him twenty-four-hour
cover. As far as I knew, Dodi was taking the tender out to
the *Cujo*. It was moored close by and it was his boat. But
I never saw Kelly Fisher.'

Debbie Gribble did see her. 'I met Kelly Fisher one
afternoon when Dodi, Kelly and another chap came on
board *Jonikal* for a very late lunch at short notice.' As
Debbie scurried around to get it organized, 'suddenly

they were coming up the ladder; I assumed they had
come over from the *Cujo*, anchored nearby. I had no idea
at the time who she was, but I felt she acted very spoiled.
I remember vividly that she snapped, "I want to eat right
now! I don't want a drink, I just want to eat *now*." It was
quite obvious that she was upset, angry or annoyed over
something.' Debbie confirms that Dodi did go over to the
Cujo on occasion, but he slept on the *Jonikal*. 'He was
our only resident guest.'

Annoyed as she may have been by Dodi's excuses for
hiding her away from the Princess and his family, Kelly
would claim to know nothing of Dodi and Diana's growing
friendship until she saw their pictures splashed across
the papers in Los Angeles several weeks later. She was
one of the first victims of the media manipulation that,
within months, would roll over both Trevor and Kez in its
obsessive promotion of a Diana–Dodi marriage myth.

Michael Cole, Fayed's PR man, made contact with the
publicist Max Clifford to help manage the explosive
potential of the Kelly Fisher affair once Fayed had seized
upon the possibility of a real romance between Dodi and
the Princess. Clifford admitted to the journalist Martyn
Gregory that he tipped off certain photographers and
press people to the *Jonikal*'s, and the couple's, where-
abouts as the romance progressed. He spoke, he said, 'to
various people, particularly friends . . . I'd known for a
long time in the media and, when they checked – "Are
they there, are they going to . . .?" – I'd say, "Yes, they
are."' When asked if he gave friendly advice, such as 'I

think they'll be down in St-Tropez,' Clifford admitted, 'Well, I did. There were times.'

Kelly Fisher was to vanish from the Fayed scene – even though her wedding to Dodi, she would claim a few weeks later, was set for 9 August. What happened to Kelly was a callous deception that seems unlike Dodi's nature. But she was not part of the larger agenda.

To Trevor's mind, Dodi's efforts to promote a romance with Princess Diana got off to a stumbling start. After dinner one evening, Dodi suddenly led the troop to a nightclub. Trevor didn't have time to recce the venue, and the media turned up almost as soon as the party had gone inside. It was a little cellar club on a back alley just off the waterfront. 'It was dingy. And there was nobody there. Dodi obviously knew the owner from his years of socializing in St-Tropez, and the owner was overjoyed.' But Trevor cringed. Dodi had rented the whole place to protect their privacy, and the little group sat alone on the small dance floor, sipping their drinks. They danced a bit in this 'empty, tacky little place. It was such an embarrassingly sterile environment. What a way to impress a Princess.'

The joke next day was about Dodi having 'two left hooves'. The Princess laughed, too. Dodi persisted and took them again, and this time it was a little livelier. Other people were there and when the children were taken home, Trevor and a driver stayed on with Dodi, Diana and Mrs Heini. 'Talk about bad security. I'm with three people now, on my own. If anyone said that was a complete shambles, I would totally agree with them.'

Dodi's father may have pushed him, but Dodi was more than willing to spend time with the Princess, and there was 'no question that the Princess and Dodi were enjoying talking to each other. I was surprised, actually, as – personality-wise – I'd have put the Princess and Dodi poles apart.' Still, she seemed to be absorbed with Dodi. When the four of them were in the club, with Trevor sitting at a table a few feet away, Mrs Heini came over, sat down and talked with him. 'It was very unusual.'

It was a shock, in fact. This was the woman who had set the jungle drums going when the family and Princess had first arrived. The lads had been sweating buckets unloading the luggage, and the Princess, as she was getting into the vehicle, had said, 'I'd like to thank the lads for lifting all the kit on such a warm day,' to which Mrs Heini had responded, 'Don't worry, there's no need.' The look on the Princess's face!

Heini sat with Trevor again one night when the three of them were having a late evening drink aboard *Sakara*. Trevor was guarding the gangplank, the only way on or off the boat. Suddenly, Mrs Heini came out to chat with him, leaving Dodi and Diana inside talking alone. It's easy to speculate that she was acting for Fayed, trying to matchmake. Who knows? 'Maybe she wanted to stretch her legs. Maybe they were excluding her from the conversation and she was getting bored.'

The Princess and Princes flew home on Sunday, 20

July. They had been due to fly back on the Friday, but couldn't resist staying another two days. They'd have to separate as soon as they returned to London, with the Princes going to Balmoral to spend August with their father. The Fayeds flew to Finland, Heini's home, while Dodi stayed on in St-Tropez with Kelly Fisher. As Diana attended Gianni Versace's funeral in Milan on 22 July, Dodi and Kelly cruised the Mediterranean. They flew to Paris on 23 July, before Kelly returned to Los Angeles, still expecting to marry Dodi in August.

Fayed told the bodyguards they could stay on for a few days before returning to England. They had a little bung money in their pockets and Trevor and a few mates went back to the nightclub. It was as seedy as he'd remembered and Trevor thought with some amusement that this place symbolized Dodi's efforts on the trip. 'Dodi was trying his best, but it was an embarrassment.' Kez, always ready with a riposte, said, 'I don't think Dodi was trying too hard. I think his father was being the matchmaker too much . . . And I think the Princess went along with it.'

Something, however, must have clicked. The last few days, the word spread through the staff that Dodi and the Princess were becoming a bit of an item. Certainly Debbie on the *Jonikal* was convinced that at least a summer romance was under way. But Kez says, 'Once our team got to know her and the Princes better, any speculation that she and Dodi were having a romance was just met with derision. I make no secret of the fact that I'm a republican. But she was a cracker – she was lovely – and her children were fantastic.' The team on the ground felt the same. 'They were thinking, "Well, she is a good lass, and they are cracking kids. It's not all front for the camera. She could do miles better than this guy, for Christ's sake."'

In its preoccupation with the millions to be made from selling photos of Diana and the raging debate over whether the Princess should or should not be the guest of Fayed, the press didn't pick up a budding romance. The media had not even commented on Dodi's arrival at the beginning of the trip. They were beginning to nibble at the edges of the story, but they didn't have it yet. Trevor could not believe there could ever really be a romance.

What the ten days had clearly shown Trevor was the differences between the two families. When Trevor heard Fayed's statements later on television about how, on this St-Tropez trip, Diana had found in the Fayeds 'a normal family she could relate to and be comfortable with, the normal family she'd never had', he responded, 'Rubbish! Normal families I know don't have a holiday with royalty, don't own villas in St-Tropez and don't have fifty-yard yachts. Normal families I know go on holiday to Majorca with inflatable lilos.'

What he took away from the trip was the scene the media never saw: the visits to the funfair. The Princess, untroubled by photographers, wandering round, joking, exploring with her sons. The Princes, throwing their heads back on the rides, laughing, teasing Trevor about his shirt. How extraordinary for her to be able to have the most ordinary of good times. In hindsight, these were probably the last relaxed and happy times she would ever have with William and Harry. Once they'd gone to Balmoral, she would never see them again.

3

The Pressure Mounts

Trevor returned to work on 6 August, after ten days' leave following the St-Tropez trip, to find his job description as 'Dodi's man' transformed. The anonymous man he'd driven alone around London had been thrust into the limelight. Now, Trevor would be running the gauntlet of the paparazzi with the Princess of Wales. As he checked in for his first shift, Dodi and the Princess were just returning from Sardinia, the second of two short trips they'd taken together since returning from St-Tropez. 'I was absolutely gobsmacked when I found out they'd been on holiday together.'

Back in London after shipping Kelly Fisher off to Los Angeles, Dodi had stepped up his pursuit of the Princess. On Friday, 25 July, he had whisked her by Harrods helicopter to Paris for their first date, dinner at the three-star Lucas Carton restaurant and an overnight stay at the Ritz.

Six days later, they flew back to the Mediterranean for a week's trip, alone, aboard the *Jonikal*.

Trevor's first assignment was to pick Dodi up at the Battersea heliport on the couple's return. Trevor was eager to see the Princess to thank her for the note she'd written him for his work on the St-Tropez trip. 'It was stuck in my pigeonhole in the Ops Room. All the lads who'd been on security on that holiday received one. A standard letter, obviously.' But it was so gracious, and at the bottom were a few handwritten words from the Princes. The embossed gold and black Kensington Palace seal appeared at the top of the letter and it was dated 23 July 1997, three days after her return from St-Tropez. Addressed to Trevor Rees-Jones Esq., it was signed in her own bold, round hand, with the body typed. In it she thanked Trevor for taking care of her and the Princes during the St-Tropez trip, and apologized for making his job even more difficult than it already was by their presence. At the bottom, William had scrawled a note from him and Harry about his loud shirts.

After the Princess had greeted him with her dazzling smile and the usual, 'Hi, Trevor, how are you?', he said, 'I want to thank you for the letter, Ma'am, on behalf of me and all the lads. It was much appreciated.' It wasn't much, really, but that note, in the months to come, would become a treasured possession.

For Trevor, it was the next day that 'the shit hit the fan'. Mid-evening of 7 August, a big dark-grey BMW pulled up outside one of the access routes to Dodi's apartment at 60 Park Lane. From security cameras scanning the entrances, Ops had reported photographers milling restlessly at the front and side entrances, waiting for action. Trevor and two other lads were hanging around just inside the doors, not wanting to be obvious to the press on the street. Alerting the Princess's driver by phone when it was clear to pull up, Trevor saw her arrive with only a driver in the front seat, and no security whatsoever.

'The photographers knew her car and the registration.' Flashbulbs started popping as they spotted the car. He dashed to the rear right door and blocked for the Princess as this breathtaking woman emerged from the back seat, still sun-tanned from the Côte d'Azur – all legs and high heels in a very glamorous, skin-tight, short blue cocktail dress. Trevor did not notice what she was wearing as he whisked her towards the lifts but the picture of the Princess wearing the blue dress and a smile of shy anticipation would be all over the papers the following morning – one of the most glamorous of all the shots taken during the romance.

The two buildings, 55 and 60 Park Lane, filled the corner of Park Lane and South Street. Discreet grey façades scarcely suggested the fashionable neighbourhood, with the Dorchester Hotel next door and the embassy of Fayed's homeland, the Arab Republic of Egypt, around the corner on South Street. They scarcely suggested the power which resided here.

Fayed had apartments and offices in 60 Park Lane, well disguised above a Lexus car dealership. The complex of offices also housed Fayed's Ops Room and security accommodation. Fayed's cousins and uncles stayed in apartments there when they were in town. Fayed and his family and Dodi's apartment were there too, and all shared a common kitchen with chef and staff. 'It was like having a hotel kitchen,' Dodi's valet would note. With a shared garage and access between both buildings, Diana would be taken first through 55 and then into 60, and up the elevator to Dodi's apartment.

Inside, the building was safe. 'The whole building is counted as secure because you've got the residence security blokes on the front door, night-time patrols of the building, cameras covering all approaches – outside entrances, access points, they're all covered.' The bank of screens for the cameras sat at the Ops desk, constantly scanned. 'As long as the blokes watching the cameras and doing the patrols are not sleeping on the job, you're secure.'

With good reason, Dodi decided to order dinner in. Next day, the tabloids reported that liveried Dorchester butlers had delivered the food, with great pomp and ceremony, on gleaming silver platters. There were photos of men carrying trays into 60 Park Lane, with captions like, 'Butlers deliver take-away food for the lovebirds'. And it was not only the tabloids. Later books would report: 'Dodi had supper sent over, on silver platters, from the kitchen of the Dorchester Hotel next door.' 'It came from Harry's Bar, not the Dorchester,' Trevor chuckled. 'And that was me! Me and another lad picked it up from Harry's Bar and had the driver pull up to the tradesmen's entrance to 60 Park Lane around the corner. We just picked up the trays from the back seat and walked in.' He laughed to himself, 'I'm not much more than a butler, when it gets down to it. But there you go.'

It was now just after midnight, and, while the couple ate, Trevor was sitting and chatting with the lad who was on stag at the desk, waiting for Dodi to ring down and say, 'We're coming down now' – the alert to take the Princess home. Someone called over, 'It's Sue, your ex-wife, on the phone.' His first thought was, 'Christ, what the hell's gone wrong?' She would never call him in the middle of work at night unless it was an emergency. He took the phone. 'Yeah, Trevor here.' Sue sounded strange, a little frantic. 'I phoned up to tell you that I'm with someone.' With someone!

'Who is it?'

'I think you know.'

Trevor had suspected for a long time that this man was on the scene. He'd even made contact with a legal firm in town, Crawford Lucas, to start the paperwork for divorce, since that's what Sue wanted. 'But I was still hoping we could patch things up. Even though we were separated at that time, she had made out that she wasn't with anyone and that she would tell me if . . . well, we'd sort of agreed that if we got involved with anyone, either of us, we'd let each other know. But when she told me, and in the middle of work, I just flipped.'

All the lads went on alert as Trevor started shouting into the phone, 'What the bloody hell are you doing? I can't believe you've done this!'

Dodi's call was about to come, and Trevor was in turmoil. There was the shock and hurt. But more than that, 'it was the fact that Sue could be so bloody insensitive as to phone me just then – to scramble my mind when I had to deal with the Princess in less than half an hour's time'. Later on he could see the irony of the situation – having his own hopes shattered just as he was going to be driving home to her palace a Princess starting her own romance.

He slammed the phone down, and punched the door to the lounge area open with his fist, startling two lads who were watching the telly. 'They'd all heard the shouting and bloody knew what was going on. We were a close bunch.'

'If you want me to get someone else to cover for you, I will,' said Andy, one of the bosses, and the assigned driver that night. But Trevor was quickly back at work, the fire under control. 'I flared up for a couple of minutes. It took a bit of pulling yourself together to do it. But once things started moving and we were taking her home, I put Sue to the back of my mind.'

This was Trevor's first London drive with the Princess. Reports were coming from Ops that a pack of photographers

were at both front and garage doors. Dodi escorted her
back as far as the car, and Trevor showed her into the
low-profile Toyota van. The garage doors opened to a
chaotic scene. Photographers everywhere. Flashbulbs
blinding you, cameras whacking against the windows.
According to reporters, a car ran over the foot of a photographer, though Trevor heard or saw nothing of the
incident. 'They were jumping out at us. If it happened,
I'm sorry it happened.'

Andy, the driver, had asked Trevor to let him take the
wheel, since he'd never seen the Princess. Trevor didn't
realize how used to the Princess he'd become in St-
Tropez until he saw Andy's reaction. 'It's funny how
quickly you get used to dealing with someone like her . . .
I was quite used to it at that stage. I don't think you can
become overawed with the situation, otherwise you let the
situation get on top of you, don't you?'

Trevor directed the driver south down Park Lane and
into Knightsbridge, past Hyde Park, towards Kensington
High Street. At the base of Kensington Gardens he would
turn right into the long driveway that leads to Kensington
Palace, and the entrance on Palace Avenue.

Just as they got to within a few hundred yards of the
drive, Trevor heard Diana's voice coming from the far
back seat of the van: 'I'm going to climb through now.'
'Okay, Ma'am,' said Trevor, trying to stay cool as he
glanced back to see long royal legs flailing over the seat,
and, embarrassed, quickly looked forward again. Good
God! She was pitching herself forward into the seat right

behind Trevor and the driver, moving herself closer to the door. The Princess of Wales!

They zoomed up the driveway with photographers waiting at the gate, but halted finally by the signs: No Admittance, Private Road, No Unauthorized Parking, and by the security barrier just beyond. As the guard, who had never seen Trevor before, said a very formal 'Good evening, sir', the Princess 'wound the window down, poked her head through the glass, and said, "It's only me"'. The barrier gate opened, the guard waved them through, and an ebullient Princess called back, 'Good night, Trevor, see you tomorrow,' as she ran up the steps of the white-columned portico and vanished through the palace door.

'I know a little pub around the corner in Mayfair. I suspect you could use a pint,' said Andy. They both could. Andy was in shock over how real and human she was – he couldn't believe it. 'No thanks, mate,' said Trevor. It would have been a great idea, if he hadn't been on duty.

Back at Park Lane, in the bodyguards' quarters, he reviewed the situation. He had returned to work to find the Princess and Dodi's romance front-page news. It was a shock after St-Tropez, where evening trips, at least, had been quiet. It was a shock after ten days in Oswestry, where the main thing filling his mind had been winning the next rugby match. 'It was the first time for many of us, that sort of attention. I don't think there has been that sort of intensity with that organization, ever. Diana was suddenly seeing someone new, and the whole world was interested.'

From then on, the building – anywhere Dodi and the Princess went – would be under siege. The threat assessment for Dodi had just gone up tenfold. Things had to change. They needed to scale up security. New protocols had to be worked out. Two-car convoys. 'But I was enjoying it.' With the new challenge, the job had just become brilliant. It was better than being bored. All the lads would be helping out, driving, whatever – he'd have 'loads and loads of help. But I was the only security person who would go to Dodi direct and speak to him. I was still Dodi's man.'

Just as the paparazzi were smelling blood, Diana left the next day, 8 August, on a short trip to Bosnia to protest against the use of landmines. Trevor was not given to commenting on or even caring much about Dodi's personal life. But it was clear that Dodi was smitten. He was so eager to stay in touch with the Princess that, although she'd only be in Bosnia for two days, 'he wanted her to have a telephone so that they could talk while she was away. We'd got a satellite phone for her, arranged through the organization. It arrived late, and I had to make a mad dash to Heathrow when she was taking off to get it to her. It looked like I wasn't going to make it. This wasn't a royal flight; it was a small private jet.' Trevor called ahead, ran to the gate clutching the phone, and handed it to an official just as the plane was ready to taxi off. Doors were unlocked. The phone was rushed aboard.

'As it turned out, she didn't need the satellite phone. The normal mobiles covered just fine.'

The media excitement so far was just a calm preamble to what was to come on the day of Diana's return from Bosnia. On the couple's most recent trip on the *Jonikal*, one photographer had been chosen above the clamouring horde and been given the tip-off of a lifetime. Mario Brenna, personal photographer to Diana's dear, murdered friend Gianni Versace, had found the *Jonikal* in a remote bay off Sardinia and brought his powerful telephoto lens to bear on two bathing-suited bodies in an intimate moment on the deck. There is still disagreement over who put Brenna on to the chase: charges and counter-charges that Diana did, or that Fayed did. The image Brenna got was hazy. It was hard to tell whether it was an embrace or a kiss. But for Brenna, it was a shot worth at least $1 million, and on Sunday morning, 10 August, the photo, exclusive in the *Sunday Mirror*, hit the news-stands with the nearly two-inch-high headline 'THE KISS' and subhead 'Locked in her lover's arms, the Princess finds happiness at last'. Even Dodi seemed, now, to begin to grasp the implications for his previously private life.

René Delorm, his loyal butler, was called to come over from Paris and arrived the same day. It was clear that the couple would, increasingly, be eating in. René had learned over his seven years of running Dodi's house-holds in Beverly Hills, Paris, and now London, to create the romantic aura Dodi liked, with every detail perfect. René was the sentimental impresario who orchestrated the silver, the crisp linen, the candles, caviar, the background music, the favourite wines and cigars – the stage set on which Dodi had entertained a host of Hollywood stars from Brooke Shields to Julia Roberts.

Trevor's problem was still Dodi's unpredictability. Unknown to Trevor, Dodi had devised a plan to whisk the Princess to the Fayeds' Surrey estate at Oxted as soon as she returned from Bosnia. By late afternoon on 10 August, the couple, Trevor and René were travelling around the M25 to the doors of the estate. Trevor could see that Oxted was temptingly private to Dodi with his father gone. Nothing wrong with that – a love affair's got to have some spontaneity and seclusion.

There was a small covey of photographers at the entrance to the grounds, but inside, Oxted was a safe and handsome haven. In Barrow Green Court, as the estate was called, Fayed had created an English country dream. Although Trevor had driven the route with Dodi often for his Sunday dinners with the family, it was always impressive. Gorgeous green landscapes of fields with grazing horses and flowering gardens surrounded a massive Elizabethan mansion. Fayed had spent millions of pounds to restore its oak-panelled rooms, to build a huge swimming pool, install horses, develop acres of exquisite gardens, and to create what has been described as 'a children's dream world' for his four young children, with toys scooped up from Harrods.

Fayed ran his empire, in all except the most bitter weather, from a white plastic tent set out on the lawn and carpeted in Astroturf-like green carpeting. It seemed a British version of the sheik's desert tent, but its purpose was less romantic – its isolation prevented bugging. 'All his other estates were variations on the Oxted theme, including the tent,' says Kez Wingfield, who was based there for five years. Through a bodyguard's eyes a different side of Oxted is revealed: a compound of 500 acres patrolled by guards. With an array of security and surveillance equipment, the estate was watertight. 'If you were there uninvited at nights, then you would have to be deemed hostile,' says Kez.

René let only the magic show for this overnight stay, as he masterminded wine and caviar under a marquee in a sort of secret garden far from the house, and then a candlelit dinner set at the edge of a sweep of garden. While enchanted with the Renaissance ruffling of the Princess's white satin blouse, René anguished over the same indecision from Dodi that frustrated Trevor. He hated having to move the cocktail-and-hors-d'oeuvre set-up from one location to another at the last minute.

Dating the Princess did not improve Dodi's sense of time. Trevor couldn't just tell him to his face that he had to start looking at his watch and living by some sort of schedule. 'But, obviously, you couldn't have this any more,' he saw. 'The good side of things was that suddenly I could put my foot down more and say *this* is the way it's going to happen, because the level of everything had increased. I think Dodi realized it as well. It just happened.'

Security plans at Park Lane were now stepped up. 'Paparazzi were taking pictures of every car they thought Dodi or the Princess might be in, and we were trying to give the couple as much privacy as we could. We didn't want to be followed all the way by paparazzi, so we put a couple of diversionary measures in – but without going over the top and, obviously, keeping it as safe as possible.' Hoping to confuse the press, they left Park Lane in two-car convoys, 'two vehicles both with darkened windows, hoping they wouldn't know which one the couple was in. We made sure it was the last minute before the garage doors went up, so you could get out at quite a speed. Our cameras were covering South Street and all the junctions, so you're on the radio to the Ops Room, them telling you, "It's clear" so that you'd be able to shoot straight out, rather than stop and wait.'

But getting the Princess from Kensington Palace to Park Lane without being hounded by a thundering herd of press cars required more resourcefulness. They devised a way to ditch the media en route. 'I'd be told, the Princess is coming this evening. I'd phone her driver on his pager and say, "Are you coming over tonight?", meaning are you delivering her? "Yeah," he'd say. We'd arrange to meet at some quiet street. We'd set a time. Our driver and I would be in a Toyota people-carrier. En route, we'd both do a bit of a recce round, make sure no paparazzi were following us. We'd arrive, park, and I'd keep an eye out for him. He'd ring us when he was approaching. "Okay, we've got you." He'd pull up, she'd get out of her car and straight into ours, and we'd drive off.' Once, her driver had to change the rendezvous place because he was being followed. An ex-Scotland Yard Protection Force officer, he was a past master at shaking off paparazzi, and regaled Trevor with how he had twisted and turned to get rid of them.

'I can't remember whether it was my idea or hers, the ducking down.' But it became their routine. As Trevor approached the Park Lane garage, he'd be on the radio to the lads. Two minutes away, he would radio in the code word 'moon'. As they were approaching their entrance, the code word 'beam' would be given, and the guy at the desk would call down to the car, 'The road's clear now, still clear . . .' so that 'we could come straight across and into the garage. As we were approaching South Street, I'd say, "Duck down now, Ma'am, we're nearly there."' She'd slip down to the floor, often laughing at the conspiracy, just as they were pressing the button to open the garage door. Timing was critical. When the photographers saw the door slide up, they'd be ready to pounce, and be on their radios to the rest of the pack. The driver would shoot down the ramp past the photographers, with no Princess in sight. The doors closed like a portcullis. 'They never ran into the car park after us,' says Trevor.

'She'd see it as a bit of a joke. She used to laugh about it. I think she was enjoying herself. Then I'd walk through 55 Park Lane with her and go to 60 and take her to Dodi's apartment.' On the way, they'd talk. 'We never got into major conversations, but the conversations I did

have were like talking to anyone. It could be anything.
One time we talked about *Men in Black*, which she'd
taken the boys to see. She didn't like it, while I'd thought
it was quite a funny film. And, a while ago, she'd taken
Harry to a film about IRA terrorism when he was under
age for the film – it caused a flap of some kind, and she
said, "I would never have done it if I'd known." She
wasn't stupid. She may not have been a rocket scientist,
but then neither am I. These were nice conversations.'

The pull of privacy and romance at Oxted was so strong
that Dodi and the Princess soon returned, starting with
a venture launched by Dodi with such flagrant disregard
for security that, for Trevor, frustration was replaced by
shock. As he and Dodi arrived at the Battersea heliport
to meet the Princess and fly to Oxted, Trevor was told
the plans had changed. The couple were going somewhere else first, and he was excluded from the trip.
Where the hell were they going? There was nothing on
the schedule at Ops other than Oxted. 'I think I should
be with you for this,' said Trevor as Dodi and the
Princess happily climbed aboard the helicopter. 'You're
not needed. We'll meet you at Oxted,' said Dodi. On the
spur of the moment Dodi was literally taking off on his
own without a bodyguard or back-up. Appalled but
helpless, Trevor called the Ops Room and said that Dodi
had departed on a helicopter with his guest to an
unknown destination.

The pilot had no idea where the couple were going

either until they were airborne. 'The man's got to plan his routes, plan where to land – this was a shambles. He took off with just him, Dodi, and the Princess. No security whatsoever,' observed a chagrined Trevor as he sped straight from Battersea to Oxted to prepare for the arrival of the helicopter from God-knows-where.

In fact, Diana was taking Dodi to visit Diana's psychic, Rita Rogers, in Derbyshire, an hour's flight from London. She was sharing with one of the men in her life the side of herself that called on the insights of clairvoyants, astrologers and therapists.

If secrecy was Dodi's goal, it was a fiasco. Dodi's growing distrust of even those closest to him was about to backfire. The pilot didn't know what he was looking for or where to land, and Diana was having difficulty identifying Rogers' house. The clattering green and beige helicopter, quickly recognized as belonging to Harrods by anyone who'd seen a newspaper in the past two weeks, hovered low above a housing estate while the three of them sorted it out. By the time it set down in a nearby field, a crowd of excited housewives and children had gathered, taking photos and home videos that appeared on the evening news.

They were spotted, too, as they arrived back at Oxted, even though Trevor and a crew of lads had worked feverishly to switch the helipad from the usual one to an old one near the house that was less exposed. Paparazzi had their telephoto lenses set up on the high ground behind the estate. 'Dodi was quite het up about the whole thing when he arrived at Oxted. Even Michael Cole, Fayed's public relations man, said in one of the news clips, in effect, "Dodi, you should know that you're the top story at the moment and they're going to be following you,'" says Trevor. 'It didn't take a genius to work out that they'd be going either to the Oxted estate, Park Lane, Kensington Palace or Harrods. They were the only four likely drop-offs.'

Trevor groaned when he heard where they'd been. But he had to admit that if the job was really about making life run smoothly for your principals, he was doing quite well. There was a sense of urgency as they darted from the helicopter into the house. 'But it seemed as if they were playing games at that stage, really.' Enjoying themselves. Once in the house, René worked his magic, with the couple having drinks again in the moonlit marquee and dining, this time, on a veranda overlooking the gardens. 'I think René saw it as a great turn-on, really,' says Trevor. 'He's very, you know, over the top with his "gorgeous, beautiful" sort of thing. He wasn't my sort of person.'

But butler and bodyguard shared the pleasure of a clean escape from Oxted next day, as they switched the couple to the Toyota van and themselves to the elegant Aston Martin – which Dodi permitted only Trevor and Johno to drive – and tricked the press momentarily as they exited the estate. At just the right moment, a big agricultural lorry inserted itself between the two-car convoy and the pursuing paparazzi, and they drove press-free back to London. 'We didn't "hoot joyously",' as René has said, 'but we were relieved.'

That night the couple went to a screening of the Harrison Ford film *Air Force One*. The Fayeds' chef cooked a simple dinner for them before the screening and secretaries had alerted Trevor to the plan in time for him to prepare. He'd done it many times before. Since the showing was pre-release, he drove over, picked the print up that afternoon from the movie studio's office – Columbia Pictures – and took it to the screening theatre. 'There were eight or nine reels of *Air Force One*, quite heavy things, you know. I dropped them off early. Dodi did not generally like me to do that because you're seeing a movie prior to release, and if you let these things out of your sight and they get stolen, then you're talking thousands of pounds' worth. But, with the Princess involved, I didn't want to be lugging the things when I was escorting her in.'

While the couple and René chatted about movies, Trevor was totally focused on eluding the media. He was in constant radio contact with the back-up car, so when they spotted a paparazzi vehicle, the back-up would cut it off and slow it down as Trevor darted and turned through the streets of the West End. As they pulled up right beside a very small screening theatre on a street no wider than the pavement, there was not a photographer in sight. 'We shook off all the paparazzi and did not get spotted going into the theatre. I parked, opened the door, had a quick check around, and we piled them inside.'

When Trevor returned from parking the car, he went through his usual manoeuvre: 'Coming in from the light straight into the dark, I'd edge my way along the wall and plonk myself down in the seat closest to the door.' This time, he almost sat in the Princess's lap.

'Oh, excuse me, Ma'am,' Trevor whispered in shock as he groped for a free seat. Dodi had moved her into Trevor's usual seat towards the front of the small theatre, but that was the only wrinkle in the evening. It had been exciting and flawless. It was the only night of the entire two-week London adventure that the couple went out. After eight days in London, security was functioning well, Trevor felt.

They dropped Diana off at the palace later. As the guard scrutinized the car, she chirped up, as she always did, 'It's only me.' They were waved in.

For all the challenges it created, the advantage of having the Princess in the car was that it diverted Dodi from nagging Trevor to 'go faster, go slower, do this, do that'. The couple were getting on very well. They were talking a lot, even though both were addicted to their mobile phones. There were no overt displays of affection in public – they wouldn't do that. 'But they seemed very close. They did seem to be enjoying each other's company. The buzz was even beginning that, if this romance carried on, they'd put a team of four on it at least.' Trevor might well be team leader. This job could be brilliant.

Suddenly, for Trevor, the action stopped. On 15 August, the Princess flew to Greece for a cruise with her good friend Rosa Monckton, a trip planned long ago, taking no security with her. Diana seemed to have accepted Fayed as her travel agent as she willingly switched from a commercial jet to his Gulfstream IV for the flight to the Aegean. Fayed's generosity was gaining him control of Diana's movements.

Dodi flew to Los Angeles, no doubt partly to try to calm Kelly Fisher after her press conference the day before. Fisher had been alerted to the romance several days earlier when the first photos and stories began to hit the tabloids, and would later tell a French judge, under oath, that 'our relationship lasted until August 7'. Until then, she claimed, she had continued to prepare for the wedding. 'The marriage was planned for August 9. Everything was fine. I had Dodi on the phone every day until the photographs of Dodi and Diana were published in the press.' Debbie Gribble, the *Jonikal*'s chief stewardess, was aware, in fact, that everything was not fine. During the cruise that spawned the 'kiss' photo, Debbie had watched René in 'muffled conversation, sweat pouring off his brow' as he took a call which, he confided to Debbie, was from Kelly Fisher. 'She had tracked René down and was demanding to know if Dodi was on *Jonikal* with Princess Di. It was quite a stressful time.'

Fisher's suspicions would develop into outrage at the global sensation of 'the kiss', and galvanize the spurned model into staging a press conference on 14 August in Los Angeles, where her celebrity feminist attorney Gloria Allred would declare that 'Kelly learned about Mr Fayed's betrayal . . . from the "kiss" photo'. She threatened to sue for breach of contract.

Trevor learned while the Princess was in Greece that the couple would be leaving on 21 August for another trip on the *Jonikal*. It would be just the two of them. For ten days. 'I was due to be off shift and someone else was going down to cover it. The bloke didn't really want to do it. He was not too happy about having to go away for two weeks.' After frantic London, the *Jonikal* would be relatively peaceful and secure. 'Sue's phone call had made it clear I had nothing really to go home for and I was enjoying working at this stage. And so I said, "Well, I'll do it. As overtime." I volunteered.'

'Is anyone else going with me?' Trevor asked. He was concerned about being on his own. He'd heard the stories about how the couple had scooted off unaccompanied on the last short trip on the *Jonikal* with only one man, John Johnson, aboard. John was laid-back, he'd never complain, but even he had got a bit stressed out.

'For God's sake, please don't tell me I'm going to be on my own. One person's not enough to look after two people, with the romance out in the news.'

'Kez will be coming,' Trevor was told. 'That's all?' he asked, astounded. I need more, Trevor argued. 'That's all,' the team leader confirmed.

But the situation had its appeal. 'In London, I'm just a cog in a wheel in a big security picture,' he thought. 'Out on the *Jonikal*, basically, I'd be in charge. Because, for better or worse, Kez and I would be the only ones there.'

Trevor had three days 'to come home and sort myself out prior to going out. Mum was my point of contact. She had the phone number. I told her I was going away for two weeks.' She'd know soon enough that Trevor was on the *Jonikal* with Dodi and Diana.

Dodi arrived back in London on 21 August. Diana was also due that day. She returned from Greece the same way she'd got there, on Fayed's Gulfstream jet, and took his helicopter to Battersea. She dashed home to the palace to freshen up and pack, and then helicoptered with Dodi from Battersea back to Stansted. It was late afternoon.

Trevor met Dodi at Stansted. He had driven up with the baggage, got it all put on board the Gulfstream, done the manifest check to make sure 'that what goes on comes off. Obviously you don't want to lose any.' They boarded for Nice. René came, too.

Already in St-Tropez with the Fayed family, now back from Finland, Kez hiked the trail down to the beach to find Fayed and pick up the several hundred pounds of bungs and floats for what he'd been informed would be just a three-day trip. He hadn't been asked, he'd been told he was going, and was feeling a bit disgruntled since his leave was overdue and he'd be missing a riding-club show. Kez had also been told that he and Trevor would be the sole security aboard the *Jonikal*. 'We'll need a few more blokes, sir,' Kez respectfully said to the Boss. 'No, no, we're going to keep it low-key. Low-key,' Fayed insisted. 'I just want to make sure that they have a good time and that they're safe.' How a man so obsessed with security could reduce it to such low levels for his own son and the Princess of Wales was beyond Kez. Still, it was only three days.

4

The Last Odyssey

Their arrival started well as Kez moved the couple from the car to the tender. The *Jonikal* awaited them offshore. With Trevor handling the luggage at the airport, Kez greeted the Princess with his usual, 'Good evening, Ma'am. It's nice to see you again,' and her reply, 'Hello, Kez, how are you?', was as friendly as ever. Moments later Dodi turned to Kez and ordered, 'Kill that mother-fucker!' as he spotted a photographer on the dock at St-Laurent-du-Var near Nice. Kez and the crewman were shocked; he'd hurled this crude bomb right in front of the Princess, and the trip had not even begun. Let Dodi's anger not infect the festive atmosphere, Kez prayed in that electric moment. Rising to the occasion, the Princess ignored Dodi's words and boarded the tender with unruf-fled poise as Kez gave her his hand. Settling Diana as swiftly as he could, Kez went across to the photographer and said, in a fierce whisper the Princess couldn't hear, 'Piss off,' which he did. The tender moved off quickly from the dock as Kez called the *Jonikal* bridge by ship-to-shore radio to alert Luigi, the captain, 'We're on our way.'

Trevor had been forced to move the couple swiftly into an armoured Mercedes at the airport, driven by one of the best chauffeurs in the organization, and send them off to the dock at St-Laurent-du-Var without him. He'd called Kez to say, 'We've landed. They're towards you now, I'm dealing with the baggage.' But it was not to his liking that he'd let them out of his sight on the ground.

There were too few blokes. 'There was me, and two of them, and all the baggage. Theoretically, yes, someone else should have sorted out the baggage. But they didn't trust anyone with their stuff. If I'd gone off with them and, say, her suitcase was left on the plane, I'd have been fired without a doubt,' says Trevor. 'But I'd not been told about any physical threat to the couple. The trip was to be low-key and the photographers were the immediate problem.'

Indeed. Six paparazzi were waiting for them on the jetty as Dodi and the Princess arrived, not just the photographer Dodi had spotted. Hours before, Kez had noted that several of the paparazzi had their tripods set up on the jetty and that there were two small boats in the harbour. 'They'd been tipped off. I don't know for certain who by,' says Kez. 'But I have my own opinions.'

The tender sped off briskly to the *Jonikal*. No press

boats could move fast enough to intercept them. They'd be aboard in ten minutes, with Trevor following shortly on the next tender trip. The holiday could begin and Trevor determined to make it just that, and to keep it 'low-key', as the Boss had ordered.

Captain Luigi Del Tevere started the engines and motored south for several hours, finally dropping anchor at nearly 2 A.M. near St-Tropez. At 9:20 the next morning, they set off on another short leg to Pamplona Bay, the closest place to the family's villa a tender could land without using the villa's tiny, exposed beach. The small yachting club there, the Pamplona Bay Yacht Club, offered a little more privacy. Trevor was told by Luigi, who'd been talking to Fayed security onshore, that the couple were going to the villa. For a late lunch with the family, Trevor assumed.

Trevor dashed to join them but was told by Dodi he wasn't needed. 'Dodi didn't want me along. Two people on holiday together, they don't want two gorillas standing over them every minute of the day, do they?' He understood, but he didn't like it. At 4 P.M., Trevor watched one of the lads take them ashore in the tender. It was just a short distance, but two paparazzi boats were following. The St-Tropez lads were waiting for them at the yacht club with vehicles to whisk them the five minutes up the hill to the villa. Trevor received a call from the ground, saying, 'We've picked them up,' and then a call reporting they'd arrived at the house.

Butler and chief stewardess, René and Debbie,

scurried to make sure everything was impeccable and
ready for the couple's return to the yacht. Aperitifs would
be prepared, music playing, candles lit. René would be
hovering close – too close, in Trevor's estimation; he felt
he didn't give them enough space.

Three hours later the couple stepped back aboard after
their visit ashore. This time there had been seven
paparazzi boats.

As they departed Pamplona Bay a few hours later, the
Jonikal moved beyond the forcefield of Fayed security.
Trevor and Kez were on their own, sole security for a
woman whose every move was worth a fortune to the photographers who could get their pictures on the market
first. Once they were aboard, Trevor deemed the *Jonikal*
'a secure environment. It was fine if they were never
going to get off the boat. But they would be getting off the
boat. It's when they set foot ashore that people were
needed.'

As Dodi's man, Trevor was in charge. And he had no
idea where they were going. 'On a trip like this, you'd
have expected to know the duration of the trip, where you
were going, the dates, the venues, whatever. We had no
itinerary.' Secrecy was the Fayed pattern, Debbie confirms: 'In this industry of superyachts, the owners usually
give the captain and crew a rough timetable of the dates
and cruise plan. But in true Fayed style, no one was ever
to know a thing about any plans, cruises, guests or dinners on board.'

The *Jonikal* would never be without company. A

relentless shadow fleet of press boats would follow them, small rented powerboats that would dog them like the albatross.

Yet Trevor felt optimistic about the trip. After London, he was confident in handling the paparazzi. You could never get rid of them. They had their job to do. They were already here, part of this trip. The best thing to do, he'd learned, was to chat with them and try to get some co-operation. You don't want to make enemies of them. 'You can't get your knickers in a twist, can you. My personal opinion of it was that it was controllable.' Kez agreed.

The second night out, he and Trevor had volunteered for an additional job: night watch. This meant checking the anchor line, scanning radar triangulation of fixed points to make sure the boat was not drifting, fire watch, and patrolling the decks. 'The crew seemed short-staffed and we felt we needed to help out. But we worked to the couple's needs, and our day theoretically finished when they went to bed.' They'd be doing the night shift from midnight to 4 A.M., with one of them sleeping in the captain's chair on the bridge for two hours while the other patrolled. 'Part of the night we had no security awake at all. There were only the two of us, and we needed to be lively in the day. We were working eighteen-hour days most of the time – a whole day's work, then the night shift, sleep for a short while, then be up for the day. I'd have liked more people,' says Trevor.

While they slept, there would be a crewman on watch

during those few hours before dawn but, to the bodyguard's knowledge, no trained professional was available
to protect the most high-profile couple of the day.

Exhausting, yes. But, Kez reminded himself, it was
only a three-day trip. Trevor had warned him on the dock
when he first arrived, 'She's going to be longer than three
days,' but Kez preferred to believe the three-day version.
He could take that. And, no matter how sleepy, he
became fully alert when the Princess appeared.

She'd be up on deck each morning around eight,
before Dodi. Most mornings, she'd see Kez scanning the
paparazzi with his binoculars and say, 'How many today,
Kez?' 'You'd pass her the binoculars and she'd have a
look, and you'd be laughing and joking about it. On occasions, she was giggling and waving. One morning, she
arrived on deck looking absolutely stunning in one
bathing suit, saw the number of photographers and went
below. Then she came back in another bathing suit, still
looking stunning.' She co-operated, made no effort to
hide. Kez observed that 'in all the photographs, you very
rarely saw her looking glum'.

Dodi was not as relaxed. As the *Jonikal* departed St-
Tropez late next morning, 23 August, their second full
day, three yachts followed them and a helicopter circled
intermittently overhead. Dodi was perturbed. He had
come up to the bridge as he usually did each morning to
talk over the day ahead with Luigi. 'What can be done?'
he demanded. Luigi took down their numbers, but
shrugged. They were not hovering dangerously close.

Luigi set a course straight out to sea, and the helicopters did not follow. But the boats were following, 'trailing us like sharks', Kez observed. Dodi wanted to outrun them.

Trevor spent much of his time on the bridge that day. You could spot approaching vessels best from there. You could also try to get information from Luigi as to what Dodi's plans were. They were usually laid out spontaneously each morning and they changed so often through the day that Trevor never called London and reported their location until they'd actually dropped anchor. At 2:55 that afternoon, he called London as the *Jonikal* moored at St-Jean-Cap-Ferrat, just west of Monte Carlo.

Two paparazzi boats were anchored nearby. But since Trevor felt the *Jonikal* was secure, he decided that both he and Kez would go ashore for a short recce. 'Two are better for recces than one.' Debbie, on a hunt for fresh flowers, joined them. 'Dodi had asked me to fill the yacht with flowers, which is not always a practical move on a yacht because everything needs to be stuck down or stowed in a safe place, and vases are never ideal. I'd bought masses of flowers in San Remo before the cruise – mainly Stargazer white and pink lilies, which always look stunning and have a beautiful smell – and displayed them around the yacht.' But Debbie found no fresh flowers in Monte Carlo – she would find none anywhere as they moved on to smaller Italian ports. So she bought a few provisions for the chef, Christiano, for his nightly *pièce de résistance*.

Late that evening, Dodi pulled another surprise.

Trevor and Kez had settled in for what promised to be a quiet evening aboard the boat when they got wind of plans for a spur-of-the-moment walkabout in Monte Carlo. In just five minutes, the couple would be boarding the tender for shore. It was a gorgeous night. They had dined on the deck, watching night fall on villa-dotted hills that were breathtakingly beautiful. You could see why the pull to go ashore could be irresistible. But Trevor knew from his very brief recce that the streets were chock-a-block. The picture-book houses were perched on very steep hills. Trevor had never been here before in his life, and the short recce had left him no time to plan – to find hospitals, liaise with police, plan a route. It was a security shambles even for a civilian operation. But, fine, it was their holiday and he'd just get on with it. Trevor and Kez yanked on shirts and trousers, grabbed their phones, radioed up, and ran for the tender.

As Luigi manoeuvred the tender towards a discreet side of the harbour under cover of darkness, the five of them – Dodi, Diana, the two bodyguards and René – couldn't believe their luck. They were apparently unseen. 'We'll radio in when we need you to pick us up,' Trevor called to Luigi as they unloaded and began walking towards the town. Then Diana gasped 'Oh, my God' and 'got all in a fluff' as she spotted a member of the paparazzi, camera poised, dead ahead. 'She knew his name. He'd apparently done a nasty batch in the papers. So we turned back towards the tender, speeding up to a run, and jumped back on.' Luigi scooted to the other side of the harbour, and, with no paparazzi in sight, they walked briskly into the anonymity of the streets. They'd escaped. The Princess's pace quickened with the exhilaration of freedom. She walked straight up the steep streets of Monte Carlo, perfectly comfortable, while Dodi struggled alongside. They both wore baseball caps, but there any parallels ended. 'They were chatting away,' Trevor noted, amused, 'but Dodi was getting a bit puffed because he wasn't very fit.'

Dodi may not have been Trevor's kind of bloke but René was even less so. He theatrically puffed out his chest and darted his eyes back and forth like a Hollywood FBI man. 'He was a complete pain in the arse, pretending to be a bodyguard, in the tightest of tight shorts with a little T-shirt on.' 'His shorts were so tight you could tell what religion he was,' Kez adds, laughing.

With August tourists everywhere in the town, they tried to steer Dodi clear of the busiest streets, as he directed, at every corner, 'right here, left here'. With Kez on point, Trevor at the rear, and René self-importantly trying to get in on the act, the five of them strode past shops, squares, cafés and bars, peeked in a few but retreated when the Princess was recognized. Trevor kept thinking, 'He'll stop here and have a drink, or get something to eat somewhere, or do some serious window-shopping around the boutiques.'

'To be honest, I needed a water stop. But Dodi didn't want to stop anywhere. He seemed so worried about them being recognized, so fearful they'd be hassled.' Dodi didn't seem to have a clue where he was going. This walk, in fact, was a haphazard replay of a walk that Dodi, the Princess and René had taken in Monte Carlo several weeks earlier, when the single bodyguard, John Johnson, had tried to cover the pair – a walk he had reported to Trevor as a hopeless mess.

Trevor and Kez kept the harbour and the *Jonikal* in sight over their right shoulders as their point of reference, in case a quick escape was required. The desultory stabs at window-shopping had stopped, and 'the Princess was striding out and they just kept walking and walking and walking'. She seemed to be revelling in this rare taste of unplanned freedom. Of course she courted the press. But, from things she'd told Trevor after her recent trip to Greece with no security, she had had enough of the media mob. He'd watched her walk past appealing little restaurants and bars, her head down, as people spotted her. 'I felt a little sorry for her, to be honest.'

The walk was fast becoming a route march. What had looked so gorgeous from the sea was, on foot, bloody steep. Sweating, Trevor was thinking ironically, 'This is a lovely little holiday stroll,' and as they broke on to the main road out of Monte Carlo the road sign gave the number of kilometres to France. They were walking to France! They'd lost sight of the harbour. 'Where are we?' Dodi asked as they stumbled on a bus stop. Here they were, the targets of every tabloid photographer in the world, totally lost, huddled at a bus stop trying to read the map in the dim street light. As a professional, Trevor was

appalled. But suddenly the Princess started giggling.
'Just paint the situation. You have to laugh, don't you?'
says Trevor. 'There's myself and Kez, the two security
blokes, and a butler, and you have the most famous
woman in the world trying to find out where she is in
Monte Carlo at a bloody bus stop! I mean it's a joke, isn't
it.' She was giggling at Dodi getting them lost, and at the
adventure of it.

Dodi led the procession downhill and towards a beach
hotel he seemed to remember, a straggling retreat from
Moscow in Kez's view. Things went silent between the
couple; 'Dodi was puffed out.' Parched and sweating,
Trevor wanted to say to him, 'Look, just relax and enjoy
your holiday. We'll look after you. We'll try our very best
to do that.'

'We got to the hotel, gagging for a drink of water. We
weren't overly dressed to go inside, but I thought they'd
go in and sit in the reception while we organized a pick-
up.' Instead, Dodi sat outside on the wall – 'absolutely
bloody ridiculous', to Trevor's mind – and ordered the
bodyguards to go off and get a bottle of Evian water from
the hotel manager. While others dined and partied
inside, the Princess waited outside, giving Trevor another
glimpse of how limiting her life really was.

Trevor phoned Luigi; thank God he knew where the
hotel was, and would be over to pick them up, if they
could get the gate to the beach open – it was locked tight
for the night.

As Trevor and Kez sat on the wall sharing a bottle of

water, waiting for the hotel manager to find the night-security man to open the gate to the beach and the jetty, Kez remarked that if he'd tried to show his girlfriend a good time like that, he'd have been dumped on the spot.

Since the crash, this walk in Monte Carlo has taken on greater significance. It would turn one of the most bally-hooed 'proofs' of a serious romance into B-grade fiction. Videos Trevor saw after the crash, at least two Diana books and any number of newspaper stories claim, vari-ously, that on 22 or 23 August, the second or third evening of this trip – or, in some versions, a week or ten days before the Paris crash – the couple went ashore at Monte Carlo, revisited the Repossi jewellery store they had first visited on 5 August, ordered a $200,000 emer-ald and diamond ring, and arranged to have Alberto Repossi himself deliver it to Paris for collection at the end of the trip, on 30 August. This was the famous 'engagement' ring Dodi was, reportedly, planning to give to Diana the night they died. The ring may be real, but the circumstances of its purchase, its purpose, and its movements during and immediately after the tragic night are lost in myth.

No, says Trevor, emphatically. There was no visit to Repossi on this trip. Kez confirms. The couple went ashore in Monte Carlo only once, on the 23rd, the third night of the cruise, and never went into a jewellery store. The only other opportunity they might possibly have had was the previous night when they went ashore at

St-Tropez. But the time-frame, scarcely three hours away from the yacht, makes it almost impossible for them to have driven the clogged and twisting coast road and back as well as visiting the shop. Also, 'I was in charge of their security,' says Trevor, 'and it's more than courtesy, it's strictly required protocol that security on the ground had to report to us any movements of our principals outside the family compound. It would have been a total violation of orders, a sackable offence. We were never informed. It is virtually impossible that it happened.'

And it simply made no sense. Why would the couple abandon Fayed and family at the villa to take a tortuous drive to Monte Carlo when they would be comfortably anchored off the town's harbour the next day?

Although Repossi has reportedly agreed that the couple visited his store 'about ten days before the accident', he personally made no sighting; he was absent that day.

Whatever may have happened on another day, the story, Trevor suspects, was circulated to promote the romance, then picked up by journalists who may not have checked the facts. This became explosive as Fayed made the Monte Carlo shopping trip for the ring during the final *Jonikal* voyage not only proof of Diana's plans to marry his son, but the centrepiece of his wild assassination theory – a conspiracy which would blossom extravagantly on the Internet, beyond Fayed, and in allegations which found their way into the French investigation after the crash, eventually naming the

British government, Prince Philip, Camilla Parker Bowles – and Trevor – among the perpetrators.

Though Dodi and Diana apparently visited the Repossi store in Monte Carlo on their earlier *Jonikal* cruise, that visit did not serve Fayed's design. The fifth of August was too early in the romance to be convincing as the date they might have ordered an engagement ring. Although 'ring' stories appeared within days of the crash, it was not until February 1998, in an exclusive interview in the *Mirror*, that Fayed revealed the full scenario. By the day of the crash, Diana had accepted Dodi's proposal, he claimed, and 'Dodi had planned to present the engagement ring to Diana when they arrived back at his apartment'. Fayed himself claims he paid for 'the stunning engagement ring . . . selected a week before the crash at the exclusive Repossi jewellery store in Monte Carlo'.

Then, in the spring of 1999, Fayed would tie the ring directly to his assassination theory, revealing the plot to the *Daily Star*: Diana and Dodi were set to announce their engagement on Monday, 1 September, as soon as she broke the news to the Princes. The CIA found out about the impending announcement by bugging Diana's call to her pal Lucia Flecha de Lima, wife of the Brazilian ambassador in Washington, on the afternoon of her death. The CIA immediately tipped off Britain's MI6, which unleashed its operatives on the Place de l'Alma. 'The plot to kill Diana was kicked into high gear as soon as British authorities found out from the CIA that Dodi had

...evor, aged about four, with his ...her. When Trevor was seventeen ... found his dad slumped dead over ... wheel of his car, an experience ... would later describe as the most ...umatic of his life.

An early shot of Trevor
the rugby player.

AFP

Army days: setting up a general-purpose machine gun in Oman.

Training for the army team: practising the back-stroke.

vor at home in Oswestry.

MIDLANDS MEDIA PICTURES

Family portrait – from left to right: Trevor, John, Jill, Ernie and Gareth.

TEGWYN ROBERTS

OPPOSITE, T
Fayed's luxury yach
the *Jonikal* – 'half th
length of a rugby pitch
Trevor reckone

OPPOSITE, BOTT
Diana and Har
jet-skiing off St-Trope
during the first tri
17 July 199

Trevor and Sue, on their wedding day in 1995.

Diana and Trevor waving at each other in the south of France. Trevor found her delightful and was grateful for the way the presence of her and her sons lightened the atmosphere among the Fayed family

MICHEL DE FOU

The American model Kelly Fisher, Dodi Fayed's former girlfriend, with her lawyer, Gloria Allred. Fisher threatened to sue Dodi for breach of contract after the publication of the famous 'kiss' photo of him and Diana.

Dodi and Diana during the second trip to the south of France.

Diana snapped from long distance aboard the *Jonikal*.

Trevor's employer, and Dodi's fathe
Mohamed Al Fayed, enjoying some water spor
off the coast of St-Tropez. Just six days lat
the idyll would be shattere

picked out . . . a ring for his future bride,' said the *Star* – the ring 'he had seen ten days previously'. 'The only reason my son and Diana were in Paris that night was so that he could personally collect the ring and propose to her,' Fayed told the *Star*. 'They deserved a lifetime's love together, and this beautiful ring was to put a seal on that.' The ring, now on display as part of the memorial to Dodi and Diana at Harrods, became the incendiary spark for the global spread of conspiracy theories that fuelled political and racist passions, clouded the investigation and besmirched the innocent.

But all this was in the future. Aboard the *Jonikal*, the cruise went on. The next day, as they left Monte Carlo and anchored at Portofino, Dodi may have had thoughts similar to Kez's after the Monte Carlo fiasco. He told Trevor, 'We're going out for a meal tonight.' It would be a challenge. Portofino was tiny, very popular, and picturesque – the Princess could lean on the rail of the boat and watch children jumping from the cliffs. The more high-profile the place, the more paparazzi, they'd noted. There were swarms of them here. But if the couple were not going to be prisoners aboard the boat, Kez and Trevor must make this evening work. They gleaned tips from Luigi on walks and restaurants.

As soon as the couple had finished their late-morning swim, Trevor and Kez went ashore. 'The couple assured us they were staying on the boat. The only bad things that could have happened were, a) the boat could have sunk, or b) they could have sailed off without us,' says Kez. They spotted a small castle. The route was steep, but it was feasible. They raced back to the boat to supervise more swimming, putting a tender between the Princess and the press boats, then went ashore to recce again as the couple settled in for their afternoon lunch on the deck.

Half an hour the other side of Portofino, they found a charming restaurant. It had a patio with a commanding view, attractive tropical plants and green and white awning. 'It would be a good place to take the missus to. It would cost a few quid,' said Kez, giving it his seal of approval. They checked the dress code: 'Are chinos okay? All we've got is trousers and shirt.' They arranged the parking, bunged the *maître d'* and told him, 'We'll call you when we're on our way.' There were no Mercedes available, limousines were too high-profile, so they arranged the two best cars they could get. They checked locations of hospitals and police – and felt delighted as they returned to the boat. People didn't know how long it took to do a good recce – a full day for a simple night at the theatre. This was the most thorough recce they'd had a chance to do on the trip.

'We get back on board and, then – nothing,' laughs Kez. Dodi and the Princess had decided to eat aboard. The reason could be seen with the naked eye, let alone with binoculars. Spread before them, on land and sea, was a landscape alive with photographers. Crowds of them on the headland and the beaches. A huge blue and white cruise ship sporting a US flag was moored in the harbour, and its tenders had been shuttling its passengers close by the *Jonikal*, the tourists leaning over the side trying to get shots of the pair. Their travel agents had never promised them this! Trevor cancelled everything ashore – losing a £100 bung. The couple never actually went out for a meal on the entire trip.

'Dodi is getting uptight,' Trevor was thinking. 'He's too desperate to have things go smoothly to impress the Princess.' You can't be tense all the time. As a bodyguard, you'd burn out and be useless. But Dodi didn't trust the crew. He suspected they were tipping off the press. The yacht manager, Mario, had been fired for allegedly leaking the news of Dodi and Diana's top-secret cruise to Sardinia in early August, although Luigi told Debbie he was certain that wasn't true. Dodi was now asking Trevor, 'Why are these paparazzi with us? Do you think Luigi is phoning them?' He suspected everyone. 'He was seeing ghosts under his bed.' To be honest, Trevor and Kez thought the crew were 'fantastic, thoroughly professional', but had never fully trusted them either. They were hastily assembled after the English crew had left – a multinational mix of Filipino, French, Portuguese, Italian and New Zealanders.

As Dodi's growing distrust led him to keep his intentions an even deeper secret from his bodyguards, they recruited two of the female crew to report any news they picked up about Dodi's plans. Not to spy, but just to give the bodyguards warning so that they could be prepared.

Both Debbie and the Reverend Myriah Daniels, Dodi's personal masseuse, had intimate access to the couple. Myriah, a vibrant young American who described herself as a 'missionary of natural spiritualism', practised what Trevor saw as touchy-feely holistic massage and healing. 'They were the English-speakers on the boat. We all chatted. I used Myriah a bit because she was a friend of Dodi's. I'd get her to gently quiz Dodi for information, and she'd pass it on. I'd also get her to push him in the way we wanted him to go. She was helpful.'

'But the crew were working their nuts off,' Kez says. 'The captain was complaining he was almost too tired to sail the boat – the skipper, of all people, is doing watches!' 'Luigi had constantly complained to me that he didn't have enough qualified crew on board. He tried to explain this by phone but never got anywhere,' says Debbie. Take the crew from the *Sakara*, he had been told, but that didn't happen. Why not use the *Cujo* as a floating barracks if there isn't room on the *Jonikal* for more crew and another two or three security, Trevor and Kez had thought earlier. The *Cujo* had been used that way before, to serve the *Sakara*'s needs. No luck. The *Cujo* was going in for a refit, they were told.

Three days into the trip, a tender pulled up to the *Jonikal* carrying Stefano, skipper of the *Cujo*. As Trevor and Kez welcomed him on the bridge, he told them, 'I'm joining the crew as well because it's going to be a week's trip.' Kez's frustrations rumbled up into black thunder. 'We're two blokes trying to do more than two blokes' jobs.

If they can send more crew, they can bloody well send more bodies!' he said. Standing on the starboard side of the bridge, he snapped his phone out and said to Trevor, 'Let's ring London right now . . . If they can send five bags of sand to Finland for the kiddies' beach, they can send us a lad or two.' But his phone was down.

As Kez remembers it, Trevor got through to the team leader at the Ops Room and told him, 'We need more blokes. We're knackered already, and now it's going to be a longer trip.' Kez could guess by Trevor's expression what he was hearing on the other end of the line.

This was the first of two calls for help from the bodyguards, calls Fayed's team would claim had never been made.

They asked for help again another evening. While the couple were finishing a late dinner on the rear deck, Trevor and Kez had gone forward to give them a bit of privacy, and were talking as they waited for the night watch. Trevor was making one of his frequent calls to London Ops when Kez says he heard him throw in another request. 'Can you give us more blokes here? The paparazzi are getting worse.' With Fayed's huge security staff at St-Tropez and a helipad on the boat, help could have been there in an hour. The answer was no. This would be their last request for help.

Even the ebullient Princess was beginning to show signs of stress from the hounding by the press. The couple went for a walk on the beach next day, at a far less popular place, Porto Venere. While they were strolling

along the beach, and Trevor and Kez stayed on the land-
ward side near the sand dunes, they spotted a single
photographer. A local lad, it seemed, who had hidden
his camera lens behind his hand. When he demanded,
'Let me take a photo,' Trevor and Kez tried to discourage
him. 'I'm going to take it anyway, or I'll really hassle
you,' he shouted back. Diplomacy was useless. As Dodi
and Diana headed back to the tender, 'her face showed
she was complaining to Dodi, "We can't even go for a
walk on the beach."' Later, aboard, Diana was 'hacked
off', and was seen crying in the lounge. It flew through
the crew that she was in tears.

Jonikal was the only safe haven. But even its 'secure
environment' was being breached from within by Dodi.
'You might want to know that Dodi's just gone swimming
off the back,' Debbie informed the bodyguards, sending
Trevor and Kez into wild activity. 'Christ!' thought Kez.
'Why the hell didn't you tell us, you idiot!' – thoughts that
would not seem destined to win Debbie as his girlfriend,
as she would become several months later. Trevor was
now totally pissed off. He knew the crew had never had
such high-profile principals aboard before. 'But I'd been
telling them, "You've got to let us know. If you see them
going for a swim, come and tell me or Kez."'

He leaped on the tender and manoeuvred himself
between Dodi and the photographers' boats. 'It had nothing to do with jumping in front of a speeding bullet. It was
the fact that he could drown. Or he could get hit by someone on a jet-ski going past – or anything.' Of course Dodi

wanted to be able to slip over the side and go swimming. But it was his choice to be here with the Princess of Wales. He didn't seem to grasp that he was no longer a private person.

The swimming episode combined with Dodi never telling him anything was the last straw for Trevor. He picked up his phone and, for the first and only time on this trip, called Fayed's chief of personal security, Paul Handley-Greaves, direct in London to complain about Dodi's behaviour, hoping it would get back to the Boss – in which case he was sure that Dodi would then get to hear about it.

Debbie had observed some of the side of Dodi that caused the bodyguards such grief. 'He loved to be in control, and really enjoyed slinging orders at people left, right and centre.' An echo of his father. Dodi came across as someone who liked to have people around him all the time, Debbie noted, confirming Myriah's sense that Dodi suffered from insecurity. In the past, he had invited Myriah to parties just for company, she told Debbie. 'I think he needed constant attention from his staff, and was very extravagant.' On one occasion, Dodi returned from a shopping-fest ashore with, by Debbie's count, five cashmere sweaters – sweaters still wrapped in plastic when he died – three pairs of shoes and two leather bags.

Twice she had seen him lose his temper with René, 'But he was never that way with me. Dodi was a nice enough person, very appreciative of everything we did.

He was polite and nice to the crew, and relaxed while on board.'

Debbie had done her job now for so many years that she sometimes lost sight of what a rarefied lifestyle this was. The Princess unpacked her own bag. But Debbie's job, and René's, was to make it unnecessary for Dodi or Diana to lift a finger, arm or foot to get whatever they wished for – a towel, drink, newspaper – so that full energies could be spent on pleasure, on talk and sunbathing, on their computers or mobile phones, or reading the news clippings on their trip that were faxed in daily. If either frowned at some imperfection, Debbie had failed at her job.

Dodi had already suggested that he might like her to join René and Myriah as part of his personal team. But until her contract was up in October, she would focus on the *Jonikal*'s interior world, viewing the romance through her unique and intimate lens, a romance played out, at Diana's request, to the theme music of *The English Patient*.

'They weren't openly affectionate. But when I was moving around the boat, I did walk into the saloon to turn the lights on and they were kissing. They burst out into giggles, but after that incident they didn't seem to care and, to be honest, I tended to ignore it. Two people don't discuss business on a cruise like this. Moonlight, champagne and caviar? I mean, come *on*.'

Annoyed with later reports that she had discussed details of their sleeping arrangements, Debbie says only

that, 'they slept in the Master Stateroom complete with
marble *en suite*, two twin cabins, dressing-room and
wardrobes, and master cabin the full width of the yacht –
all closed off by a hallway and two doors. They used all
three cabins for luggage, showering, sleeping and dressing.' End of story.

The crew – especially the personal staff – seemed
oblivious of the frustrations of the bodyguards. 'They
were enjoying the couple,' Kez could see. Glimpsing the
romance from close quarters as it unfolded within the
interior of the boat, immune from the outer world Trevor
and Kez dealt with, they felt only minor frustrations – a
change in the choice of wines, an unavailable flower. To
René, the days were 'a festival of sunshine, sea water,
candlelight and starlight, one indistinguishable from
another'.

An interest in that side of things was simply gossip as
far as Trevor and Kez were concerned. 'We were far too
busy to notice any of that rubbish, even if we'd wanted
to,' says Kez.

'The crew pictured us as a couple of real uptight
blokes,' Trevor knew. 'They couldn't understand how we
worked a shift,' Kez adds. 'If it was lunch, Trevor would
typically be on the bridge with his binoculars, and I'd
rush down to the galley, get as much food on my plate as
I could, eat it as quickly as I could, and run upstairs.
Then Trevor would rush down and repeat the performance.' For the bodyguards, midday was when the
couple could still jump off and go for a swim, or decide to

go ashore. For the crew, the midday meal was a major event of the day, and they would watch the British body-guards, aghast. 'They'd condemn us for putting pasta and meat and everything on the same plate. They'd say, "These English, they're barbarians." If things were calm and peaceful, Dodi thought we weren't doing anything,' Kez later learned from Myriah.

As they watched the crew drink wine with their dinner, the two of them would have loved a beer, 'but we bloody well never would. Can you imagine talking to your prin-cipal, and he catches a whiff of alcohol? You'd be sacked.' They had to stay on their toes, but they weren't the dull lads the crew thought they were. 'We're not saying we were on holiday. But we were enjoying our work. You've got to enjoy it,' says Trevor.

In the evenings, the differences between the crew's and the bodyguards' priorities mellowed. Most of the time. Kez, a passionate reader of the occult, would relax in the galley getting into lively discussions with Myriah on matters spiritual and psychic. But Trevor saw it as 'mumbo-jumbo'. 'My mother's compassionate and caring. But to link it to some invisible blooming spirit!' 'I'm a pie-and-pint man, myself,' he'd say, if Myriah tried to embroil him. But she'd lose even Kez when she responded to some casual question like, 'Are you enjoy-ing dinner?' with 'But is the dinner enjoying *you*?'

As they left Porto Venere in the early afternoon of 25 August, bound for Elba, three boats were following them.

Two had been shadowing them for days, with five or six photographers in each – Germans and Italians, they thought. They'd spoken to port authorities, but the boats had ignored the warnings. 'Try to do something about it,' Dodi demanded. Luigi and Trevor took the tender out to one of the boats to have a talk, and Luigi gave them hell in Italian. The Italians hurled back, 'We're not doing anything wrong, and, look, we can get worse – we can phone the English press if you want!' Back aboard, Dodi wanted to know, 'What was said?' 'No result,' Trevor reported. 'We asked them to keep their distance. They claimed they were not invading our personal space. Just doing their job. You can't stop people travelling the same sea lane as you.'

Kez had been excited about going to Elba, the place of Napoleon's exile, but when they dropped anchor in the early evening, he was disappointed. The island looked forbidding. A mistral was blowing. Dodi and Diana, too, had been driven to Elba against their will. With the *Jonikal* battened down against the wind, the outdoor salon cleared of its cushions, they all stayed aboard that evening and night.

And yet, next day, things were better – the idyll might be realized after all. On Tuesday, 26 August, at the tiny island of Molara off Sardinia, Dodi had his first, in Trevor's estimation, brilliant idea of the trip. Very late in the evening, with everything prepared and tables set for dinner on board, he told René, 'The Princess and I have decided to have a barbecue tonight – on the beach.'

René's and Christiano's hearts sank when they heard, as the chef grabbed chicken burgers, baby-back ribs and smoked sausages from the freezer. Debbie and René rushed to assemble the silver, crystal, wine buckets and half a dozen little folding tables from the deck. This was not to be a sand-in-your-face jam-sandwich sort of picnic.

Kez had recced the site that afternoon and had told Trevor, who had relayed it to Dodi, 'Not advisable for walking at night.' It was the most desolate place they'd found yet. A few deserted huts and goat trails. But it was secluded and private, and the bleakness would be obscured by the dark.

Luigi went ashore first to find a good site and light a bonfire on the beach. The first tender went ashore at about 9:30 or 10, René in his full butler's gear with black bow-tie, and Christiano in his tall chef's hat – 'It's like a Monty Python sketch!' thought Kez.

As the staff set up the barbecue, it became more like Fellini. René was in his element, conjuring magic from a place so uninhabitable that even shepherds had abandoned it to their goats. He spread blankets over the area, smoothing away every twig and pebble, and hid three small tables under a damask cloth to create a full-sized dining table, aglow with candles. He uncorked Dodi's favourite white Loire wine, chilling in buckets nearby, and served the Princess's favourite caviar as Christiano fired up the coals on the big metal grill. Trevor checked out the periphery. It was rough and coal-black. There would be no strolling here. But no one could creep up. It was secure.

After the couple had eaten, Luigi picked up the staff in the tender and took them and the equipment back to the boat while the couple stayed on to finish their wine. Only Trevor stayed with them, sitting discreetly in the shadows on a rocky outcrop only twenty feet from the two people a thousand paparazzi would kill to find. 'All that remained was the bonfire, a bottle of wine, glasses, and Dodi and Diana,' Trevor reflects with something uncharacteristically close to sentiment.

Sitting there with his hand-held Motorola two-way radio and Europager, 'with the Princess of Wales and a yacht in the distance – there could be a worse job. You could be digging ditches somewhere,' he was thinking. He might be 'bleeding to death from mosquitoes', but Trevor had to admit that, at times, the job could be great. They had survived Dodi's behaviour without serious mishap for six days, and Dodi had finally done what Trevor called 'giving a girl a nice time'. 'I couldn't pass comment on whether they were happy or not. But I could see the point in a nice barbecue on the beach.' Looking at her, Trevor still marvelled, 'How in hell has he ever scored with this woman?' – this beautiful, lively woman he had come to value for her human touch. He'd been close to them for six weeks now, and he still would never have put them together in a million years.

Starting their watch later that night, Trevor and Kez saw the last light of the beach fire die as they did their rounds. Their mood was good. The couple wouldn't be on deck until at least ten, they predicted, which meant an extra hour or two of sleep. These were the most peaceful hours of the trip. You'd pad around the deck in your bare feet, keeping everything quiet. Even the paparazzi were asleep. They'd fish a little to help stay awake – even caught a few – and check the radar every fifteen minutes. The ladder was pulled up. It was like a house all locked up for the night.

The peace didn't last for long. Three times the next day, 27 August, helicopters hovered low over the yacht, driving the Princess from the deck. Previously, Dodi had directed, 'Take down their numbers. Call the police.' They'd done that. Now, in a fury, he ordered, 'Shoot them down.' Dodi had wanted to camouflage the *Jonikal*'s name, cover it over, as if that would make any difference. You couldn't miss the boat. Now he wanted to wage war! He told Trevor 'to ring London to see if we could get some kind of night-vision laser device that, if cameras are pointed at us, would destroy the optics of the camera'. 'He may have read something about the laser range-finder they had in the army – if you flashed them in someone's eye, it would damage their retina,' Kez guessed. 'Basically, he read too many comics.' But the two pacified Dodi with the usual, 'Right, we'll get on to London to see if they can do anything.' All he wanted was an answer – and he never asked again.

Next day, ashore, Dodi was recognized for the first time. Oh, God, thought Trevor. He'd been anonymous before, but 'now Dodi was famous because of her'. While

Trevor tried to stop the photographer, Dodi disappeared, just vanished, and Trevor had to search the streets to find him. Watching Trevor, Kez realized that a shift was taking place in their two roles. 'At first, it was me that was getting annoyed, and Trevor who always had a nice calming influence on the pair of us.' As the days went by, Kez was growing a little more resigned, while Trevor's frustration had built. 'Within a few days, I would be off that job and going on leave. Whereas Trevor, I could see, was looking to the future and saying, "Well, bloody hell, I've got another X number of years working with this guy."' He could quit, of course, but if you did, it haunted you, Kez had seen. 'So as we moved towards the end of the trip, the rules had sort of changed. It was me, the bitter little dwarf, who was calming down the gentle giant.'

Both Trevor and Kez agreed that if Dodi and the Princess did get together it would be 'a recipe for disaster, security-wise, if he didn't start trusting us and giving us more information'. Rumours had begun before they left London that, if they remained a couple, Trevor would be team leader. 'In our civilian side of things, you can't get a more prestigious principal than her, can you?' But Dodi had to grow up. 'I've got to sort it out with Dodi,' Trevor told himself. But not in front of the Princess. He would seize his moment. Perhaps back in London.

Trevor had no idea if they would stay together. A comment the Princess made to Debbie suggests that Diana may have had her own doubts about how well she knew

Dodi. 'Once, after Dodi had been very dramatic about something daft like the mosquitoes, she said to me, "Debbie, what are these Arab men like?"' But Debbie didn't have a clue. 'I really don't know, Ma'am,' she responded, thinking to herself that Diana obviously didn't know Dodi that well, and was a little naïve.

As they dropped anchor at Cala di Volpe, an elegant and private Sardinian resort, you could feel the trip winding down. The mood had changed. The couple seemed a little restless. It had always been open-ended, but now the bodyguards could sense that the holiday was reaching its natural conclusion. 'They'd enjoyed themselves a lot of the time,' Kez felt. 'You've got to have a good time sailing around the Med, haven't you,' Trevor adds. But the two bodyguards had seen them, and the fabled journey, up close, 'warts and all. There's not a lot of people wake up looking beautiful. It's life, isn't it. Just because people are famous and rich, they're still people.' The bodyguards had seen the growing strain as had no one else.

They spent the second-to-last full day of the journey dropping into several small Sardinian ports, as if making one final, desultory effort to find the freedom that had eluded them. But the paparazzi never left them alone. They returned to Cala di Volpe and put down anchor for the last time.

On Friday, 29 August, there was a buzz from the crew that they were moving tomorrow. That they were going home. 'Home meaning the UK. We were overjoyed,' says

Kez. After dinner, the couple, the bodyguards and René went ashore for a stroll. They were too big and intrusive a group to go into shops or cafés, so the men held back as the couple found respite from the stares in a charming little garden within the resort's grounds.

Late that night, there was another buzz. We're going to Paris tomorrow. There had been no word from Dodi. No chance to prepare with Ops or to co-ordinate with Fayed's flagship in Paris, the Ritz, which would do their on-the-ground planning. Trevor was now thoroughly annoyed as Dodi continued to withhold information. He and Kez both packed their kit, ready for whatever the next day might bring.

They had told London of the possible move to Paris, so a contingency plan had been organized. 'We found out early the next morning [or it could have been very late the night before, Trevor thinks, his memory imperfect] that Paris was the next venue. Both London and the G4 [the Gulfstream jet] were informed, and we were given our take-off slot. London would arrange transport at the other end and inform the Ritz.'

A trip to Paris was a nice way to finish, the two mates agreed.

5

Prelude to Tragedy

Trevor led the Princess down the steps of the plane into heat that made the breezes of the *Jonikal* and the Côte d'Azur seem a distant dream. Parisians abandon their city to the tourists in August. It is always an uneventful month.

The Gulfstream had arrived without fanfare. The airport had not received a Sigma signal, which alerts that it is a state or VIP flight; no special instructions of any kind had been given. The Princess had not advised the British Embassy of her presence in France and had not requested any particular protection from the French authorities, the French investigation would later report.

The paparazzi, though, were waiting. Tipped off again – by their colleagues in Sardinia or by Fayed's people were the best guesses – they were grouped at the private terminal, their giant lenses recording every movement of the party as they exited. Trevor led his charges down the stairs and felt confident that, for this one last overnight stay, they could manage. He could see several *gendarmes* and motorcycle police standing by – airport police, he guessed. There was the back-up of the Ritz security, too. 'The Princess and Dodi were happy to be in Paris, were not at all anxious,' he felt. But here they faced a new and frightening dimension to the chase. In London, the paparazzi hunt by car, but in Paris they choose motorcycles and scooters as well. A shiny battalion of Hondas and Mitsubishis was parked alongside the Peugeots, ready for the chase. As Diana appeared, their engines started up. The tensions between the Princess and her pursuers that had built up, like the heat, over the summer, were ready to boil over.

Ordered by the Ritz, two vehicles, a Mercedes and a Range Rover, waited at the bottom of the ramp with their drivers. One was Philippe Dourneau, Dodi's regular driver in Paris and a licensed chauffeur of Étoile Limousine; the other, Henri Paul, a thinning-haired forty-ish man with glasses, was the assistant head of security for the Ritz. Dodi walked directly up to him, shook hands and chatted. Trevor had met him before. 'But he didn't click with me as a person. He was perhaps a little too chatty . . . But obviously Dodi had lots of faith in the man, the way he went to speak to him straight off.'

Trevor could see that the couple were eager to leave. They loaded up the two vehicles, with Trevor, the driver Philippe, Dodi and the Princess leading in the Mercedes, and Henri Paul driving the Range Rover as back-up, with Kez, Debbie, Myriah, René and the luggage aboard. They took off into a scene that made the chases in London seem tame. They were surrounded by screaming motorcycles, darting around the target vehicles, sometimes two to a bike so that the photographer could wield his camera and focus the powerful zoom lens. From the Mercedes, Trevor saw the escort of police outriders fall back at the boundary of the airport. They were on their own. He heard the Princess express her concern, not about the harassment, but that one of them might fall under the wheels and be killed. He could feel the good mood slipping away. Dodi gave Philippe orders to put his foot down and lose them and Philippe succeeded, skilfully manoeuvring past and out of reach of the bikes.

Having briefly shed their pursuers, they raced off to the Villa Windsor, former home of the Duke and Duchess of Windsor, and now leased by Mohamed Al Fayed. The bodyguards spent the night there when in Paris – in the security quarters. Dodi told Trevor to phone Kez and tell him to join them at the villa after dropping the others and the baggage off at his apartment.

Kez and Henri Paul were greeted by Ben Murrell, one of Fayed's British security men posted to the villa. Chatting with Henri Paul, Murrell noted that he smelled as if he'd had a very good lunch. If he did smell of the wine and garlic of 'a good lunch', it was disguised for Kez, a non-smoker, by the offensive smell of Henri Paul's cigars. They stayed at the Villa Windsor for no more than thirty or forty minutes, Trevor recalls. Fayed's own security video cameras recorded twenty-eight minutes. Hardly the long and leisurely stroll through their future home later claimed by Fayed's PR.

Before they left, Trevor managed to ask the Princess, 'What's the programme for the evening, Ma'am?' 'Well, eventually we'll be going out to a restaurant,' she replied. He couldn't very well do a recce on that scrap of information, could he?

The restlessness that had begun the last few days on the *Jonikal* became almost manic over the next few hours. From the Villa Windsor, the couple moved on to the Ritz. After a smooth de-bus by the bodyguards into the hotel's Imperial Suite, Diana – in safe territory within the Ritz, where the hotel's security personnel covered for the bodyguards – had her hair done in the beauty salon while Dodi drove with Trevor in the Mercedes the few hundred feet to the Repossi jewellery store, one of a series of famous jewellers which circle the Place Vendôme like a necklace. That Dodi decided to drive the short distance is a measure of the threat he now felt. Kez and the acting hotel manager, Claude Roulet, followed on foot, and they waited outside the store with Trevor for no more than five or ten minutes as Dodi went inside. He did not tell Trevor what he was doing but was apparently completing arrangements for 'the ring' to be delivered to the Ritz – the ring Dodi and Diana were inaccurately reported to have chosen and ordered in Monte Carlo on the just-finished *Jonikal* trip. Although

Trevor has a vague recollection of Dodi leaving the boutique carrying one of those small elegant shopping bags with strings, it has been continually reported that the ring was picked up and taken back to the Ritz by Roulet, and given to Dodi later.

As Kez walked back, pretending to be studying the column made by Napoleon from the melted-down bronze of 1,200 cannons captured at the Battle of Austerlitz, he was studying the paparazzi. There were several scooters. Several motorcycles. Tourists gathering.

Trevor got a call saying the couple would be going back to the Rue Arsène-Houssaye, just off the Champs-Élysées, to dress for dinner. Deciding to give them some privacy to counteract the growing tension, Trevor put the couple in the lead Mercedes with Philippe at the wheel, with Kez and himself following in the Range Rover. 'We could see the situation was winding them up, and we thought we'd just give them a bit of privacy, but within the bounds of our brief, which was to let them enjoy themselves and keep them safe,' says Trevor. They were followed by journalists, but Trevor saw his technique of reasoning with them paying off. 'We'd asked them not to take any photos during the journey, especially at junctions and traffic lights. They did what we asked.'

The calm was broken as they arrived and the paparazzi, who had been waiting outside Dodi's apartment, surrounded the entrance door as the Mercedes nosed into the street. They had become aggressive, and an incident was unfolding as Gérard, a security man at the apartments, confronted a photographer and pushed him. The fragile truce between bodyguards and paparazzi threatened to disintegrate. The Princess was shaken, Dodi angry. As soon as they got the couple upstairs in the apartment, Trevor and Kez came down to try to calm the photographers – in fact the reason Kez was on the trip in the first place, the only one he was given, was that he spoke some French. 'We know you've got to do your job,' he said to them. 'Look, get your shots as they come and go without hassling them, and hold off from any pictures while they're in transit.' Trevor shook hands with several of them, hoping he'd defused the situation, and that he'd bought a little privacy for the couple on the way to dinner – wherever that might be.

René had laid out Dodi's clothes, a casual brown suede jacket, blue jeans, a fine-checked grey shirt and cowboy boots. He claims that it is here that Dodi confided his plan to propose to the Princess that night, and showed the breathless butler 'the ring, a spectacular diamond-encrusted ring – a massive emerald surrounded by clusters of diamonds, set on a yellow and white gold band' sitting in 'a small, light-grey velvet box from . . . Repossi'. 'Make sure you have the champagne ready,' René reports Dodi saying, 'as he carefully closed the ring box and pocketed it'. Given René's devotion and obligation to Fayed and to Dodi's memory, his recollection may be coloured by, at the least, a vivid imagination and wishful thinking. As René set out chilled wine and caviar before they left for dinner, Diana changed into the casual kind of style permitted in late August in Paris – skinny white jeans, high-heeled black Versace sling-back pumps, and a sleeveless top under a beautifully-cut black blazer. She put on the gold earrings she loved to wear, and a pearl bracelet Dodi had given her.

'Where are they going?' Trevor asked René, again and again, while the two were dressing, desperately trying to find out what their evening plans were. 'I'd just had it. Zero information was coming from Dodi. I couldn't go knocking on their apartment door saying, "Hey, where are you going tonight?" You can't do anything more. You can't walk up and grab the butler by the scruff of the neck and say, "I need to bloody know." It was so frustrating.' René went in and out of the apartment. If he knew, he never shared it with the bodyguards. It was the Ritz's Claude Roulet who had made reservations for 9:45 at the fashionable Chez Benoît restaurant near the Pompidou Centre. Roulet waited for the couple there.

They were forty minutes late coming down, and on edge when they saw the number of paparazzi. But Trevor trusted the deal he'd struck and, again, put the couple up front with Philippe and followed with Kez in the Range Rover. As the two vehicles drove off, Kez called London on the car phone: 'We're on the move.' 'Where?' 'We have no idea!' The photographers raced along in escort, but honoured the deal, giving the couple a few minutes of privacy. Trevor hoped they could hold the lid on.

Inside the Mercedes, a decision had been made to

abort the plan to eat at Chez Benoît – it would be too public – and Trevor got a call that they were heading for the Ritz. Christ! No preparation. The paparazzi and tourists, by the time they'd left the Ritz last time, looked like a street fair, cameras everywhere, with a crowd of several hundred jostling at the entrance, like people waiting for a parade. As the excitement over where the couple would spend the night heightened, it would only get more intense.

It was 9:50 P.M. as the two-car convoy pulled up close to the front entrance of the Ritz. The mob was waiting. Trevor raced to the car's rear door and opened it, ready to block for the couple as they rushed through the revolving doors and inside. Once inside, the hotel was deemed a secure environment.

Dodi paused. The couple didn't move. Inside the car, it was like a freeze-frame in the movies. No action. For Trevor, 'this was the limit'. What was Dodi bloody doing? Trevor swiftly closed the car door again as the paparazzi zoomed in on the car. The delay was no more than a few seconds. But it was all it took for a successful de-bus to turn into a disaster. By the time Dodi moved, and things began to happen again, cameras were all over the car. The couple were engulfed. Dodi's hand went up to shield his face, the Princess looked anguished as she took a running stride towards the door. The results of Dodi's hesitation had enormously bothered the couple, Trevor saw as he pushed the photographers back. In the mayhem, one photographer slipped through the revolving door. Trevor got rid of him straight away, but Dodi turned on Kez and gave him 'the mother of all bollockings'. 'How the fuck did this fiasco happen? Why didn't you have the reception arranged?'

'You never told us where we were going. If you had, we'd have been able to phone ahead and get it sorted out,' snapped Kez, close to losing his temper, and at that Dodi wound his neck in a bit. Kez was trying to keep Trevor out of it.

They got the couple settled into the restaurant at the end of the long lobby. 'I'm going to sort it out with Dodi tonight,' Trevor muttered to Kez as they returned to the front of the hotel. Trevor got the journalists pushed back to the other side of the service road leading to the Ritz, and got the police to cordon them off far enough away so at least there couldn't be any physical assaults. At last, a chance to get a sandwich in the bar. They hadn't eaten since breakfast on the *Jonikal*, which seemed years and a million miles away.

They'd barely ordered their fizzy waters when they saw the couple walking through the foyer. They had left the restaurant for some reason. The Princess was crying, Kez noted. It was probably a combination of things, he guessed – being pursued by photographers that day, being looked at in the restaurant. At 10:01 P.M., the two hustled the pair up the grand staircase to the door of the Imperial Suite. 'We'll be eating in, go get yourselves some food,' Dodi told them as he closed the door. Back at the bar they sat at a table near the entrance where they had

a view of the staircase. At last, a club sandwich. 'The
food is great here,' thought Trevor. The next job would be
to get the couple back to the apartment after dinner – if
that's what Dodi decided to do. They'd eat, then wait for
them outside the doors of the suite.

Henri Paul came through the revolving doors of the
Ritz just a few seconds before 10:08, in suit and tie, a
jovial smile on his face and his ubiquitous cigar between
the fingers of his left hand. Although he was off duty he
had been phoning in frequently for reports on the
couple's movements and had received a call just before
ten o'clock from the Ritz's night-security manager,
François Tendil, telling him that the couple were going to
eat in their suite. On his own initiative, Paul had returned
to the hotel.

He turned up at the bar and joined Trevor and Kez,
who assumed he was on duty as they briefed him on the
couple's status. Kez chatted with him a bit as Trevor ate
his sandwich in silence, thinking, 'He does go on a bit,
doesn't he?' Kez had 'the distinct impression that Trevor
didn't like Henri Paul. I'd just met him that day, didn't
even know he was the second-in-command of Ritz security. I thought he was just a chauffeur.' Kez was
disgusted, again, by the smell of the cigars Paul was puff-
ing. As Paul ordered a yellow drink – juice, Kez
assumed – Paul made a joke about it being '*ananas*' –
pineapple, and the two had a crude little laugh over the
'ass' part of the word. 'Like a soldier's joke. I know it's
pathetic. But we were giggling away,' says Kez.

It was turning to nervous laughter. 'Things were getting a bit tense because Trevor wouldn't speak to him, and then Henri Paul was telling us that we shouldn't be eating here because Mr Klein, the hotel boss, wouldn't like it.' The nerve! There was no coffee shop; they couldn't leave the hotel. 'Well, I couldn't give a toss, because we work for Mr Fayed. Nobody else,' Kez snapped back. Trevor had been sitting there, staring at his food or looking outside. 'I have to admit that I lost interest very quickly,' he says. But as he heard Henri Paul 'get adamant' that Mr *Klein* was his boss, Trevor put the issue firmly to rest. 'Klein works for the Boss, and so do *you*!'

'We gobbled our sandwiches and left,' says Kez. The time spent with Henri Paul in the bar had been very brief – 'only five minutes', as Kez recalls. He went 'to and fro on the ground floor, walking around, while we were having our meal. I didn't know what he was up to. It wasn't my problem,' Trevor remembers. But he did not seem on edge. 'I assumed he was trying to organize things to do with the hotel.' Neither Trevor nor Kez knew him well, but there was nothing in his behaviour that raised a red flag.

By the time Henri Paul left the bar, the barman had served the hotel's assistant head of security his second Ricard *pastis*, a high-alcohol liquorice-flavoured aperitif popular in France. Those two drinks would soon be revealed as the top-up to other drinking during the time between Paul's arrival home from the afternoon's airport pick-up and his return to the hotel. As he finished his *pastis*, Paul's bloodstream carried a concentration of pure alcohol 'far superior to the legal level', as an autopsy would state, combined with a cocktail of two prescription drugs – an anti-depressant and a deterrent to alcohol dependence – and low enough levels of the protein transferrin to indicate 'chronic alcoholism over the course of at least a week'.

As Trevor searched his memory later for details of this brief scene in the bar, he knew that it never crossed his mind that the drink might be alcoholic. Paul was speaking in English, and was not slurring his words. He was perfectly entitled to have a drink if he was off duty, although Ritz employees were not permitted to drink in the hotel's bars. 'But it was clear to me that Henri Paul felt he was on duty,' Trevor recalls. With the Princess and the Boss's son in the hotel, why else would he be there? Drinking on the job was such a deep taboo for Trevor that it would never occur to him, especially with such a senior and, apparently, trusted man. 'I'm not saying people shouldn't enjoy a drink. I like a good night out. But I would never drink the day before I'm due to go back. If you're going back Tuesday, you don't drink on the Monday.'

At 11:07, both bodyguards arrived upstairs and sat outside the Imperial Suite, waiting for word. The two cars were out front, with Jean-François Musa, a director of Étoile Limousine, and Philippe Dourneau awaiting orders. Trevor and Kez did not know what was happening next. Nor did they know that, while they had been eating, Dodi had made a phone call that would change their lives. He had called the hotel's night manager, Thierry Rocher, to report the paparazzi mess at the door and, hearing that Henri Paul had returned, asked Rocher to tell Paul that they would need a third car for him and the Princess at the back of the hotel. The two cars they had used that day would stay at the front, in the Place Vendôme, as a diversion.

As Trevor and Kez waited outside the suite, Henri Paul came by several times, up and down the stairs, and seemed very busy chatting with hotel staff. Photographers report that he was agitated and sociable to an unusual degree as he moved around the entrances. He'd seemed a bit of a showman the few times Trevor had seen him; it was nothing new.

Twenty minutes before midnight, Henri Paul turned up at the door of the suite, still stinking of cigars, Kez noted, and told them, 'The plan's been changed. We'll be leaving from the back of the hotel, with just one car. He wants me to drive. The two other cars will leave from the front, to divert the paparazzi. Dodi doesn't want a bodyguard.' They'd be leaving in half an hour.

This was a terrible plan. Henri Paul was a security man, not a chauffeur. They needed a two-car convoy. And a bodyguard! Trevor shot back to Henri Paul, 'No fucking chance is he leaving without a bodyguard – no way in a million years it's going to be without me . . . I'll be coming with you if we go with this.'

The bodyguards announced that they'd have to report this to London, only the second time in the trip they'd felt Ops should be told about a bad plan of Dodi's. But Henri Paul confirmed, 'It's been okayed by Mr Mohamed.' Kez is sure of this, the phrase 'Mr Mohamed' standing out from the ubiquitous 'the Boss' of the lads. He had heard the second-in-command of security at the Ritz say this plan had been okayed by Fayed. But he knew that employees often took Fayed's name in vain, since there was no way to check without causing offence – or worse. And the plan was still a hopeless one.

'It wasn't Henri Paul driving that bothered me,' says Trevor. 'He'd already driven that day – it would have been like challenging Paul Handley-Greaves about driving the Boss.' It was the plan itself that disturbed.

Minutes later Dodi popped his head out of the suite and confirmed it all. They'd have a third car behind the hotel, and the two in front would serve as decoys while the couple escaped out the rear. Paul would be driving, he told them. Trevor was forceful. 'You aren't leaving without security – I'll be coming.' The photographers and the crowd had been moved back across the road. They weren't close. It would be quite safe to leave from the front, Trevor argued to Dodi. But Dodi insisted that the party should leave from the back – with one car only.

Still in stage whispers, Trevor was saying very forcefully, 'It's not going to happen. There's absolutely no way you're going without any security.' This was non-negotiable.

'Okay, one of you can come in the car, in the front,' Dodi finally relented.

'We need a back-up car as well. I'll bring one of the cars around from the front to the back,' said Kez, pushing it. But Dodi was resolved.

'No, no, then people will know. Wave the cars forward so everybody will think we're coming out the front, while we go out the back,' he said, and vanished back into the Imperial Suite.

Trevor was of a mind to finally grip Dodi and say, 'Look, this can't be allowed to go on.' He was basically going to tell him, 'We can't do this job without more information from you.' Kez cautioned his mate: 'We're on the last day now, speak to him when we get back.'

Trevor had argued against the decision, but now he had to put it into play. Quickly. The couple wanted to leave in a few minutes. He went downstairs to find Henri Paul. The extra car was to be ordered by the Ritz while Trevor was organizing the chauffeurs. He called Philippe and Musa, on stand-by at Étoile just across the Place Vendôme from the Ritz, and told them to come over to the hotel. He briefed them and asked them to help find Henri Paul. Fast.

It was six minutes after midnight. Now alone with Dodi and Diana, Kez gave it one last try. 'But two cars is best . . .'

Then Dodi evoked the magic words. 'It's been okayed by my father.' Was he telling the truth or not? Kez had no way of knowing.

Fayed would later admit to talking to Dodi fifteen minutes before he left the Ritz, but stated that, with regard to the decision to ask Henri Paul to drive, he knew absolutely nothing about it. Rather, he said, he had cautioned Dodi to be careful and to spend the night in the hotel if necessary.

Kez saw he was in a no-win situation. Ringing Fayed at midnight, doubting his son's word, wasn't a way to stay employed. 'You can respectfully suggest that a plan is crap. But if they don't listen, your hands are tied.' And, after all, they were taking photographs here, not posing a threat to the Princess.

As Trevor briefed them, the two chauffeurs had no idea why Henri Paul had been summoned to drive the car. Clearly, Trevor was carrying out orders from the Ritz.

Almost immediately after Trevor's directions to the drivers about Henri Paul, Roulet, acting manager of the Ritz in Frank Klein's absence, turned up, and asked Musa to put another car at Dodi's disposal. According to Philippe, he reiterated that the car was to be driven by Henri Paul and that the couple would come out by the Rue Cambon, the back entrance.

Trevor did not know that Henri Paul was not licensed to drive the commercial limousine which Musa ordered. Musa claims that he offered to drive, but they were working in a situation of urgency. No one had time to think. Between the moment Trevor asked the chauffeurs to come and the car starting its engine, fewer than ten minutes had elapsed. And the Ritz was virtually Étoile's only client. How could Musa refuse Roulet's order?

The car would be a Mercedes S280, bought by Étoile, second-hand, in 1994 for 114,666 French francs. It carried the registration number 688 LTV 75 on its licence plate. A standard car, it had no darkened windows or bullet-proof armour.

Étoile also owned the armour-plated Mercedes Fayed always used, but they had not been asked to send it to the airport earlier, or to use it for Dodi's royal guest. 'Dodi had never used the "heavy" as long as I'd been with him,' says Trevor.

Why had Dodi insisted upon Henri Paul driving? That mystery can never be solved, but Trevor believes Dodi made the choice because he trusted Paul, as he trusted Philippe, who would drive the decoy car at the front. After the tension of the trip, Dodi was trusting an ever-smaller band of people.

Shortly after midnight, a Ritz 'car-jockey', Frédéric Lucard, received word to bring up the car from the underground garage and round the Place Vendôme to the discreet rear entrance of the Ritz on the narrow Rue Cambon.

As Dodi and the Princess left the Imperial Suite, she seemed happy, as opposed to the crying earlier, Kez observed. They both were. It was obvious they'd had a glass of wine or two. 'But if you've had a glass of wine, you can go both ways, can't you? The happiest guy on earth or a little bit angry and nasty.' Chatting with the couple, Kez said, 'It's just a ten-minute drive. I'll see you back at the apartment.' Then he slipped in lightly, 'So it's straight back then. Not to a nightclub?' 'No, straight back,' said Diana, laughing.

As the Princess and Dodi turned away, Kez grabbed Trevor's arm. 'Look, mate, I'll get in the car, because he's not going to bollock me if it all kicks off. And if he does, I couldn't give a toss anyway because I'm going home tomorrow.'

But Trevor insisted, 'I'm Dodi's guy, so I'll go with him. I'll see you in ten minutes.'

'I'll beat you back,' Kez joked to Trevor as they split up outside the door of the Imperial Suite.

Dodi's plan had backfired even before they reached the rear door on the Rue Cambon. As the four left the suite, turned right and walked down the one flight of stairs to the back entrance, a handful of paparazzi had figured out that a ruse was in play and lay in wait. By 12:19, the four stood in the narrow service corridor, Dodi and the Princess facing a staff bulletin board as a smiling Henri Paul chatted to them, animatedly using both hands to make his points. Trevor, to the couple's right, checked outside. Where was the Mercedes? Ordered just minutes before to deliver it, the young Ritz driver was still en route, manoeuvring as fast as he could. Dodi and the Princess huddled side by side, waiting, with Dodi's left arm around her waist as Paul chatted on. Trevor remembers that they seemed very relaxed.

As Trevor looked out at the back entrance, 'just down

the road was a small, white hatchback type of car – a three-door car which was either white or light in colour, with a boot which opened at the back – and perhaps a scooter, or a motorbike, I believe . . . with two or three journalists'. He was relieved that there weren't more, but knew it was a hollow victory. They would soon be on their phones to their colleagues at the front. The pack would be upon them within seconds.

As the Mercedes arrived, Henri Paul pushed open the metal-grille door and stepped towards the car to make the switch of drivers. Observers and video tape reveal no hesitancy on his part. His confidence in his powers was far greater than his condition warranted. Carrying enough alcohol in his bloodstream to make him more than twice over the drink-driving limit, along with traces of other prescription drugs, Henri Paul slipped into the driver's seat.

Had Trevor seen any sign of impairment, he knows he would have stopped him. He would put up with orders just so far, but safety was sacred. There were discreet ways to ease a driver out without embarrassment or a scene. 'I could have made some simple excuse. "I'm afraid he's taken sick."' Trevor could have called François and Philippe, poised just around the corner at the front of the hotel, and returned to the two-car convoy, or called Lucard, the car-jockey. It might have delayed Dodi's planned departure and given the paparazzi a bit of a field day, but Trevor would never have knowingly let a drunk man drive. He would never have knowingly let an improperly licensed driver drive.

Why didn't Paul disqualify himself, knowing how much he had drunk? Trevor reckons that, 'His error was in not saying, "I can't drive. I've had too much to drink."'

The moment passed. History moved forward. Trevor preceded the Princess out the door, followed by Dodi about ten feet behind. Flashbulbs popped as they walked around the back of the car to get to the rear right door, the Princess taking huge strides in her delicate high heels, eyes down, as Trevor briskly ushered her into the back seat.

Kez took Trevor's call on the hotel's internal phone just inside the front door of the Ritz. 'We're about to move now.'

Kez went to the front and flashed the sign to the two drivers for all the paparazzi and tourists to see. Five minutes. Meaning, bring the cars forward so that all attention would focus on them. While the two vehicles appeared to be waiting for the couple to come out, Dodi and Diana would be slipping away at the back. The Mercedes and Trevor were on their own, with a driver Kez scarcely knew. This Henri Paul had driven well enough from Le Bourget airport earlier that day, though. The only two things you can't prepare for are a nutter and an accident.

The plan called for Kez to wait five minutes before moving out. But he'd seen the paparazzi move off – the plan hadn't worked, so he cut it to a minute and a half. As he drove off in the front Mercedes, he called London from the car phone – his mobile was still down. He got Martin Quaife, a good lad who was on the Ops desk that

night. 'They're on the move.' Okay. Immediately, he
called the Champs-Élysées apartment. 'They've been on
the move for two minutes, towards you. You can expect
them in about six minutes.'

In the Rue Cambon, the paparazzi were shooting
photos as the Mercedes' doors closed and Paul pushed
the gear into drive. Perhaps the most famous of this final
series of photos of the couple was taken now from the rear
right, the Princess's blonde hair towards the camera as
she looks to the front, and Dodi leaning over Diana's
back, peering anxiously out of the window.

What is arguably the last photograph taken before the
crash was of Trevor. Snapped by Sygma photographer
Jacques Langevin, it is a close-up of Trevor pulling his
sun visor down, looking intensely out of the window as a
round white flash fills the black background. The back of
the Princess's head is clearly visible, her head turned
away, looking towards the rear. Using his zoom lens,
Langevin had positioned himself right in front of the car,
about three metres away. Trevor speculates that 'I'm
trying to shield them in the back, putting a block between
them and the photographers, just trying to make it more
difficult to take a photo, really'.

Seconds before 12:20 A.M., the Mercedes left, at
speed, from the back of the hotel.

Trevor's clearest, and last, memories of the night are of
the Mercedes pulling away. He again saw the white or
light-coloured car that 'crossed the road and followed
us . . . I do not remember if the motorbikes followed us,

but I do know that journalists were following us'. He remembers mentioning it to Dodi and the Princess: 'There's a couple of photographers at the back, but not many.' His memory will always be fallible. But he places his trust in the earliest memories that came to him in hospital, memories he shared with the judge and which have endured. These are memories that emerged untainted by the barrage of reports that would confuse and compromise even an undamaged memory. In summary, they tell a single consistent story of events immediately before the departure from the Ritz: Henri Paul seemed normal. It was Dodi who changed the plan. Trevor's memories cease as the car pulled away from the Ritz.

'My last memory is of moving off . . . I do not remember anything more.'

PART II

IN THE EYE OF THE STORM

6

The Crash

Henri Paul manoeuvred the car along the fastest route back to the apartment on an August Saturday night, wisely bypassing the late-movie crowd on the Champs-Élysées for a diversion to the left along the Seine. He would then wheel right on to Avenue George V and whisk his very special cargo direct to the apartments near the Arc de Triomphe. A six- or seven-minute drive on a good night. The primary delays would be traffic lights. As they reached the first set at the end of the block they had already acquired an aggressive escort of motorcycles, with more converging.

They moved swiftly through the next corner, Rue de Mont Thabor, which was free of lights, but were then halted at the Avenue de Rivoli, where they turned right and proceeded a short distance to the Place de la Concorde. As the traffic from Rue St-Florentin crossed in front of them, merging into the frenzied wheel of traffic that circled the Place de la Concorde's Egyptian obelisk, and Henri Paul prepared to turn left on to the northern flank of the Place de la Concorde, the Mercedes was stopped by the first of several traffic lights along that side – an alarming chance for the paparazzi to catch up.

A witness, M. Bonin, was stopped at the next light, the base of the Champs-Élysées, when he spotted the Mercedes. He had been driving home from a restaurant on this warm night, windows closed, and had seen a crowd in front of the Ritz hotel and thought, 'That must be a star.' Following the same route as the Mercedes around the Place de la Concorde, also heading for a right turn at the Quai, he found himself next to 'a very big black Mercedes off to my left'. Then he noted 'a big black motorcycle registered in [*département*] 75, Paris, with two people on it. The person on the back . . . was carrying a camera and was literally taking pictures continuously with a flashlight into this car – it was not a darkened window.' Paparazzi, he thought. No photographic images from this rare photo opportunity, however, were found on any of the photographers' confiscated film.

'Then I recognized Dodi Fayed.' He'd seen his picture in the papers. Dodi's left hand was holding on to the hook above the window and, although his right hand was in front of his face, one could still identify him. 'On his right sat Princess Diana, who was trying to hide in the car. Behind the wheel was a man of forty-five years of age. He wore glasses . . . and a blond young man next to him I assumed was the bodyguard. The bodyguard seemed irritated, turning his head very often' – wanting the car to move off, Bonin guessed.

The witness also observed that Dodi and the Princess did not have their seat-belts on. He couldn't tell about the two in the front seat. As the light turned green, Bonin drove straight ahead and noticed that there seemed to be a black car in front of the Mercedes which did not start, blocking the Princess's car. 'Then I saw in my mirror that the Mercedes . . . had swerved over to the right and the engine made a lot of noise.' As Bonin drove a few metres and approached his right turn on to the Quai, 'I saw the Mercedes pass very quickly by the right-hand side.'

He lost sight of the Mercedes as it sped along the straight, unobstructed expressway along the Seine. This is where Henri Paul could, and did, pick up speed to try to outrun the motorcycles. It is where, given Dodi's pattern of frustration with the paparazzi, he could have urged Paul to accelerate and get away. The Mercedes entered a long tunnel under two bridges, the Pont Alexandre III and the Pont des Invalides, emerging on to a leafy stretch with trees overhanging the Quai on both sides. They were less than ten seconds from the crash. It is here, immediately on exiting the first tunnel and just before entering the descending curve to the left which leads into the tunnel under the Place de l'Alma, that Henri Paul had almost certainly planned to exit the expressway to the right. The last exit before the tunnel, it would have given him a straight shot up the Avenue

George V to Dodi's apartment off the Champs-Élysées. It was just three minutes away.

Controversy will always shroud this moment. Trevor's best record of events – the most reliable substitute for his own memory – has to be the findings of the French criminal investigation's rigorous fourteen-month technical examination and reconstruction of all the evidence. One of its conclusions – that Henri Paul may have been forced into the Alma tunnel because motorcycles blocked the exit he intended to take – is still a leap of faith unsupported by hard proof. But the facts that lead to that conclusion are as accurate a reconstruction of events as history will ever have.

The Mercedes, as it approached the tunnel, was travelling at a speed between 118 and 155 kilometres per hour – between 73 and 96 miles per hour – in a speed zone limited to 30 mph. Five paparazzi motorbikes were in pursuit – a Honda, a Yamaha, and three BMWs. Though witness accounts vary as to how close and in what relation to the Mercedes the bikes were, both the Honda, with a top speed of 155 kph, and the BMW, of 196, could have kept up with, or even passed, the Mercedes, through the final mile of acceleration.

What was the bodyguard doing as Henri Paul pressed the accelerator? All he knows is that he'd have felt the usual frustration, stripped of the professional control he needed to do his job properly.

'But if Henri Paul was going so outrageously fast that it was going to cause an accident, I think I would have made a comment.' He would not have grabbed the wheel or put his foot on the brake – that would have compounded the danger. 'Discreetly, I'd have said, "Take your foot off the pedal" or "Slow down, we're going too fast."' Dodi might not have agreed. If Paul had heard two competing orders, who was he going to obey?

Anyone who has driven through that, or any other, Paris tunnel knows that speeds in excess of the legal limit are routine. But special circumstances were coming into play. Just as Henri Paul was simultaneously faced with navigating the left curve and substantial dip which lead into the tunnel, he was confronted by a small white Fiat Uno blocking the right lane. The Uno was probably just outside, and about to enter, the tunnel as Paul first saw it. The small car, after a heroic nationwide hunt in which 3,000 owners of Fiat Unos were questioned, has never been found. But paint chips, dents, glass, marks on the Mercedes and its damaged rear-view mirror prove without question that Henri Paul had a minor collision with a Fiat Uno as he raced by.

It is here that Trevor's reactions may well have come into play – here that he might have grabbed for his seatbelt and pulled it part of the way across his chest. But if he did, events were moving too fast and violently for him to complete the buckling.

With contact with the Fiat Uno, the crash sequence had begun.

The condition of the car itself was not a contributing

factor. Exhaustive tests over two years proved that the
Mercedes carrying the couple was, in fact, in perfect
working order. But other factors now compounded each
other. First, Henri Paul's exit may have been blocked by
one or two of the pursuing motorcycles as the police
report claims, giving him no choice but the tunnel.
Second, with speed too high to navigate the smallest
curve, the car became difficult to control. Third, there is
the contact with the Fiat Uno. Three dangerous, virtually
simultaneous events, each to be interpreted and resolved
in split seconds.

Henri Paul could well have been tired. It was late, he
was supposed to be off duty, the pressure of the high
responsibility was enormous. And he was drunk. The
final, determining component was alcohol, and a brain
suddenly confronted by more danger signs than it could
sort out.

The immutable laws of physics take hold.

Just as the Mercedes reaches the curve to the left, it is
pulled irresistibly to the right by centrifugal force – and
also, perhaps, by Paul's plan to exit to the right at that
point – and he faces a Fiat Uno in his path. As he pulls
to the left to try to avoid it, he swipes the Fiat's left rear
end, a minor collision, but forceful enough to send the
front of the smaller car to the left as the rear is pushed to
the right, shrinking the Mercedes' driving space.

Paul is now racing down a narrow canyon, a row of
concrete pillars to his left, the Fiat so close on the right
that, for a split second, the two vehicles tear along in

tandem, the Mercedes' right wing-mirror shattering against the Fiat's side as he tries to swerve around the car. He skids to the left for nineteen metres, one wheel off the ground, and just as he passes the Fiat and turns to the right to get ahead of his nemesis, his path is blocked by yet another car just ahead of the Fiat, a Citroën BX.

He turns the wheel left, too hard, and skids inexorably towards the pillars dividing the tunnel in two. Tall, square, white and unforgiving, the pillars have, for thirty years, been an invitation to tragedy. This tunnel has already taken eight lives, and left another eight people severely injured in thirty-four accidents. Still fighting for control in this final second, Henri Paul instinctively reaches for the gears to shift down from fourth to third to slow the breakneck speed. But errors in judgement are now cascading upon him. He has forgotten, perhaps, that he's driving an automatic car, thinks he is changing the gears of his Austin Mini, and throws the gear into neutral – free-wheeling instead of slowing. It is too late now for any attempt to compensate. He finally hits the brakes just sixty-four metres before impact. Too late. The Mercedes has become a hurtling death capsule, still estimated to be travelling at between 100 and 110 kilometres per hour – over 60 mph. At 12:23 A.M., just three minutes after leaving the Ritz, the Mercedes ploughs head-on into the thirteenth pillar, the right-angled edge of the pillar carving a foot-deep 'V' into the radiator grille, crumpling the shiny steel skin of the bonnet like a handful of cellophane in a giant's hand.

On impact, both front airbags deploy in less than 20 milliseconds. Performing perfectly, they explode into two white-skinned balloons of carbon dioxide, buffering Trevor and Henri Paul from the engine structure being driven towards them as their own bodies continue to hurtle forward. On the driver's side, the airbag holds Paul back momentarily but cannot stop the steering wheel, engine and radiator from being thrust back against his body, killing him instantly. As the airbag pops, carbon dioxide is released with explosive force, pressing into his lungs, raising the levels of carbon dioxide in his blood to 20.7 per cent – the equivalent of two packets of cigarettes.

Trevor's airbag saves his life as the entire front of the car concertinas into a chaotic tangle of ripped and twisted metal, protecting him from instant death. The impact has left him almost unscathed. But now, as the Mercedes rebounds from impact, it rotates clockwise at high speed and crashes against the tunnel wall to the right. At the first shock of deceleration, Dodi and the Princess were propelled violently forward in the same trajectory and speed as before impact, smashing into the front seats. But now the whirling car compounds their bodies' stubborn momentum, pivoting around them, hurling them, at high speeds, against the car's interior.

The impact and extreme deceleration leave Diana's heart displaced from the left to the right side of its cavity, and with injuries so serious – the severing of the vital pulmonary vein and rupturing of the pericardium, the heart's protective sac – that 'there is no example in international medical history where a person suffering from such an injury survived', the judge's medical experts would ultimately report.

And then they come to rest.

The Mercedes was now facing back towards the entrance to the tunnel. Henri Paul's head was back against the seat, his face holding the same smile he'd had most of the day. Several threads of blood traced lines across his forehead and cheek. There was no breath, sound or movement.

Dodi's crushed ribs had become dangerous inside his chest, puncturing the lung and blood vessels, creating internal bleeding that – with a ruptured aorta and spinal fracture at the neck – would be named the cause of his death. His fine-checked shirt was torn open at the throat. But his face, too, was peaceful, with a trace of benign smile, the only overt signs of the assault on his body, like Henri Paul, the several long, neat lacings of blood across his forehead.

The Princess was slumped on the floor, leaning against the back of Trevor's seat, facing in the direction the car had originally been going. Her legs were twisted, one under her, the other on the seat. Traces of blood came from a cut on the forehead and trickled from nose and mouth. But her face was almost intact. With her chin down on her chest and her eyes closed, she looked beautiful, serene, asleep. The internal trauma could not be seen. Copies of *Newsweek* and *Time* were still visible in the seat pockets behind her, the mass media ironically present even here.

The horn blared under Henri Paul's body, the same chilling wail Trevor had heard as his father had slumped, dead, over the wheel ten years earlier. Smoke rose from the front of the car. There was some incoherent mumbling and arm movement from the Princess. A few signs of sound and movement from the front right passenger. But it was an eerily calm, quiet and almost bloodless sight the first witnesses stumbled upon.

Except for Trevor. Trevor had survived the first impact with little damage. But he lost the protection of the airbag as swiftly as he'd gained it, and as the car turned on itself — as it spun right and hit the wall, instantaneously draining itself of momentum — his body kept flying forward, smashing his face and chest against the dashboard and windshield. The left side of his face bore the brunt of the impact. The sight of the bloody gashes and loose flaps of flesh horrified early witnesses as Trevor slumped semi-conscious, his face pressed flat against the dash. 'The lower half of his face was ripped off and hanging loose' was one of the graphic descriptions that shaped the global image of Trevor's condition. Another, 'His mouth and tongue were ripped off,' launched the rumour that swiftly spread that Trevor's tongue had been severed. It had not.

The paparazzi had skidded their motorbikes to a halt and run with their cameras to the scene. A photographer

named Romuald Rat was the first. Leaping from a motorbike driven by Stéphane Darmon, he ran to the Mercedes
and instantly snapped three photos. Trained in first aid,
Rat claims that he then opened the rear right door to try
to help the Princess, and told her, in English, to stay
cool, hold on, help would come. He claims to have heard
someone shout, 'I have called the emergency services.'
Then he and the others went aggressively about their
business, shooting a total of 118 pictures, which were
taken from as close as one metre from Diana's head, and
as far as ten metres – from three to thirty feet.
Photographer Serge Arnal did call the emergency
number, 112, before calling his senior editor and racing
into the tunnel to shoot sixteen pictures. His call – the
first recorded alert – came at 12:23 A.M., seconds after
the crash.

A dentist, James Hutte, heard a 'very heavy brake
noise and a triple impact of great intensity' from his
nearby balcony, and ran to the tunnel, where he heard
'the continuous sound of a horn', saw 'a bit of smoke'
and photographers' flashbulbs as people converged on
the scene. Running back to the cars stopped at the tunnel
entrance, he grabbed the mobile phone of a man in a
Jaguar and, calling on his memory as a professional,
dialled the SAMU rescue number – the Service d'Aide
Medicale d'Urgence ambulances – 01 45 67 50 50, and
reported the crash. He then called 18, the main Fire
Station, which had just received its first call from a
witness, Paul Carril.

The first competent report of Trevor's condition comes from Frédéric Mailliez, an off-duty doctor with a Parisian rescue team who was returning from a private party. Turning on the flashing blue light of his car, he did a swift mental triage of the four people he found in the car. The driver was so incarcerated he could hardly see him. 'But I had no illusion . . . I knew he was dead.' The back left passenger was dead. The front right passenger seemed to have a severe facial trauma. Even this emergency doctor was shocked by the 'gruesome' sight: 'The left side of his face was just hanging down – it was horrible.'

He turned his attention to the woman. 'She seemed to be in the best shape.' He raced back to his car through the sea of paparazzi and witnesses who were 'in a state of panic' to make some calls from his mobile phone – to call 18, to order ambulances and to order a 'mobile can-opener', for it was clear that Trevor could not be treated until the car roof was removed. Grabbing what sparse medical equipment he had with him, he returned to find that the first *pompiers*, firemen, had arrived, and were caring for the front passenger as he focused on the woman. He gave the Princess her first emergency care. With not even a blood-pressure cuff, there was little he could do. But with easy access to her through the open door, he carefully raised her chin, freed the upper respiratory passages by bending her head back slightly, and put an oxygen mask over her face. She was semi-conscious, but talking, though he could not understand what she said, and seemed to respond to easier breathing with more movement and agitation. He had no idea who she was. When more rescue crews arrived to take over, this Good Samaritan left.

The first police to arrive also instantly determined the Princess to be in better shape than the bodyguard, and that the two on the left were dead. Picking up a radio call at 12:30 and racing to the scene, arriving before the rescue teams, policemen Lino Gagliardone and Sébastien Dorzée had to struggle to get through the photographers taking pictures from every angle. Even though they said 'the Princess was bleeding from her mouth and nose and had a profound wound on the forehead', she was very much alive, 'mumbling something in English, maybe "My God"', as Dorzée spoke to her and pressed the wound, trying to keep her from slipping into unconsciousness.

He prayed the rescue teams would arrive as Gagliardone tried to hold back the photographers, who were using their cameras 'as if they were machine guns'. A photographer said to him, 'in an arrogant manner, that if I had been in Bosnia I would not take it so tragically . . . One of them said in a very vulgar manner, "Leave me alone. Let me do my job. In Sarajevo the policemen usually let us work. You just have to have people shoot at you and you will see."' Then, at last, with the arrival of the rescue teams, the police could control the paparazzi, set up cordons and extend the secure perimeter of the crash site.

Trevor's care had begun with the arrival of the first two teams of *pompiers* aboard emergency rescue vehicles 94 and 100, which pulled into the crash site at 12:32, two minutes after receiving the call. In their familiar blue trousers and T-shirts, ten *pompiers* descended on the scene and went to work. In command, Sergeant Xavier Gourmelon swiftly evaluated the passengers, and saw that Trevor was 'alive, incarcerated, conscious, with a facial trauma'. Standing near the woman, Gourmelon heard the words in English, 'My God, what's happened?' and saw her move her left arm and legs as he issued his orders.

Kez had just put the phone down after his call to the Ops Room in London when, to the left, he saw flashing blue lights and heard sirens. 'There's been an accident,' he commented to Philippe Dourneau. 'Is there any way around this?' 'No, we're too late. We're committed now.' There was already a massive backlog of traffic. Kez redialled the security desk at the apartments. 'Are they there yet?' No. 'Well, they might be a bit late because there's been an accident. Stand by on the doors because they're going to be coming in quickly. But with the accident, you're going to have to wait a couple of minutes.'

Kez phoned Trevor to find his position. No reply. He thought, 'Shit, they've done it! They've nipped around the corner and gone into a club, and he can't hear the phone.' His nightmare was that Dodi had got the sudden idea to go to a nightclub, and Trevor would be the sole bodyguard – with no back-up car or extra bodyguard.

He paged Trevor, but there was no answer. It was now

six or eight minutes since they had departed from the
Ritz. 'Are they there yet?' he asked the apartments again.
No, said Gérard, the security chap who'd had the flare-up
with the photographer earlier that evening.

There were more sirens and ambulances as they nav-
igated slowly through the clogged streets. Now Kez was
annoyed. 'I don't believe it. We've beaten them back.
They've turned off. Gone to a club,' he thought as they
circled part way around the Arc de Triomphe and parked
on a nearby street to the Rue Arsène-Houssaye. Walking
back with Philippe and Jean-François Musa, Kez
stomped in, told Gérard to stay in the office just inside
the door to catch any calls from the car, and rushed to
prepare for the arrival. 'François, move the car in to hold
a spot for the Mercedes. Give me a shout as soon as you
see the car turn in.'

By land-line from the office, he called the Ops desk in
London. 'We've beaten them back. There's a possibility
they've turned off. But there's been an accident, a couple
of roads are blocked off, so they're probably trying to go
around it.'

As Kez ran ahead to get reception set, Philippe had
walked back to the building with Musa, and noted about
ten journalists waiting, and, just inside, two of the Ritz's
security agents, who asked them if Dodi's Mercedes had
arrived. 'I was surprised that they hadn't arrived because
they'd left before us, and I myself had driven slowly.'
They all waited around worrying about what had happened when the mobile phone of one of the journalists

rang. 'This journalist answered and I saw his face become white and suddenly very excited,' which got Philippe's attention. 'He continued to talk and at the same time went to his car and I followed him with Musa because we suspected something had happened.'

'Tell us – what's happened?' the drivers demanded. The journalist wouldn't answer, but looked tense and nervous and they saw him grab his jacket. He still wouldn't talk and Philippe became extremely worried.

'There's been an accident.'

'Where, where?'

'In the Alma tunnel.'

He didn't need to tell them it was Dodi. They ran for the Range Rover, leaped in, and drove as fast as they could to the tunnel as the journalist, too, drove off.

At the security desk, Kez had seen a commotion outside, seen Philippe bolt away, and thought, 'Well, he's getting home before the backlog of the crash.' But he was preoccupied trying to reach Trevor, redialling his phone, letting it ring and ring, getting annoyed, thinking, 'I don't care where he is. He's going to answer this.' Then – it couldn't have been more than three minutes since he'd seen Philippe dash off – he grabbed a call from Philippe, on his mobile. Where in hell . . .? 'There's been an accident. It's Dodi.'

'Shit! How bad is it? Find out as much as you can and call me back.'

Philippe and Musa got the car as close as they could to the tunnel and ran towards the blue lights of the emergency vehicles. Kez ran through the options in his mind. Are they going to need another car to get them out of there? They'll be stuck and Philippe will get them into his vehicle and come back. They'd been right, him and Trevor – if they'd had a back-up, he'd be getting them out now. Shit, that's what a back-up is for.

Kez redialled London. 'There's been an RTA [road traffic accident] here involving the principals' car. Don't know any details yet. I'll get back to you as soon as I can.'

'Okay,' said Martin, 'I'll shake Dave.' Dave Moody, the on-duty team leader, was one of Kez's good friends. Trev will be in the thick of it, doing what he can, Kez thought, relieved.

Gourmelon assigns two firemen to Trevor, and orders them to hold his head up, liberate his breathing, attach a cervical collar in case there is spinal damage, and apply oxygen. Several on the scene report a fireman cradling Trevor's bloody head in his hands, keeping the crushed face lifted up from the dash. He is the last person in the crash to be rigorously helped. It is not just that he is of secondary interest compared to Princess Diana, once her identity is known. He is 'incarcerated' – trapped inside this mangled cage of metal – and cannot be given extensive first aid until Diana is extricated from the wreckage and he can be 'disincarcerated'. The car's roof must be removed. The *camion de désincarcération* left the station at 12:32, and is on its way.

Gourmelon assigns another member of the No. 94

team, Philippe Boyer, to care for the Princess. He gently attaches a cervical collar around her neck while checking all vital functions and specific traumas, and hands over her care, while she is still in the car, to a SAMU physician when he arrives. Several men from the No. 100 team remove Henri Paul's body from its grotesque metal shroud, lay him on the roadway, make the final confirmation of death, and cover him with a blue plastic sheet. Grasping any chance that Dodi might be revived, two from No. 94 carry Dodi's body from the car and stretch him out on the concrete and, for thirty minutes, try aggressive external heart massage. They then cover him, too, with a plastic sheet.

The *camion de désincarcération* – the 'can-opener' and spotlight van – arrives under the command of Arnaud Forge at 12:44. Responding to Gourmelon's orders, Forge turns on all spotlights, wedges the car in place, and starts removing the roof, cutting first across the back, then through Trevor's seat and through the door. With his charge, the Princess, now in the hands of the SAMU, Boyer begins to extract Trevor from the car. He finds him sitting in his proper position in his seat, slightly elevated, with his chest pressed on the dashboard. His seat-belt is stretched out and stuck, and he must cut it before Trevor's limp form can be eased out and strapped to a rigid *olivier* board to keep him immobilized as he is carried into an ambulance for the blue-light run to the hospital. A police photo, taken just as his chest and head are being pulled up from the dashboard, a shot of his profile, reveals a

shocking fact – Trevor's face has been flattened, his nose
and eye sockets pushed back so far that, in profile, his
nose scarcely protrudes beyond the lips.

Although the earliest hands-on work on the victims was
being done by the *pompiers*, all medical action was supervised, from his arrival, by Dr Arnaud Derossi, the
designated SAMU rescue physician for the accident, who
had been told only that one of the victims was 'a high personality'. He quickly surveyed the scene, ordered
additional help, and soon found himself in charge of
three firemen rescue teams and three SAMU ambulance
teams. As he focused on the victims, he assigned his
partner, Dr Marc LeJay, to handle radio and telephone
communications; it was LeJay who learned from emergency services that Diana and Trevor were to be sent to
La Pitié-Salpêtrière hospital. It was not the closest, being
about four miles away, but it was the best-equipped unit
for this kind of trauma.

Derossi, in his swift survey of the condition of the four
passengers, saw – like others – Diana's shape as 'severe
but not critical'. The words he heard her say were confused, but she was speaking. As she was finally freed
from the wreckage at 1:00 A.M., Derossi had supervised
the firemen taking Diana from the car and saw her go into
cardiac arrest as she was being lifted on to a stretcher.
The extreme fragility of her condition was becoming
clear. 'I had to intubate her, give her respiratory ventila-
tion and a heart massage to revive her,' he reported,

before she could be placed in the ambulance for more extensive care prior to leaving for the hospital.

As, at last, Diana could be given a medical evaluation, the police report would describe her condition as 'falling into coma, multiple fractures of right arm, bleeding wound on the head and right back, and chest trauma – very severe state'.

French rescue vehicles are equipped like mini emergency rooms, and do far more initial care – stabilizing, emergency procedures – than their American counterparts, who practise the 'scoop and run' system. There will always be debate over whether Diana might have survived had she been rushed to hospital. Although she was trapped in the wreck for nearly forty minutes while her life-blood flowed out from the torn vein, many physicians concur with the French report that 'no other surgical, anaesthetic or resuscitation strategy could have prevented deterioration in the condition of the patient'.

As Trevor, the unidentified bodyguard, was finally extricated, his condition would be evaluated in the police report as 'facial trauma, fracture of the left arm, head fracture and stressed trauma'. He was in 'very severe shape'.

From 12:45 A.M. until nearly four that morning, Kez never left the phones. He was manning three at once, two mobile phones and the guardian's phone, the information lifeline between the crash site and the Ops Room in London.

'Hello, hello.' It was Philippe. Kez heard chaos in the background. Sirens. French voices shouting. Philippe trying to be heard over them.

'It's Dodi. It's Dodi.'

'How is he? What is it?'

'He's dead.'

'That's when everything, like in parachuting, just dropped out of me.' For a millisecond, Kez was stunned, empty. Once on his birthday, they'd said, 'Your mum's dead.' She wasn't – it had been a mistake. But he'd felt the same disbelief that he felt now. There's no phrase really suitable for these overwhelming moments. He would have loved to have passed the ball to someone who outranked him. Then his training clicked in. 'Right. Calm down. Confirm it.'

Kez could hear Philippe shouting, 'Wait, wait!' across the police cordon to the paramedics or police. In French. Too fast for Kez to pick it up. He came back on.

'Dodi is dead.'

'How's the Princess?'

'She's awake. She's hurt her legs. She's okay.'

Thank God for that, thought Kez.

'What about the others? Find out. Ring me straight back.'

But Philippe didn't hang up, he just kept his phone open for what seemed like minutes, Kez hearing the sounds, picturing Philippe fighting his way to near the car, seeing Dodi on the ground, being pushed back behind the police tape.

It was time to drop all code names. 'Martin, I'm going to send it all in clear because the shit's hit the fan. Dodi's dead in an RTA. The Princess has injured her legs but she's okay. About the others, I don't know.' Then Dave Moody, the team leader, was on the phone, probably the most professional man Kez had ever met in his life. Yanked from his sleep by the emergency, sitting at the Ops desk in his underpants, Dave said, 'You're doing fine. Just keep telling me what's happening.'

Gleaning what he could from Philippe's crash-scene reports as they were passed on, cross-channel, by Kez and clinging to the sketchy reports that Trevor was alive, Dave called to reassure the Rees-Joneses in Oswestry, and called Fayed's chief of personal security, Paul Handley-Greaves, to tell him of Dodi's death.

In Paris, Kez was taking another call from Philippe, saying, 'The front two are dead.'

Humbly aware that, to the world, this crash was about Diana, Trevor would later say, 'Media-wise, of course, the most important person was the Princess. The driver and the security bloke were secondary. It would be just one sentence on the news, a driver and a security man are injured.' But to the lads, Trevor, right now, was the focus of their universe.

As Paul called Kez to confirm Dodi's death before telling Fayed, his father, Kez told him, 'Henri Paul and Trevor are dead, too.'

With the arrival of supervising rescue personnel like

Derossi, and the police, the crash was transforming into an official event, placed in the hands of a criminal prosecutor. As soon as there is a car accident – as soon as anyone dies violently in France, whether murder or car crash – the prosecution must be informed. Within minutes of the report of the crash to the prosecutor's office in the Palais de Justice, the heart of the French judicial system, Mme Maud Coujard was appointed prosecutor. She went into action immediately, arriving at the scene in a leather jacket on a BMW motorcycle driven by her husband. She immediately expanded the case bureaucratically to include senior officials of all involved departments – the head of the Criminal Brigade, Assistant to the Director of Public Security, Director of the Judiciary Police. They all rushed to the scene. Through the ensuing chaotic night and day, Coujard had to sign the dozens of official documents that would launch an investigation, declare deaths, and permit corpses to be returned to their homes and families.

This expansion paralleled the global expansion of the case as a news story as the first fragments of information about the accident reached the wire services and television stations. It expanded in other ways, too: personally, as, at shortly after one in the morning, Dodi's father, Mohamed Al Fayed, learned of the crash and of his son's death; and diplomatically, as, at 1:45, British Ambassador Sir Michael Jay was notified while Diana's ambulance was still en route to the hospital. He would call the royal family, with Prince Charles the first to be informed that the Princess had been seriously injured.

While this crash of crashes swelled out on levels that would make it one of the major news stories of the late twentieth century, an unidentified British bodyguard's tenuous hold on life was still in the hands of a small group of French firemen.

The same firemen were still hovering over him as, at 1:30 A.M., the ambulance carrying the Princess moved slowly off from the Alma tunnel towards the Pitié-Salpêtrière hospital across the Seine. The trip was not announced on radio, so as not to alert the media, or the public, about the route. Diana's heart was now so frail that twice the doctor ordered the ambulance to stop so that she could be stabilized. Just past the zoo, they stopped for five minutes to give her complete immobility. Across the Pont d'Austerlitz, just metres from the hospital, they had to stop again, then drove straight up the Boulevard de l'Hôpital and turned left as a red and white barrier raised to let them into the hospital grounds, a vast and sprawling campus of yellow and red-brick buildings. Blue lights flashing, they moved past the eight-storey modern grey-green-and-steel panelled emergency medical building and turned right into the emergency entrance.

In Trevor's ambulance, the medics inserted a tracheal tube down his throat to keep his breathing going, monitored vital signs, got a drip into his veins so that his brain and vital organs would not be starved of blood and oxygen, and controlled the facial bleeding as best they could. But without scans and X-rays they had no idea what damage had been done internally, or to his crushed, bloody and swiftly swelling head.

The bodies of Dodi and Henri Paul were transported to the morgue next door to the hospital. Paul underwent an autopsy. Dodi did not, as his body would be returned to England that day for immediate burial, as Islamic custom requires. Paul and Dodi had both been dead since the crash at 12:23, but their deaths were not declared until 2 A.M.

Minutes later, Diana's ambulance pulled up under the covered entry, with Trevor's ambulance arriving twenty minutes after hers. Their stretchers were wheeled through automatically opening doors, 100 feet along a glass-walled wing to the elevator which took them up one floor to the *Réanimation* unit – intensive care, equipped with the sophisticated equipment and doctors of a major Parisian hospital. In physical terms, Trevor had been closest to the Princess as the doomed Mercedes came to rest – just the few inches of the passenger seat had separated them. Now, a few rooms apart, they would share the upcoming fight for survival. The battle for the lives of two vibrant and strong young people – a Princess and a bodyguard – had moved into its next, decisive, stage.

A male nurse, Dominique Hagnère, had been the first to give intensive care to the Princess after she arrived at the emergency gates at 2:06 A.M. and was whisked into

Réanimation. She was being given oxygen to help her breathing. 'I am positive the Princess was totally unconscious when she arrived and, in my presence – and I never left her – she never became conscious again.' X-rays were immediately ordered, since she had no external wound and pulmonary injuries were suspected. In *Réanimation*, she was being continually monitored for heart level, pulse, oxygen readings.

By luck, two leading surgeons were on duty as the Princess arrived. Alerted to prepare as the first ambulance left the tunnel, cardiovascular surgeon Dr Alain Pavie and anaesthetist Dr Bruno Riou were scrubbing for surgery when they were told who their patient would be.

'As soon as we got the X-rays, we understood that she suffered from extensive internal bleeding,' Hagnère reported. 'The surgeon opened her chest to get into the lungs and find the source of the bleeding.' The thoracic cavity was awash. The discovery that it was the pulmonary vein, the major line between lungs and heart, was devastating. The drainage of blood for more than an hour and a half ensured that irreversible damage had been done to organs and had almost certainly damaged the brain. 'We immediately tried to evacuate this bleeding with a pulmonary drain so that the lungs were not compressed too much,' says Hagnère. 'We transfused her with massive amounts of blood – both donated and her own,' but it was not enough. Diana's heart kept stopping. To keep her alive, the nurses injected 'enormous' amounts of adrenalin – 150 injections of 5 milligrams each – direct into her heart. In a desperate, last-ditch effort to save her, doctors massaged the heart by hand for many minutes. Their skills could not save the Princess. At 4 A.M. the doctors admitted defeat and declared her dead. The announcement would not be made until 4:30.

Checking other arrivals while the drama with the Princess was unfolding, Hagnère observed the *pompiers* working over Trevor, whose identity was still unknown to the rescue and hospital staff.

Dr Luc Chikhani is on call, in bed at home, when he receives the call from the junior doctor in intensive care at La Pitié-Salpêtrière. He is told what most of the world does not yet know: there has been a crash involving Diana, and there is another wounded patient, Diana's bodyguard, who has just arrived and needs maximum care. It is one of the worst days of Trevor Rees-Jones's life, but also one of the luckiest, as one of the finest facial surgeons in Paris throws on his clothes and rushes by car to the hospital. Just thirty-five, a handsome and ebullient man whose prep-school years in New Hampshire have given him near-perfect command of English, Chikhani is one of the elite one-in-a-hundred Paris physicians to do his surgical training as a fellow of the prestigious Internat de Paris.

But he cannot get into the hospital. At least ten large Mercedes with diplomatic plates block the entrance, and one door of the hospital has been completely closed. Photographers, cameras, press, police, officials are everywhere. He circles the building in his car, with its doctor's ticket on the windscreen, but has forgotten his identity card, and police rebuff him. He knows he has an urgent tracheotomy to do. He races the half-mile back to his office in a distant ward, grabs his white coat with the official name tag, dumps his car 'in the middle of nowhere' and runs to the entrance again. Guards are about to impound his beeper as a camera when the chief of the intensive-care department finds him and berates the guards, 'You bastards!' as they rush up to the second floor.

Chikhani runs a gauntlet of armed men as he makes his way to the emergency operating room, offended that he should be waved along the hall by unsheathed guns. They are Secret Service from England, France, Egypt, he is told.

As he enters the emergency operating room, he shuts off the clamouring world outside the door. The patient – this bodyguard whose name he does not know, whose face he has never seen – is unconscious. Chemically asleep, sedated. But their relationship has begun.

What he sees is a '*fracas*' – a crashed face. The nose is not a nose. There are massive lesions at the left eye and across the left lip and cheek. It is not the face the media will soon report as 'hanging off'. But it is one of the most crushed and shattered faces he has ever seen. Even the intensive-care doctors who've seen everything are coming by to look at this extraordinary case. Strangely, the skin, except for the two big cuts, is roughly preserved. But it is like . . . What? . . . A bagful of nuts and you crush the whole thing, and the lumps and bumps are pressing up against the bag. As Chikhani touches the skin, everything is moving all over the place and there is a sort of grinding sound, a '*grrrrrkkkk*'. Underneath the skin, he knows, it is mush.

He orders X-rays. A CT scan. The scan shows extensive bleeding around the skull – oedema, but there is no skull fracture or gross damage to the brain, the first good news in terms of Trevor surviving at all. But the scan reveals a broken left wrist, internal injury to the chest, and so many broken and displaced bones that it will require massive surgery to try to piece a face together again.

Fractures, though, are the secondary emergency. The first is to make Trevor breathe, to keep him alive. First, Chikhani must do the tracheotomy. Then, pay attention to internal bleeding and lesions – bladder, liver, kidney, heart. No reconstruction can be done until the swelling and bleeding of the head are reduced, if he survives this day. Chikhani asks a neurosurgeon, an ophthalmologist and an orthopaedic surgeon to evaluate, as an anaesthetist prepares the patient for emergency surgery.

Before sunrise on Sunday, 31 August, two surgeons descend on the shattered body. Urgently, Chikhani does the tracheotomy while the team puts the patient on a ventilator, which will breathe for him while his punctured right lung heals, and inserts a drain into his chest cavity. Orthopaedist Dr Ramare sets the fractured left wrist as Chikhani turns to the face, the canvas for this reconstructive artist's skills.

He closes the wounds, suturing the largest flaps of skin and flesh torn from the bone across his upper lip, left cheek, and a major wound to the left eyelid where tissue has been ripped off, and cleans it all carefully, with infection a constant fear. He wires the right jawbone joint temporarily back in place – 'reduces' it, and, on the spot, invents a technique for taking a casting of his teeth. All that can be done for now.

But as he works on this face, he feels exhilaration. Only rarely has Chikhani seen, or had the chance to rebuild, a face this damaged. He has seen cases as challenging as this – faces ravaged by cancer and violent trauma, but the patients have died. If this man survives, Chikhani will be lecturing about him for years; young doctors will learn from this case. He is mentally planning the surgery ahead. Laying out his strategy, step by step. The two things he must have are photographs and anatomically reliable data – he must get family photos and dental records, immediately. Chikhani knows he can do it, technically.

But far more important to this young surgeon, if this patient survives, is that he can give him back a real life. 'My aim is to give you back your function, which is breathing, looking at things, eating, chewing, opening your mouth, speaking, and having your social place – to be socially comfortable with living, going with a girl, and getting married,' he was mentally telling this nameless young man.

'You are the only living witness – the VIP of the world this day. But the journalists do not care about you as a person,' Chikhani feared. It was the money, the story. They would do anything to get a picture. In the coming days they would be caught in the ward and expelled. They would offer some of his colleagues 300,000 francs! Chikhani knows that creating a relationship with Trevor is vital to his survival. He may be unconscious, but he is not absent. This man is central to his own recovery. Chikhani initiates the physical relationship. He reaches out, touches him, and tells him, 'You will not die. You will not die.' If this patient is to survive and become himself again, he must have extraordinary will. He must do his own healing.

Kez, still on the phones at the apartments, was continuing to function even with the most recent news that his mate was dead, when he got a call from Paul Handley-Greaves in London at about 2:30. 'Jack up some cars from the Ritz,' Handley-Greaves tells him. 'Fayed's arriving at Le Bourget at five o'clock.' Kez, and two cars, would be there, in place, at 4:20 A.M.

Back in London, Dave knew two families would be desperate for news if they stumbled on any television or radio bulletins. Trevor's and Kez's parents. In Hull earlier, Kez's mum had been watching the National Lottery, 'and my mum had been doing the numbers like most people do. She hadn't got even one, and she was dripping like hell to my dad. Then they got the call when they'd gone to bed later on that evening, and my mum's peering at the telly, thinking something's up with the lottery. My dad went to get it, and got the news from Dave, "There's been a crash, it will be on the news, but it's not Kez. He's okay." My dad asked Dave, "How's the other lad?"

'My father's a bit of a cold fish,' Kez reflects. Shows little affection, or pride in his son. 'But he walked in to my mum and said, "We've just won something that I think's better than any lottery win."'

As Kez left his post in Paris and drove to Le Bourget airport, Claude Roulet, the hotel's acting manager, drove with him. They pulled the cars up close to the helipad. It was 4:55. The aircraft was in hover, just about to touch down, when Roulet took a call and passed it to Kez. 'It's the British Consulate, for you.'

'The Princess is dead.' That was it, then.

'Right, cheers,' was all Kez could muster as he pushed the antenna down on the phone and looked up to see Mr Fayed and two bodyguards stepping out of the helicopter.

He'd never touched the Boss before. But now he put his arm on his shoulder and said, 'Look, Sir, I'm sorry for your loss.' Fayed mumbled something, disconsolate.

'I'm sorry, Sir, I've got some more bad news for you.'

'The Princess?'

'I'm afraid they're all dead.'

Five of them drove into Paris to retrieve Dodi's body, Kez in the front, Fayed in the back.

'I hope the British government is satisfied now,' Fayed suddenly erupted, in a burst of emotion.

'Nobody could have wished this, Sir,' said Kez, shocked, grasping for a reply. Then the Boss just sort of slumped back in his seat.

The terrible announcement of the deaths had just been made in another wing of the hospital as Fayed and Kez arrived at the front steps. This plain, unadorned entrance with two granite steps and simple automatic glass doors opening into a small lobby with a few plants and sofas had become the centre of the world. Fayed was met on the steps by a hospital official. Though Fayed would soon claim that, inside, a nurse had delivered to him Diana's last words: 'I would like all my possessions in Dodi's apartment to be given to my sister Sarah, including my jewellery and my personal clothes, and please tell her to take care of my boys' – a claim decisively repudiated by the hospital – Kez always knew it had not happened; Fayed never went into the hospital, not even the foyer. They were only there about ten minutes. Kez was beside Fayed, on the steps, the whole time.

The hospital official – he was wearing a white coat, Kez assumed he was a doctor – seemed to be looking for someone. Then he spoke to Kez in broken English. 'Are you one of the bodyguards?'

'Yes, what do you want?' Kez snapped, heavy with grief. 'I know I sound like some kind of heartless animal,' Kez thought, 'but if he'd said to me, "Three of them have got to go. Who's to survive?" I would have said Trevor. Because he's a mate.'

The man said, 'Your friend is alive.' Kez grabbed him. Shook him. What did he mean? What did he mean? Maybe he meant Henri Paul.

'The bodyguard is alive.' Suddenly, Kez was terrified that they'd had to amputate, left him mutilated. 'Is he okay?'

'He's got head injuries.'

'Oh, well, that's fine. He can handle that,' said Kez, grabbing a radio phone. He said it in clear, for all the lads to hear. 'Trevor's alive. Trevor's alive. Call London.' He told Fayed, who was pleased, but the Boss had just lost his son. Then Kez looked out at the two security blokes across the way, and 'just saw massive morale sweeping their faces', like a wave.

They went on to the morgue to claim Dodi's body. Kez felt compassion for the Boss, as Fayed had to stand waiting while keys were found to let him in. He just stood there in shock, looking at the doors. They picked up luggage at the apartment, where Debbie had packed the Princess's clothes. By the time they were driving back to the airport, Fayed was in command again, detailing his people off to do this, do that. Hunting for people to blame. All Kez could see were the lads, giving him the thumbs-up and grinning. Trevor had survived.

7

Rebuilding a Face

London responded to its disbelief and grief over the tragic death of Princess Diana with flowers – acres, tons of flowers. The first cellophane-wrapped bouquets laid at the ornate gates at Kensington Palace before dawn were fast becoming a flood, with notes, photos and mementoes that would swell, night and day, and fan out across the lawn into a fragrant floral lake. Throughout the world, churches and embassies became spontaneous shrines. Football matches were cancelled, while trains, buses and the Underground filled with ordinary people coming to Kensington Palace.

How could it end in a car crash? Fate wouldn't choose such a crude and ordinary death for Diana. Who was to blame? By sunrise, the hunt for culprits had found its target. Millions had seen the television images of a forlorn group of photographers hauled off to jail from the crash site, seven slumped, dishevelled men mercilessly exposed in the brightly lit police van to the despising eyes of the world. Eye-witnesses were describing their callous behaviour – offering no help, descending on the crash like vultures, flashbulbs firing like machine guns, obstructing emergency care. 'Loathsome creeps,' Fayed's PR man Michael Cole condemned them in a press briefing that day as the paparazzi became public enemy number one. Within two days, nine would be named as suspects in the French criminal investigation.

Another cause had been named within minutes of the crash, out of view of the tabloids and networks: assassination. Conspiracy. At 6:40:59 A.M., two and half hours after Diana's declared death, the first Diana website went up and, thirteen minutes later, the first conspiracy website. Conspiracy theories would eventually rage worldwide on 36,000 websites, charging MI6, the CIA, and others, as agents of death for the British government, the royal family, and even for arms dealers who had feared Diana's anti-landmine campaign.

The Egyptian press, which had fanned national pride in Dodi's summer romance, instantly seized on the conspiracy theory, recruiting even its most distinguished writers and journals of record to charge assassination as a British tactic to prevent a royal marriage between the Muslim son of a famous Egyptian and the mother of future kings. Libyan leader Colonel Gaddafi joined the chorus. Racism, a Diana pregnancy, a payback for

Fayed's role in the fall of a government – all were grist for the North African conspiracy mill.

Though low-key at first, Fayed's own conspiracy theory was born at news of the crash. At 1 A.M. he had been told the tragic news. By 5 A.M. Fayed was bursting out to Kez in the car: 'I hope the British government is satisfied now.' Rumours were already spreading among Fayed drivers and security men in Paris that Henri Paul had been drinking. Could the conspiracy theory be a response? At 4:30 P.M. Ritz boss Frank Klein went to the Paris judiciary police to report 'suspicious circumstances' surrounding the crash, and John Macnamara, Fayed's senior security chief, was assigned to a full-time world-wide investigation. Next day, 1 September, another essential building-block of the conspiracy theory – the engagement and imminent marriage of Dodi and Diana – would be put into place as Michael Cole gave reporters the breathless headline: 'DODI AIMED TO SPEND REST OF LIFE WITH DI'.

All these external threads would lead to Trevor's door.

'Oh, Trevor, why is it always you?' Jill whispered as she entered Room 107 of La Pitié-Salpêtrière and approached an unrecognizable puffball of bandages and swelling attached to life by a tangle of tubes and wires.

They were strange words to come from a mother's lips as her son's life hung by a thread. But they expressed the love Jill Rees-Jones felt for this middle son, the one who, all his life, had been in and out of trouble compared to his brothers – always trying to do the right thing, always standing up for the underdog. She'd had heartaches, but few hugs, from Trevor – a family trait. Jill had never seen Colin, Trevor's father, show more affection to his own mother than a handshake. But the love was there between them.

She and Ernie had been in stunned shock since Sue's call in the middle of the night alerting them to the crash. Since they'd picked up the first television reports at 3 A.M. and heard that 'Diana was seriously hurt, the driver and Dodi were dead and the bodyguard was seriously injured', they'd been on a rollercoaster of conflicting reports over Trevor's condition – he was badly injured, dead, alive. With the Princess declared dead and the world's focus on her, they could glean only scraps of news on the bodyguard. At about 7:30 A.M., Fayed's people in London had urged them, 'Don't believe the report that he's dead. We know that he's still alive.' They must get to Paris – somehow. 'When we contacted Park Lane again, they offered to arrange a flight for us. We didn't realize at that stage that it would all be paid for, and didn't even think about it, to be honest – we just needed a flight.'

Sue called, wanting to join them, and they said, 'That's fine,' though Jill felt anxious about the effect it might have on Trevor. But she was still his wife. She had a right. Booked to fly out of Manchester mid-afternoon, somehow they'd packed overnight bags, a distracted Jill 'standing in the bedroom, putting a pair of knickers in my bag, then taking them out again – I just didn't know what

I was doing', while Ernie changed into his black suit. 'I never thought for a minute that he was going to die,' says Jill.

Shaking with cold in front of a blazing fire on a hot August night, Jill had to reach the boys. 'It was hard not to break down on the phone. I reached my eldest son, Gareth, in Birmingham – he didn't have a clue what Trevor's job was.' What admiration she felt for Trevor; he'd kept it all to himself. They called Ernie's son, Chris, in Oswestry. The boys were in 'shock, deep, deep shock', as they turned on their televisions to track their brother's fate. Jill tried to reach her youngest son, John. 'I couldn't contact him. He was away for the weekend. I couldn't just leave a message on his answerphone.' Jill was frantic. What if he heard it on the news? John, as it turned out, would follow the news of the crash for most of the day without knowing the bodyguard was his brother.

Ernie packed up Sooty, the dog, with her food and her basket, landed at a neighbour's doorstep, saying, 'I'm ever so sorry, but can we leave her with you?' and drove off.

Word that Trevor Rees-Jones was the injured body-guard was racing by word of mouth through Oswestry before most newscasters knew his name. Oswestry was facing the double shock of the death of the Princess and catastrophic injuries to a young man who, they suddenly discovered, worked in close protection – for Mohamed Al Fayed. 'He never talked about his job,' Mike Owen, the rugby club vice-president, would say to the media. As flowers began to build at the memorial gate at Cae Glas Park for a Princess who had never visited this borderlands Shropshire town, there were prayers and tears for Trevor, too.

Sue could not find her passport, the only delay they encountered as British Airways moved the three swiftly through a protected cocoon of VIP treatment – no check-in or queues, First Class seats. 'They just took us under their wing and marched us through,' says a grateful Jill. Sue's impending divorce from Trevor hung like a wall between them on the flight as they sat in silence. 'We were just so wound up in our feelings and emotions and the whole stress of the situation, wondering what was happening in Paris.' At Charles de Gaulle airport, 'The stewardesses gave us a hug and said, "I hope everything's okay,"' as they were ushered into a Ritz car, 'a big, long, black car with blacked-out windows – unbelievable', Jill observed, as was the sight at the hospital – 'the number of television crews and reporters, the main entrance road just covered in satellite dishes and television vans cheek by jowl, everybody's flashbulbs and cameras going off as we drove to the entrance of the hospital, and immense, absolutely immense, crowds of people, just wanting to be there'.

Like celebrities, they were hustled through the sea of clamouring media to the hospital steps and entrance where ten hours earlier Fayed and Kez had stood and where, now, France's leadership gathered to say a ceremonial farewell to the British Princess who had died on their soil. President Chirac and his wife waited for the silver-grey Jaguar flying the royal standard that was carrying, in a speeding convoy of ten vehicles escorted by police outriders, Prince Charles and the British Ambassador to France, Sir Michael Jay, and, following, Diana's two sisters, Jane and Sarah. 'Stand by,' Jill, Ernie and Sue were told, 'Prince Charles wants to meet you when he arrives.'

'At that point, a coffin arrived, covered by a deep crimson sort of heraldic flag, and it was taken up in the lift,' Ernie noted, shaken. It would carry Diana home to England. They and the Prince had been hurled on to the same nightmare stage.

They were led by doctors into the elevator up to the intensive-care unit, on the first floor. They moved through a heavy French police presence guarding Trevor into the sterile corridors of *Réanimation*. Jill was stirred by the word. 'Re-animation . . . what a wonderful word,' she thought. 'They're going to re-animate Trevor.' There, at the door to the ward, 'we were greeted by a reporter from our local newspaper'. They were appalled. How had she got in? How could she intrude on them now? 'I'm from the *Shropshire Star*, I speak French, and I'm here to help you through this terrible ordeal,' she said, as the couple, intuitively knowing that speaking to the media would be the last thing they needed just then, snapped, 'Go away. We do not want to talk to you.' 'But I can speak French,' she insisted, as the police escorted her off the premises.

Jill knew she had to 'take off my motherly head and

put on my medical head', or she'd never be able to handle what lay ahead. She had to find out before she saw Trevor what the scrambled television reports could not tell them. 'I had to know what was going to happen, what the prognosis was' – what the likelihood was of him having brain damage or paralysis? Could he, would he, survive? The veteran nurse ran through her list of questions with Dr Puybussent, the emergency medic who had been caring for Trevor since Dr Chikhani had completed his emergency surgery at dawn. 'If anybody looked at me, they'd think "what an uncaring mother", but it was the only way I knew how to cope with it.' Ernie, a retired hospital technician, had worked in hospitals too many years, seen too many of these types of injuries, to have any illusions. Showing them X-rays, Dr Puybussent gave them a swift summary of the fractures, contusions, bleeding within the skull. The injuries were appalling.

'Every bone in his face was broken,' Jill could see. But there was no skull fracture, thank God. The 'penetrating wound in his lung' held the risk of collapsing the lung, with infection and pneumonia in the pleural cavity; it had to be drained constantly. The lethal risk was from the swelling in the brain. They'd done a lumbar puncture and found blood cells in the cerebral spinal fluid, which meant that the violent jostling of the brain at impact had torn the meninges, the leathery membranes that surround the brain and hold in the cerebro-spinal fluid that cushions and protects the brain. Meningitis was only one of the threats.

Trapped inside the skull, the swelling – cerebral oedema, as doctors called it – could put such pressure on the brain that it could cause breakdown of the vital functions and organ systems controlled by the brain, and kill him. 'You could have heart or respiratory arrest,' Jill feared, 'or failure of liver or kidneys.' The thing that could trigger cerebral catastrophe was agitation – the great physical and mental agitation caused by this building pressure and irritation on the brain. Trevor must be subdued by heavy sedation. If he woke up, he was in danger of damaging himself. The doctors were not yet able to say if there had been brain injury from the crash itself.

Great urgency hung over his condition. The desperate effort to reduce the swelling and stabilize his functions was driven by time. The surgery that would rebuild Trevor's face 'must be done', Jill knew, 'before the bones had begun to fuse. They either had to operate quickly – within five or six days of the crash – or leave it for three or four weeks until you could re-break the bones where you wished.' If you had partial fusion, you could not break the bones cleanly and precisely, and you ran the risk of random shattering.

As they were taken to Room 107, they were prepared, in Ernie's words, for one of three scenarios: 'If he didn't die, he was going to be brain-damaged or paralysed.'

'You may not recognize your son,' the doctor warned as they approached. Trevor's left wrist was in plaster, a familiar sight for a nurse with many years in the operating theatre in Oswestry's orthopaedic hospital. But nothing could prepare Jill for the head. 'A round ball with tubes coming out of it – a face like a football, almost spherical.' Through the blood and bandages, she could see a face that 'looked as though it had been hit with a frying pan, like a Tom and Jerry cartoon. It had been smashed back, widened and flattened. The whole contours of his face were just demolished.' Eyes were hidden behind the swelling, the left socket gashed and sagging. Rough sutures held flaps of flesh together. He was unrecognizable.

The life-support equipment that was maintaining and monitoring his existence spoke eloquently of the fragility of his condition – tubes up his nose, an arterial line, a drip in his right arm, a lung drain that came out between his ribs. An ECG on his bare chest gave a heart trace, a ventilator breathed for him through the tracheal tube stuck into his windpipe. There was a pulse monitor on his finger, a cervical collar to immobilize the cracked vertebrae in his neck. Trevor had been transformed into graphs, traces, oscillations and electronic heart beeps. The nurse in Jill was alert to any irregularities or racing in the beeps. They seemed normal.

She knew him by his legs. And by his ears, battered by rugby. 'Oh, his ears were very personal to Trevor.' The happiest of memories were now unbearably bittersweet – the Saturday afternoons she and Ernie had cheered him on, with Trevor always in the thick of things, 'always at the bottom of the ruck'. He was sedated, and more out of consciousness than in, but the doctor was shouting at

him, trying to get a response. 'Trevor! Open your eyes!
Trevor!' He was getting a small reaction from Trevor's
right eye, and fitful traces of movement in Trevor's arms
and legs. He was not paralysed – he even seemed to want
to get out of bed! Good signs, but the agitation was dangerous. His mother touched his arm, willing him to live.

They had been with Trevor for less than ten minutes
when an official came up and said, 'Prince Charles is
arriving now. Would you come with me, please.' How
could they tear themselves away? Reluctantly, the three
of them followed him to the lift and down to the lobby.

The surreal drama swirled around them. Security,
police, hospital personnel everywhere. They were led
towards the entrance door. A twelve-man honour guard of
the Garde Républicaine flanked the entrance. As they
were about to be ushered into their audience with the
Prince of Wales – this grieving man still able to care
about them, doing his duty – a nurse rushed up, excited:
'Your son, he has awakened.' 'We left the official group –
stood up His Royal Highness – as we belted back to the
ward,' says Ernie, their words of regret and thanks to
Prince Charles echoing in the polished hallway behind
them as they rushed to Trevor's bedside. Gathered round
him, jubilant that an eye had opened, they held his hands
and talked to him. They picked up the chorus, 'Trevor!
Open your eyes,' and he responded. 'We're not sure he
could focus on us, but without a shadow of a doubt, he
knew we were there,' says Jill. They were permitted just
five minutes more with him. They rushed downstairs

again, but Prince Charles had departed with Diana's coffin.

On the hospital steps, Jill and Sue were given a hug by British Consul General Keith Moss, with tears in his eyes, and were moved quickly into a waiting limo to be taken they knew not where. 'We didn't have a clue.' The chauffeur was instructed to take them to 'the apartment' and could tell them nothing more. At the Arc de Triomphe, the car pulled up to the doors of Fayed's apartments on Rue Arsène-Houssaye, where Trevor had been just twenty-four hours earlier, and they were met in the foyer by a 'very burly, strong character' – the security guard, Gérard, who had scuffled with paparazzi. It was strange. There was no one representing Fayed, only the building's caretaker, to meet them.

He took them up to the fourth floor in a wonderful old lift with marble walls and ornate metal gates. The doors opened on to 'a scene of luxury we had seen only in stately homes – it was on that scale', Ernie marvelled. Jill, Ernie and Sue walked around, gasping at the lavishness – 'a splendid upstairs lounge big enough to hold a dance, with huge vases, all in red and gold, a dining room with massive marble fireplace, antique French furniture everywhere, wonderful carpets, silk tapestry wall coverings'. Checking the other rooms, Jill found 'three double bedrooms, two *en suite* with big circular baths and marble this and marble that . . .' It was like living in a museum.

They walked on to a balcony whose filigreed black iron railing overlooked the Arc de Triomphe and

Champs-Élysées. 'We'd thought we would be lucky if we could reside in a small flat,' Ernie felt. 'But to see an apartment of such opulence,' says Jill, picking up Ernie's words mid-sentence, as both so often did, 'I just could not believe my eyes. I'd never been anywhere that was so over the top.'

And food, Madame, the caretaker explained to Jill in French – anything they wished could be ordered from the Ritz. They'd not eaten since the day before. 'Well, perhaps we could do with a bit to eat . . . *un peu à manger*,' Jill responded in halting French. Shortly, food arrived in elegant cream and gold boxes – enough for eight or nine people. Smoked salmon, cold lamb and beef, pâté, fresh bread rolls, salad and a lovely French dressing. Wine had been sent over, and a display of fruit that looked like a seventeenth-century still-life painting.

They couldn't face the food. The apartment was air-conditioned, but they felt stifled and breathless. Jill was haunted by having to tell Trevor that he was the only survivor. Would he be able to bear it? How, when would she tell him? Jill and Ernie had to get out of the apartment, so they decided to go for a walk, leaving Sue in the flat. A casually dressed couple in their early fifties, they could have been tourists. In every one of the few snapshots they took, there is Jill, a slim, pink-cheeked woman with naturally waved sandy-brown hair, wearing the same loose white blouse and tan slacks she would wear to the embassy or penthouse. Right now, clothes couldn't have mattered less.

Near midnight, they walked down the Champs-Élysées. Suddenly, as they circled the Arc de Triomphe, a car was skidding and screeching towards them, giving Ernie a split second to push Jill out of its path. In his rage, he kicked the car and shouted as it braked and tore away. He had to strike out at something. As they headed for a pavement café, Jill burst out laughing. She suddenly had a vision of her being in a hospital bed beside Trevor, with Ernie stuck in the Bastille. Even black humour helped. They ordered a beer and were stunned to discover it had cost them £8! They wouldn't last here for more than two days. But they felt better. Only one thing mattered, and they toasted it with beer, establishing a ritual. 'To Trevor's total and complete recovery.'

The heat was still smothering, oppressive. They were drained. They called the hospital for a report on Trevor, and went to bed amid the grandeur, but were sleepless. Disbelieving. Profoundly grateful to Mohamed Al Fayed for looking after them. He even gave them a chauffeur, Philippe Dourneau, who regularly drove Dodi and Mr Fayed. A few days later, 'Philippe leaned over the back while driving us to the hospital, handed us a brown envelope, and said it was from Mr Frank Klein. We opened it, and found 2,500 French francs. Then, when we met Mr Klein later, we said, "Thank you very much, but why?" Klein said, "Mr Fayed wants you to have this for your expenses."'

*

That evening Kez was at Park Lane, being debriefed by
Paul Handley-Greaves. After getting Mr Fayed and
Dodi's coffin under way by helicopter to Battersea heliport, Kez had flown back to London in the Gulfstream jet.
Met by family at the heliport, the Fayeds were caught up
in the ceremonies at Regent's Park Mosque and burial
that day. The lights that ringed Harrods like a cruise ship
at sea had been turned off, and a shrine to the couple had
been installed in a window. Back at Park Lane, the lads
had greeted Kez like someone back from the dead. 'You
okay, mate?' 'Yeah, yeah, I'm fine.' 'How's Trevor, then?'
'He's in good hands.' Kez went through his debrief with
Handley-Greaves, told him everything – harassment by
the press, Dodi's idea to have Henri Paul drive and leave
from the back – but he was too numb and tired to feel
much emotion or the scale of what had happened.

'It's best if you go home on leave,' Handley-Greaves
told him. He was planning to anyway. It would be 'the
first sort of holiday I'd had in five years in the organization . . . I thought it was prudent to get away for a bit.'
He'd hang around Park Lane for a day, then go to Ireland
for a while, as planned, with two friends. To Kilkenny, to
the annual Goresbridge horse sales. Now, after all that
had happened, he wanted only to get on the ferry to
Rosslare, buy a horse, perhaps, and get as drunk as a
lord. 'I wanted to get as far away as possible from the
papers and TV, just to be among real people again.'

Along with the whole of Oswestry that Sunday, lawyer Ian

Lucas was watching television. It seemed a long time ago
that he had been woken up by his six-year-old daughter
who had come shrieking into her parents' bedroom.
'Mum, Dad, there's been some terrible news. The
Princess of Wales has been killed!' Half asleep and not a
strong royalist, he was, however, 'quite a sentimentalist,
and I do get a tear in my eye on occasions like this. I
thought it was very sad, intensely sad.' Like everyone
else, he felt the tug to the television set, and, late in the
morning, heard that a bodyguard had survived – may
even have heard his name. But it didn't register.

Later that day, his phone went; a secretary at the
Crawford Lucas law firm on Upper Brook Street, Tessa
Lloyd, called her boss at home. 'I think you should know
that we act for the bodyguard.' Ian didn't get it at first.
Then she said, 'Trevor Rees-Jones', and he remembered.
Ian had never met him, but recalled that his firm – the
young woman solicitor who specialized in matrimonial
work, Linda Hill – was handling his divorce, and that
Tessa's friendship with Trevor was a strong bond with the
firm. For Ian, 'at this stage, it was difficult to know what
to do. I knew immediately that the focus on him would be
monumental. We wanted to do something. But I was torn
between wanting to help and, on the other hand, not
appearing to be in any way ambulance-chasing.' He took
no action that Sunday.

David Crawford, the previous owner of the firm, knew
nothing of the connection until he came into the office on
Monday morning, climbing the 200-year-old stairs to the

third-floor office he now occupied as a partly retired consultant. His old office, directly below, had been taken over by Lucas, to whom he had sold the firm a few months earlier. 'Are you aware that we've acted for Trevor Rees-Jones, the bodyguard?' Linda climbed the stairs to ask.

That he would have a link with the tragedy seemed quite unimaginable, but actually, David Crawford had known Trevor's father, Colin Rees – had counted him a good friend. A fine and respected general practitioner and surgeon, he'd been his doctor. The son of a prosperous dentist and with Welsh roots himself, Crawford felt a connection with this medical man. He'd never met the son. But if he was anything like his father, it would take some injuries to keep him down. 'Colin was a great bloke, a very strong personality – nobody would dream of messing with him. An ex-military doctor, full of vim and vigour. He had lots of friends,' Crawford reflected. In recalling the father, he was describing the son more closely than he could have guessed. Colin's heart attack – in his prime – had been a tragic loss. What must the family now be enduring?

Crawford knew the rugby crowd well; he'd often handled legal matters for the club and its members. They must offer help. He immediately discussed it with Ian, and they agreed that, with an event of this magnitude, the Rees-Joneses would need someone to advise them. They jointly composed a letter to the hospital, saying, in effect, that they were 'the lawyers of Trevor Rees-Jones, who

was currently in their hospital . . . [they were] available
should the hospital wish to, in any way, communicate
with [them] . . . and would they, please, send this letter on
to him or his family as soon as possible'. Thank you, they
said, for all you've done for our client 'as well as for other
victims of this terrible accident'. It went off by fax to the
director of La Pitié-Salpêtrière hospital at 12:35 P.M. on
Monday, 1 September. Given the chaos surrounding the
crash in Paris, they had no idea if anyone would even see
it.

The two solicitors who, with this fax, had tossed their
calling cards into this highest-of-high-profile accident
cases were high-street lawyers who had chosen to do
country law – wills, divorces, personal-injury law, small
claims, business disputes. But they felt no intimidation in
the face of this extraordinary event. Ian Lucas came from
a working-class family in the industrial north-east, and
his brains had led him to Oxford University to study law.
That had cured him of any awe he might have felt for the
Establishment. He was just thirty-seven, and had run as
North Shropshire's Labour Party candidate for Parliament
in the last election, doing better than any previous
Labour candidate in this traditionally Conservative rural
seat. The campaign had taught him a few things about
handling the media.

From continental travel and schooling, Crawford
spoke, read and wrote French fluently and had the time
and resources to offer himself to help, if need be.
Crawford followed up the fax with a call to Sue's parents

in Whittington. He was a friend of her father, Ieuan Jones; they'd shared a trip to Spain. 'If you're in touch with Jill and Ernie Rees-Jones, perhaps you could just mention to them that we represent Trevor and would be happy to help in any way they think we could. I'm a fluent French speaker and am available,' he told the Joneses.

In Paris that morning there was a knock on the apartment door, and there stood a young woman. 'I'm Myriah, I was on the boat with Trevor. Can I be of any help?' It was Dodi's holistic masseuse. She had this wonderful energy within her, she explained, that could be of benefit to anyone who needed it. She had tremendous charisma. She claimed to have been a good friend, a confidante, of Trevor's, Jill noted: 'At that time, we felt that any support at all, as long as it couldn't hurt, could do some good. I'm all for anything that makes you feel better.'

So the four of them drove to the hospital in what would become the daily midday visit to Trevor, and gathered round Trevor's bed. Jill and Ernie each took a hand as Sue hovered in the background commenting that there were really not enough hands to hold on to. Ernie sensed that she felt left out, as Myriah lay her hands on Trevor's head and appeared to pray for him. There was no response.

Then, as the three pulled back, Sue leaned over Trevor and talked to him. He responded immediately. 'He responded totally to her. He knew her voice,' Jill saw. A good sign. But she felt a flaring of protective concern. 'It made me realize that until we knew what his memory situation was, it could be detrimental for Sue to be around.' Would Trevor remember that they were separated when he woke up? She'd noted that he wasn't wearing his wedding ring, but, clearly, he still loved her. What if he wants and needs her – and she's not there? Sue had absolutely no intention of coming back, Jill knew – in fairness, she'd been perfectly honest about that.

Sue went home that day, at Jill's urging. 'Maybe it would've been better for Trevor if Sue had stayed – who knows,' she would always agonize. It was never, ever a personal thing against Sue. But right now, semiconscious, Trevor was just too vulnerable.

'We had to bring him back to the real world, Dr Puybussent had advised us.' Jill began speaking to him, trying to reach that flicker of consciousness he had shown as he responded to Sue. She told him the four things she would repeat, like a mantra, each time she visited. 'There's been an accident. You're in Paris. You're in a hospital. You're going to be all right.'

Back at the apartment, they met Ben Murrell, the security man based at the Villa Windsor. He felt himself to be a good mate of Trevor's, and was assigned to provide Jill and Ernie with anything they might need. He would bicycle in each day. With a chauffeur and now Ben at their beck and call, they were free to focus solely on Trevor's recovery.

The press were a hovering threat. Whenever they looked from the balcony, 'there were film crews everywhere, just filming the apartment block, God knows why . . . We think they'd got wind of the fact that we were there, and were in wait,' Ernie noted, dismayed. This anonymous Oswestry couple had become a prime target for the paparazzi. Whenever they tried to leave the apartment, 'everybody was pushing in on you – you felt you couldn't breathe. We felt besieged.' Ernie was seething with resentment at this 'pressure by the press, just the sort of pressure which might have caused the accident. I feel they are very much to blame.'

Nine photographers and a motorcycle rider had been swiftly named as targets of the French investigation. Wielding the French 'Good Samaritan' law, which requires people to help unless they would endanger themselves doing so, the investigation would be for the crimes of involuntary homicide, failure to assist people in danger and involuntary wounding of the survivor – Trevor. If charged and found guilty, they faced up to five years in prison and a massive fine.

Amazingly, Jill and Ernie had avoided capture by a camera so far. Yet the world wanted to know about the bodyguard. The British Embassy was being flooded with requests for interviews with the Rees-Joneses, and had asked Jill and Ernie to come in for a meeting on the Wednesday after the crash to discuss the handling of the media as well as to introduce them to the Ambassador. Things were becoming complex. Sue's parents had told them, by phone that day, about David Crawford's offer to advise them. That evening, Monday, Jill called him in Oswestry.

'How is your son?' he asked.

'He could be better, but he could be worse,' said Jill, showing Crawford what he would come to know as 'the phlegmatic down-to-earth approach which was to shine through from her and Ernest throughout this ordeal'.

Crawford could see nothing that required immediate legal attention. With Trevor still unconscious, Crawford and Lucas could not yet speak on his behalf, but he urged Jill to call him if things changed at the Paris end. 'We're there if you need us.'

As he and Jill chatted, Crawford referred to the remarkable news he had just heard on British radio: that the driver of the car had had the equivalent of three times the legal limit of alcohol in his blood, that he had been drunk.

This was incredible news. A drunk driver! It threw millions of mourners into denial as they struggled to transform an epic battle between the hunter and the hunted into something as common and stupid as a drink-driving accident. It threw the guilt of the paparazzi into confusion, and pointed blame at an employee of the Ritz.

Jill had not heard the news. David was astounded. 'Are you being looked after by the Fayed family?' he asked. Yes, they were. She could not disclose the address, but gave him a telephone number. Fayed's people were caring for them solicitously, David was sure.

But he sensed that this first call from Jill might have been triggered by a growing need for input from elsewhere.

The news had set his lawyer's mind to work. He saw that possible issues of conflict with Fayed and the Ritz might arise for Trevor. Trevor had been injured in the line of duty, an innocent victim – he had interests and rights that must be protected. Crawford saw, also, the urgency and value to Fayed of learning what Trevor had to tell. The only one alive who could know what had happened in the three minutes before the crash was Trevor. It did not take an overly suspicious mind to see that, with the news of Henri Paul's drunkenness implicating a senior Ritz employee in the cause of the crash, Fayed might well have an interest in gaining early and exclusive access to Trevor's memories.

The media had seized on the importance of Trevor's memories from day one. Frustration with his inability to speak surfaced early. Monday's headline, 'POLICE WAIT TO HEAR CRUCIAL TESTIMONY', was followed, three days later in the *Mirror*, by 'The criminal inquiry has been brought to a standstill because of Rees-Jones's condition'.

But Trevor had to be kept heavily sedated until after his massive facial surgery. On 2 September they moved a step closer to that day when Jill and Ernie met Dr Chikhani for the first time. He came in to check on the swelling, hoping, needing, to do the surgery as soon as possible. The swelling was still too great, Trevor's temperature from chest infection too high. But Chikhani was exuberantly upbeat. The ballooning head *was* deflating, and new tests were being taken that day to see if he was operable. 'He can't wait to get his hands on Trevor, to put him together again like a Meccano set. He believes the surgery will be successful,' Jill and Ernie thought. They were charmed and impressed by this 'very keen, excitable, enthusiastic character – a young man in his mid-thirties who wears a wooden bow-tie . . . and speaks excellent English'.

Chikhani established, from the first, that he would have no communication with the press. He was a doctor, not a performer. Each time he turned on the radio or television, Trevor's face was there. The reports were outrageous – and wrong! Trevor had lost his tongue, he heard, the very first afternoon. It was a rumour that came from hearing that he could not speak, because of the tracheotomy, he guessed. But Trevor had a tongue!

Making a connection with his patient, though, was vital – it was everything. He must transmit trust, will, hope. Yet Trevor was not yet operable. Until he was, Jill would be Chikhani's sole path to Trevor. He would work through Jill with the same intensity and focus he brought to his contact with Trevor. Ernie, others, might be there, but they were invisible as he spoke only to her, explaining everything in technical, and in human, terms. Jill Rees-Jones would be absolutely perfect in taking care of her son, he saw. She was a nurse, but she acted as a mother. He marvelled at his luck. How rarely do you find such a perfect conduit to the patient?

The contract is between you and me, he said silently to Trevor. You cannot speak, but your mother has said, 'I believe in you. I trust you. You can take care of my son.' She had become vital to Trevor's recovery, part of a tight team of three: himself, Trevor and Jill.

There had been a strong suggestion from the Fayed organization very early on that Trevor should be moved to the private American Hospital. Fayed's concern for Trevor's welfare never seemed to cease, Jill and Ernie noted gratefully – perhaps Fayed felt he could protect Trevor better there from intrusion during this critical phase of his recovery. They resisted the pressure as they were very happy with the team at La Pitié-Salpêtrière. They had total confidence in them, and Trevor was in no fit state to be moved.

Chikhani saw this pressure from Fayed at close range. 'Since Trevor was a VIP and so on, this hospital was not good enough for Mr Fayed,' Chikhani mused. 'So he asked some doctors from the American Hospital, which is very select as far as money is concerned, to come. But when they came and saw the situation – when they *saw* him . . .' – Chikhani chuckles at the memory – 'they hurried to say, "This is very good. Yes, yes. He should stay here."' As surgeons, they knew you had to do many, many of these major reconstructive cases to be really good. Perhaps they felt they hadn't done enough.

These were the cases Chikhani lived for, though. He loved the traumatic cases. He loved his patients.

Since the contours of Trevor's face had been destroyed,

Chikhani needed photographs. Jill and Ernie had brought some, but they were not good enough. With calls to Oswestry they initiated a frantic hunt for pictures. Anything that showed his face clearly. His wedding pictures. Yes. Trevor's friend at the law firm, Tessa, feverishly collected the best that could be found, and sent a batch of photos off to Paris.

The day ended well. A new CT scan showed 'important regression of cerebral oedema'. *Réanimation* staff had agreed to the operation. It was set for two days later, Thursday, 4 September. Chikhani was jubilant.

That Wednesday, the day before surgery, Jill and Ernie went alone to their midday appointment with the Ambassador at the British Embassy. Collected in a very large limousine at the Hôtel Crillon on the Place de la Concorde, a convenient place for Philippe to drop them off from the hospital, they were driven the few hundred yards to the embassy on the Rue St-Honoré – for Jill and Ernie, just a brisk three-minute walk. A horde of media milled around the front, so they were driven through the back gate into the garden, where they were met by Sir Michael and Lady Jay, and served a wonderful tea. Jill and Ernie saw no reason why, just because they were at the British Embassy, they should not give their customary toast. Jill explained, 'Every time we have a drink, wherever we are, we always toast Trevor's recovery.' The Jays were delighted. In the garden, limp with the heat, they toasted, in tea, 'Trevor's total and complete recovery'.

Following tea, they were given their first stack of press clippings. Jill and Ernie were astounded by the coverage of the crash, and of Trevor. It was just too upsetting to read it all but they agreed to scan the stories flagged by the embassy. They had not said a word to the press, and Trevor couldn't speak. But that had not stopped the newspapers from turning Trevor into a military hero. Jill and Ernie knew he would be embarrassed to death – he'd never been to the Gulf or the Falklands, never served in the 'close-protection team of the Royal Military Police' or 'escaped from Kuwait as the Iraqis invaded'.

While Jill and Ernie were well aware that Trevor's survival was still tenuous, a British paper reported that 'the ex-Royal Military Police officer will make a full recovery'. And yet the day of his surgery, the *Mirror* would report that he had 'lost his tongue and half his face in the dreadful accident'. That rumour would soon lead to a well-meaning company in the US sending Trevor a talking computer to compensate for the loss of his tongue – a fantasy from the outset. It was nonsense. And irresponsible. They would read no more, unless they had to.

Jill and Ernie felt a pang of helplessness. 'The embassy wanted us to speak, to make an appearance, but we refused,' says Ernie. 'I think the embassy felt . . . what was coming across to them from the media was that our not speaking had something to do with Mr Fayed, that we were acting on Mr Fayed's instructions. It wasn't that at all. It was more that we were so emotional at that time that any one question could've triggered the response they were looking for, which would have been . . .' Jill completes the sentence, '. . . a breakdown.' So the embassy settled with the agreement that Jill and Ernie would write their own press releases, and the embassy would send them out. No interviews.

As they left the embassy, they were urged to take a mobile phone. They would need it later that day: Prince Charles would be calling them between 5:30 and 7 P.M. on that number.

They would miss Charles again. They left the mobile phone in the car because, with the hospital's sensitive electronic equipment, they were not permitted to use it in the ward, and they were at the hospital on their regular late-day visit when his call was supposed to have come in. 'We felt terrible about it. We'd stood up HRH twice. We often wondered if our driver had actually spoken to the Prince in our place – and what he might have said.'

The next morning, Dr Luc Chikhani lifted his scalpel and, following the path of an old rugby scar, made an incision across Trevor's face, from inside the mouth just above the upper teeth, then another, from jaw to jaw below the lower teeth, and began to peel back half of his face to the chin. At 7:30 A.M. he had entered the surgical theatre for the most exciting challenge of his career – the total reconstruction of Trevor's face. Although there were some lesions here that he had never seen before – some dislocation of the temporal mandibular joint he had never even seen published – most of the technical challenges

he at least knew could be dealt with. What was extraordinary – unique! – was to see them all together, at the
same time, in a patient who was still alive.

Each day, Trevor's vital signs had grown stronger. An
anaesthetist, checking his heart, had deemed him strong
enough, this morning, for surgery. Yet it would be gru-
elling for doctor and patient, a medical marathon of at
least eleven, perhaps twelve or thirteen hours of non-
stop surgery. If successful, it would give Trevor a face,
give him the chance of a life with some semblance of
normality. It would let him go out on the street without
humiliation, and give him back the anonymity and privacy most people don't value until it is lost.

Chikhani liked to operate with natural light coming
through the windows. But because there were journalists
everywhere, with long lenses, they had to hide the whole
thing. They covered all the windows with screens, and
the medical chief warned every member of the surgical
staff, 'You'll be fired if you say a word to anybody.'

An array of Trevor's wedding pictures was taped to the
walls, two metres away from Trevor's sedated body. What
an irony to have, as a guide, pictures of the best day of
Trevor's life – this broadly smiling man, in tails and top
hat, ecstatically happy beside a beautiful smiling woman.
Chikhani could see that, before the crash, this was a man
everybody looked at. Not because he was a bodyguard to
Diana, but because he was impressive from a facial point
of view. He was good-looking. You think anatomy, of
course, but you think aesthetics, too. And yet you cannot

be arrogant; he must not make the face that he, Chikhani, might want the patient to have, but the face he had had before.

He had one aim: 100 per cent return not only of his face, but of his function – to have Trevor as he was before. His secondary goal was to fix it all in one operation. It was much more difficult to do a further operation later. More difficult, with a lower chance of success.

The atmosphere was very tense. But the tension fell away, for Chikhani, as he began. The operation was already done in his head. He had had three days, and knew what he was going to do, step by step. It was completely clear. He had only to recollect it.

First, he told Trevor everything that was going to happen. And again, he told him, 'You will not die.' Through a very long day, he would struggle to regain symmetry and a likeness to the man in the wedding pictures.

If Jill's first sight of Trevor evoked the imagery of a Tom and Jerry cartoon, the surgery was more science fiction. Once he made his incisions, Chikhani would painstakingly peel the skin back to the chin – an extraordinary process that would expose his entire face, one half at a time. Though a shade less sensational than Hollywood fantasies like *Face/Off*, which shows a whole face being peeled off one person and attached to another in an identity switch, it is still one of the most astounding procedures in the medical repertoire. It was not like peeling an orange, but what Chikhani called 'undermining'.

The aim was to make no visible scars, so you never cut anything. You exerted no force. Skin was layered in many planes, skin under skin under skin — epidermis, hypoderm, muscle, intermeshed with blood vessels — spurting veins, oozing capillaries — and tangles of sensitive nerves. You went in with a pair of exquisitely sharp scissors, progressively snipping through the layers, undermining, uncovering, freeing the nerves and the tissues from their bone hold, exposing the bone itself. You must be precise, and economical. Severed nerves could leave Trevor with facial paralysis. You must limit the bleeding — twelve hours of bleeding. Since it was still attached to the face, blood continued to pulse through this large flap of flesh during surgery, keeping it alive.

The 'peeling' of the bottom half of Trevor's face took only half an hour, or at the most an hour. As Chikhani laid bare the entire mid-face — the mouth, chin, lower jaw — he faced a scene of devastation. As he had expected, it was a landscape of fractured, free-floating bones and masses of bone debris, of teeth cracked and skewed crazily from their orderly rows. It was mush.

It was vital that the jawbone joint be re-established, and that the upper and lower jaws and teeth fit together. 'We are going to do intermaxillary fixation now, Trevor,' he explained. Chikhani secured wire at the outer ends of the cheekbones, then stretched it, top and bottom, across the upper and lower jaws, creating two wire arcs. Then he wired the jaw — wrapped wire around each tooth, attached it to the wire arcs and fixed the two jaws together with many other wires, locking the mouth closed. The skin was rolled back up over the mouth, and clamped – but not yet sewn – into place.

Chikhani was not even halfway there. He was the only senior surgeon in the operating room. He had some juniors to help him. They, and the nurses, rotated every three or four hours, giving him fresh help. Usually, you let the juniors assist you with the operation, so that they could learn. But in Trevor's condition this was out of the question. One senior surgeon helped him for about an hour. But Chikhani could not stop. You do not have the luxury of operating for forty hours – the patient could not survive it, you dare not risk it. As he completed the lower face, he paused for twenty minutes to eat a little, his only break.

And then he turned his attention to the upper half of the face. The longest, most dramatic part of the surgery still lay ahead. The eyes. The nose. Repeating the process of the lower face, he now made an incision across the top of Trevor's head, from ear to ear through his hair – careful not to sever the vessels that feed the hair, which could leave Trevor bald – and delicately, delicately peeled the flesh back to below the eyes, the technical limit of the technique. As he bared the facial skull, Chikhani saw for the first time the shattered terrain he knew so well from careful study of the X-rays and scans. The mid-face had been severely displaced – pushed back and spread. The distance between the two eyes had been expanded from 36 millimetres to 56 millimetres – from roughly 1½ inches to 2½ inches. He looked oriental. And his eyes were going in all directions. The eye sockets had been depressed a full inch; in profile, the bony bridge of the nose sat far back from the mouth and teeth.

A stack of titanium mini- and micro-plates, with screws and washers, sat at hand, this carpenter's tools. Titanium was lightweight, strong, and adapted to the face. With special pliers, Chikhani could twist and shape each plate to the bone it was to be attached to. He would position disconnected pieces of bone together, put plates on both sides, then screw the plates together, reconnecting the pieces. He would be rejoining the articular surfaces of the jaw joint to the skull, fusing cleaved cheek and chin bones, rebuilding the shattered bottom floor of the orbital cavity – the eye sockets, and the whole orbital wall on both sides – and pulling the entire mid-face forward.

As they now were, the eyes were grotesque. Yet, as he explored, he found that Trevor's eyes, though pushed back an inch and spread apart twice their normal distance, were, miraculously, intact. 'We're going to fix your eyes in a good position, now, so that you don't have diplopia – double vision,' he told his patient. 'Your eyes will be fine.' For hours, like a mechanic, he gently moved shattered pieces of bone around and, when they were in position, drilled tiny holes, attached the plates, and – using the tiniest of screwdrivers – tightened the titanium screws, gently forcing the pieces of bone together, where they would knit. If the lower face had been a monument to wire, this would be a monument to titanium plates! He would use thirty or forty of them.

'Trevor, I am going to rebuild your nose now,' he said, speaking to the inert form. He would take some bone from the back of the skull and graft it to the cheekbones to create a new bridge. Then, with flesh and cartilage grafts, he would fashion a new nose.

After five more hours, he had completed the top half of Trevor's face, the mid-face – eyes, nose, cheekbones. The skin was then rolled back over the bones and re-attached to the head skin with staples.

At 6:30 P.M., after more than eleven hours of surgery, everything that could be fixed was fixed. The mouth was the last to be sewn up. Full of bacteria, most prone to infection, its incision was the last to be closed. Chikhani and his assistants pulled the skin of Trevor's lower face taut to meet the top half, and sutured the two together. It was over. If there were scars on this face, they would be from the accident itself and from rugby, Chikhani felt sure. They would not, he hoped, be from his scalpel.

He would not know for perhaps a week if he had done it all in one operation – or if he would have to go in again, which he would feel was a failure. But as Trevor's swollen head was swathed in bandages – as Chikhani took off his surgical greens and dressed for the street, as if coming home from some ordinary office job – he felt satisfied that he had done the best he could, today. Now

Trevor must find the courage for the daunting job of recovery. Chikhani must call the parents.

For Jill and Ernie, the world had shrunk to the walls of the apartment and thoughts only of Trevor. For eleven hours, they could not leave. It was the first time in the last four unreal days that Jill had had time to reflect. Ernie found his therapy, his way of making sense of the chaos, by organizing the daily events into notes and writing them down each night. Now, Jill found her catharsis in writing a letter to Helen, her good friend and colleague at the surgery where she worked.

My dear Helen,

As today is the day of Trevor's mammoth facial reconstruction, we are staying here in the apartment by the phone all day . . . Firstly, and without doubt, the major consideration is Trevor – as yet he hasn't been totally conscious at any time. Yesterday we did feel that he was aware of us and I think he knew it was me . . . He is being kept sedated . . . and they will not wake him up until after his operation. When he does wake, we have no way of knowing what his mental state will be. The doctor is confident that the trauma to his brain is minimal and he should therefore not suffer any long-term deficit. However, what he will remember of the accident, the hours and days before the accident, we have yet to discover.

I feel strongly that the people who are here when he

wakes up must be the ones who are his closest family, as we will be there for him through the coming months. To this end, I have, I hope, dissuaded Sue from being here, as if she is around one moment and then not around it would be too confusing for Trevor – he may not even remember they have separated.

Gareth, John and Chris are flying out on Friday, and so we will all be with Trev over the weekend, when he is allowed to wake up. The information that Diana and Dodi are dead will be a tremendous shock to him and that will have to be done very carefully as he was very close to them both.

If that were all we had to cope with, it would be quite enough, but due to the circumstances, we suddenly find ourselves in a situation of which we have had no previous experience and instead of our quiet private life, we are suddenly the target of the press pack. We have been looked after incredibly well by Trevor's employers and are protected as far as possible, but the sudden change from cycling to work in Oswestry to being whisked around Paris in big black limousines with darkened windows is a little hard to take! . . . We are learning as we go along . . . At present I'm fine – Ernie and I are propping each other up . . . We have seen some press clippings and get the *Telegraph* each day but neither of us are able to read any of the accounts as we get very emotional – so we are keeping clear of things that upset us . . .

On a more lighthearted note – this apartment is so big, Ernie keeps losing his shoes!

We can't wait to get back to normal – I promise I will NEVER think my life dull and boring again . . . All our love . . .

Chikhani called in the early evening. The surgery had been a success. Trevor was stable. Recovery would be total. Jill and Ernie escaped the apartment, jubilant, drained. They went to the flashy neon-lit Virgin record store a few blocks down the Champs-Élysées. Jill put on earphones to listen to a CD of Bach Cantatas, and was powerfully moved. She bought the CD, but was never able to listen to it again. 'I tried once, and it just finished me off.'

8

The Sole Survivor

Jill desperately needed to connect with home – needed to see the boys. Friday night, after seeing Trevor, she and Ernie picked them up at the airport, her oldest and youngest sons, Gareth and John, and Ernie's son, Chris. Their flights had been arranged and paid for by Mr Fayed. There were hugs, and the range of responses Jill could have predicted, with each of them so very different. 'Gareth, appearing to take things in a very light-hearted fashion.' A dentist, so like his father, physically.

John had made the family's love of sports his profession, teaching sports education at a college – 'a very serious and emotional chap' who, as Jill expected, showed the most emotion as they met. Chris, Ernie's son, perhaps because he lived in Oswestry, 'is very involved in having organized everything at home – he's taking responsibility, making sure the house is all right'.

Jill and Ernie had planned a family meeting around the dining-room table. The dining room had become the one place in this vast luxurious apartment that felt anything akin to their own home, and the dining-room table was where they gathered to talk and eat and plan. They had prepared an agenda for the meeting, and they ran through it: Trevor's condition. A warning to the boys about the horrendous Paris traffic – and the high living costs. They explained about the money from Mr Fayed for out-of-pocket expenses. 'We don't want to take or use any more than we really have to, but we're very grateful and appreciative for all that Mr Fayed and his group have done.' The embassy, too, 'was there for us' and was helping with the press releases. Of great importance, the boys must know that 'we don't feel pressured by either the Fayed group or the embassy – we feel we're able to make our own decisions'.

Only the boys' wives or partners – 'only Heather and the two Helens' – were to be told of 'our situation, the apartment, where we're staying'. It was really to protect the Fayed group. 'We don't want them to feel that we've let them down by telling everybody we are living in such luxury while we are in Paris – you can imagine the headlines in the *Shropshire Star* if it got out. And tell everybody at home: don't believe what you read in the papers; just read the official statements. We wrote one today about Trevor's surgery and the embassy are

releasing it.' With news of the drunk driver, they told the
boys, 'the situation regarding the accident is getting more
tense, but Trevor was very highly regarded by Dodi and
his family and the whole organization'. Ben Murrell had
reassured them on that. If Trevor should need legal rep-
resentation in France, the embassy would help. And
Oswestry lawyers were standing by.

'You are very, very important to Trevor, and to us. We
need you,' Jill and Ernie told them as the meeting wound
up. The boys must know that, though their parents might
seem preoccupied with Trevor, they had not been forgotten. 'We all need each other. We are forging ahead as one
family, together.' The future? Jill would ask for a leave of
absence from the surgery. 'And we're going to have the
family Christmas party. If Trevor's at home, we'll have it
at home. If he's elsewhere, we'll go to him.'

They followed the meeting with what became the weekend's ongoing game of gin rummy, letting off the tension
with 'a lot of laughs'. You had to laugh to stay sane, Jill
and Ernie had quickly learned. They laughed at the little
things, at the ludicrous ironies of it all – the caretaker's
wife snatching Jill's bit of hand-washing from her as she
rinsed her undies and one blouse in the bathroom sink
and, from then on, insisting on washing, pressing and
folding her knickers as if they were royal ballgowns. Well
past midnight, the whole family went for a walk. And
laughed some more. They suddenly discovered a new
threat: hordes of in-line skaters scattering pedestrians on
the pavements of the Champs-Élysées.

But they could not watch Diana's funeral the next day. It was not bearable.

Diana was buried on Saturday 6 September after a service at Westminster Abbey with the pageantry of a full royal funeral, forced upon the royal family by a public demonstration of affection that far surpassed any previous royal death in record or memory. Fifty-nine per cent of all adult Britons watched on television, along with an estimated two and a half billion people around the world. As Charles and the two Princes walked in procession behind the coffin, change walked with them. After staying, silent, at Balmoral, while the nation fumed, the Queen had shown the first signs of listening to the new Prime Minister, Tony Blair, and the people the day before. As Jill and Ernie's sons flew to Paris, the Queen returned at last to London and appeared before her people, doing a walkabout outside Buckingham Palace. She spoke at last, paying tribute to Diana in a compelling television address. The Palace flag would fly at half-mast for the funeral. She had appeased the worst outrage of her subjects. But if the monarchy was to survive this crisis, it could no longer offer hollow ceremonies without human involvement. It was William and Harry's walkabout amid the sea of flowers at Kensington Palace that had touched and broken hearts. A sobbing woman reached out to touch William's hand. 'Your mother lives on in your face, lad. God bless you.' Mohamed Al Fayed could be glimpsed among the mourners, wearing a dark suit, a look of anguish.

As the preparations for the funeral gripped the world, the Rees-Jones family went to the hospital together. 'Trevor's a bit of a mess. They're keeping him sedated,' Jill told the boys, to prepare them for the still grossly swollen, unresponsive person they were about to see. John was so upset as the reality, the enormity, hit, that, for some time, he stood looking out of the window and couldn't look at Trevor directly. Chris and Gareth, typically, were very stoic. Gareth – so different from Trevor that they could go a month without talking – went direct to Trevor's bed and chatted to him about his wife's pregnancy, about their optimism, after two miscarriages, that they'd have their first baby to show him soon. John joined his brothers at the bed, as each, in his own way, willed Trevor to heal.

   That afternoon, they went for a walk – the usual routine. Jill and Ernie had developed 'a game of hide-and-seek with the press. We'd have a look outside, wait until the photographers had moved round the corner, then we'd rush out of the apartment,' says Jill. 'Once we were out, we were anonymous again – we could walk without being recognized.' When they returned, they'd hide across the street until the coast was clear, then run in to safety. They took the same route, Champs-Élysées, Place de la Concorde, down to the Seine and, this time, to the accident site. 'Paris seemed empty, so quiet it was unbelievable – every-body must have been watching the funeral,' Ernie noted. They went to the gilt flame at the Place de l'Alma, just above the tunnel, Diana's shrine in Paris. An enormous flow of people had been placing flowers, taping on poems and cards. Notes were written in many languages. 'It finally got to us, here, how many people have been struck by this event.'

Jill shared the sense of personal loss the world felt. 'I had a great regard for her and was terribly upset that she had died. I felt she'd been badly used by the Establishment and that she'd have done her level best to make a life for herself, and to be of use to society. And yet, we felt strangely detached – we were involved, and yet we were looking in on them, not part of them.'

From their unique vantage-point, they were witnessing the transformation of the flesh-and-blood Princess who had laughed with Trevor into a legend, one of the charis-matic women who endure in the pages of history. Diana was being enshrined as 'The People's Princess', her legend burnished by the briefness of her life, her unknowable future. Had she – like Charles's great-uncle Edward, the Duke of Windsor – ultimately married a for-eigner, she might, the *New Yorker*'s Tina Brown would speculate, have lived 'a life of luxurious exile, of mean-ingless wandering from one pleasure spot to the next', an ageing beauty whose only hope of redemption would be 'the thing that has redeemed her in death: her earnest, utterly unironic efforts to ease a bit of human suffering.

Now she is frozen into bas-relief, forever kneeling to comfort some hurt.'

Here, at the flame, the Rees-Jones family began to grasp how big and how long an impact this death would have on their own lives. As the durability of Diana's flame became apparent, anything that attached to her became more important. Trevor – almost alone in the Western world – had no idea that the Princess with whom he had so recently shared a Sardinian beach and paparazzi-dodging was dead. And yet her death would touch the rest of his life.

Walking back around the Arc de Triomphe, the family ducked the cameras of the street photographers who took pictures of tourists before pestering them to buy. 'Non, merci. Non, merci,' they said as they deftly escaped, laughing that all these hustling photographers had the shot of their careers, the shot all the paparazzi in Paris were trying to get – and had missed. 'They could have made a fortune – thank heavens they don't know who we are.'

The boys visited Trevor on Sunday, before leaving Paris. They gathered round him. Ernie held his right arm, Gareth his left, and John and Chris each had a foot. Jill was at his head and placed her hands on Trevor's chest to see if he was still burning hot and fevered with infection. He was cool. His temperature was down. He had broken the infection that threatened pneumonia. The doctor on duty that weekend, Dr Poett, came by. 'We will wake him up on Monday, and hope he is not too agitated.' Ernie and

Jill 'bade a sad farewell to the boys' after they left the hospital.

When Jill and Ernie arrived next morning, there was already great excitement in the ward. With sedation reduced, Trevor had awakened during the night. The intern who had been with him, a German student, had asked Trevor, in English, if he remembered the accident, and Trevor had become so agitated, the intern reported, he'd had to struggle to calm him. Trevor had opened his eyes and responded well to his commands. Trevor would remember nothing of this event, and would later, typically, downplay its significance. 'It was probably no more than the flicker of an eyelid. It's not like I would sit up and have a chat.'

It was Monday, 8 September, nine days since the crash. 'The change,' Ernie recorded, 'is dramatic. His dressings have been reduced and he's no longer wrapped up like the Invisible Man – we have a look-alike Trevor with us again!' Above all, 'his eyes are open, he responds to Jill by moving a cheek muscle and an eye – several times. He knows that we are both there with him.' 'We were absolutely over the moon,' says Jill. 'A very positive day,' Ernie summed up, with his usual understatement.

Earlier that morning, Jill and Ernie had gone to the Ritz hotel, at the invitation of the hotel's president, Frank Klein, to meet a lawyer they assumed to be one of Mr Fayed's legal team, Jean-Pierre Brizay. 'The purpose of that meeting,' as Ernie saw it, 'was to express concern for Trevor and to suggest the names of suitable lawyers in

Paris – in particular, Theo Klein of Klein Goddard.'
'Trevor has Mr David Crawford available to represent
him,' they told the hotel manager, as he handed the
couple their second float of 2,250 francs. They took it
with no sense of obligation to Mr Fayed; Trevor, a valued
employee, had been working when the accident had happened. As David Crawford would later say, 'It was the
least he could do.'

The Ritz meeting was a fading footnote compared to
the good news on Trevor, as Jill and Ernie had their daily
late lunch of beer and camembert sandwiches at the Café
Tilbury. They toasted Trevor at the simple little red-
canopied café, close to the apartment, that had become
their club, their sanctuary. Each day, between the midday
and early evening visits to Trevor, they ordered the same
45-franc sandwich and felt comfortable. Anonymous.
Safe to pour out the day's events to each other. And
delight in their own small conspiracy: the owner had no
idea who they were.

At 7:30 that evening they met their MP, Owen
Paterson, in the Yellow Drawing Room of the
Ambassador's residence. 'Wonderful news on Trevor
today. He's woken up,' Jill reported. 'Ah, this calls for
champagne,' said Sir Michael. They toasted Trevor's
recovery, this time, from crystal flutes.

The celebratory mood dropped to silence when – as
Jill and Ernie glanced through a new stack of press clippings – Fayed's name came up. They had both noticed,
from the beginning, the embassy's sensitivity to Fayed's

name. There was a 'strange feeling and the tone of the
conversation went cold if we mentioned Mr Fayed. No
comment would be made, but we'd be moved on to a different subject. They never told us why. We wished they'd
tell us what he had done,' Ernie reflected. 'Fayed had
simply not impinged very much on our consciousness in
Oswestry,' Jill observes. Sensing the embassy's discomfort with them staying in Fayed's apartment, Ernie,
always frank, took the occasion to ask them, 'If we were
to stop using Mr Fayed's apartment, is there anything
that you can do for us in that regard?' No, they were terribly sorry, there was not. The consulate would love to,
but had no accommodation to offer, nor a car willing to
drive them to the hospital sometimes three times a day.

While Jill and Ernie studiously avoided reading crash
stories, the embassy, Britain's face abroad for both the
government and the crown, read them avidly. Just as
Trevor had passed the survival crisis, there were signs
that the monarchy, too, might have passed its crisis. Cries
in the press for abolishing the monarchy were being
replaced by cries for reform. In *The Times*, David
Dimbleby's article 'Hard Lesson the Queen Must Learn'
saw 'a changed nation crying out – not for republicanism
but for a new style of monarchy that better reflects the
Britain of today'. The *Financial Times* had followed Tony
Blair's Sunday lunch at Balmoral with the headline,
'"ROYAL FAMILY MUST EMBRACE CHANGE" SAYS BLAIR'.

With the news of Henri Paul's alcohol levels, Fayed's
charges against the photographers had been dramatically

diluted. But he continued to keep up the pressure on them. A story in that morning's *International Herald Tribune* quoted one of Fayed's lawyers, Bernard Dartevelle, as saying that the crash had been caused by harassing paparazzi cars and motorcycles reported by witnesses, and that the police were hunting for a car that 'might have been trying to slow down the Mercedes so that pursuing photographers could get a shot of her through the window'.

The 'ring' story broke in Paris on Tuesday, 9 September. The *International Herald Tribune* picked up a *Washington Post* story quoting the jeweller Repossi that 'the couple went unexpectedly to the Monaco branch of his store about ten days before the accident . . . and together picked out the diamond ring he gave her hours before they died'. The story spread like a virulent cancer, backing Fayed's claims of an engagement. But, as Trevor and Kez knew, part of it, at least, was untrue.

The day the ring became part of the legend, Trevor came off the ventilator, breathing for himself for the first time. He was 'awake and responsive'. He couldn't talk because his jaws were wired shut and the tube in his throat permitted no sound. But Jill and Ernie were encouraging him to respond to them with signs. They asked him questions, and said, 'Trevor, if it's yes, just squeeze my hand.' Or shake your head. Or try to open your eye. They'd made a chart on the back of one of the cream and gold cardboard boxes that delivered Ritz food, and written a small alphabet, hoping it would help him talk to them. If he opened an eye, they pointed to letters and tried to interpret his tiny reactions to form a word. Could he still think, reason – and remember?

On that day, he was very agitated, and the twitches and movements had increased. 'He wants to cough to clear the airway, but he cannot. He wants to tell us something,' Ernie saw. Do you want to ask us something? The hand squeezed. Yes. What is it? They sense his frustration. The chart. The muscle twitches. It was all so painstaking. So painful. He was close to communicating – anxious about something. But he was so disturbed they did not dare push it any further that night.

Back at the apartment, Paul Handley-Greaves and John Macnamara, Fayed's two heads of security, were waiting for them. It was Handley-Greaves's second visit, Macnamara's first, from London. The two had been denied access to Trevor by the hospital staff, and asked many questions about the crash. Jill and Ernie, of course, knew nothing. 'What they really wanted to know,' Ernie could tell, 'was whether Trev had remembered anything.'

They arrived at Trevor's bedside the next morning with the chart, and started pointing to letters that spelled names. He looked more human. His hair had been washed, his face had healed a little. But he was violently agitated. Showing his enormous strength, twisting, trying to move his lips. The fight was still there, Jill saw, elated – the powerful swimmer who'd come within seconds of winning the Welsh National Championship, the rugby player who'd, a thousand times, fought his way out of the pile of bodies at the bottom of the ruck. Trevor was still there. 'He's amazingly strong,' Ernie noted, 'and he wants to get out of bed. He can put his foot up on to the metalwork above his bed and twist his body over. He holds his mother, and puts his good arm around her. He held Jill.' To get more leverage? To show affection? Jill guessed that his struggle was against the realization, at last, that he was badly injured.

She was wrong. Trevor believed he was perfectly well. 'As soon as I woke up, I started remembering things, and I thought I was perfectly all right, to be honest. When your brain starts working, you think you're fine, don't you. I didn't think I was as bad as everyone was making out. I thought I was fine. I could get up and go home.'

Jill and Ernie had work to do. 'Do you want to ask about Sue?' they asked. No, said Trevor, pointing to the chart. About your boss? No. Is it about Helen, your sister-in-law who's pregnant? No.

'Is it something to do with the crash?'

Yes.

'Is it the driver?'

No.

'Do you want to ask about the people that were in the car, the other passengers?'

Yes.

The time had come to tell him. But he was exhausted, too drained by this effort to go any further, and the nurses put him back on the ventilator. They said, 'We'll try and find out what happened to the passengers, and tell you tomorrow, Trevor,' and he seemed quite happy with that.

Inside his head, Trevor had just had his first conscious recollections. 'I knew there was a crash.' He remembered that Dodi and Diana were in the back seat as they left the Ritz. He remembered fighting, struggling with someone to get out. He didn't remember the crash directly, didn't know who the driver was, but he had finally understood what his mother had been telling him, 'There's been an accident . . .' He had not had long, unbroken hours of clarity. Just fragments of memory. 'I was off, and then back on, the ventilator that day, and I must have been sedated for that. I was in and out of consciousness,' he speculated later. But he was re-entering the world.

Jill and Ernie searched out the hospital psychologist, desperate to know 'if we would be doing the right thing by telling Trevor of the deaths so early – or should we wait? We didn't know.' The psychologist was very helpful. 'He made a wonderful comment: "Listen to the rhythm of his responses." We must listen to what he was trying to say to us and respond accordingly.'

Not wanting to intrude unless he was asked, David Crawford had not notified the Rees-Joneses of his trip to Paris until a few days before his arrival with his mother the night of 9 September. The trip had come up spontaneously, in any event. He had seized on an out-of-the-blue opportunity to take his mother on their annual holiday together, using half-price First Class train

tickets offered him by a travel agent friend. He'd been
eager to go, hoping he might be of use to Jill and Ernie.
And, frankly, he found the electricity surrounding events
in Paris a compelling magnet. He checked his mother
and himself into the Apollo, the closest hotel he could
find to the Gare du Nord, where they had arrived on the
TGV. Early next morning, he called his office in Oswestry
and learned that the Rees-Joneses had called, and
urgently wanted to meet him.

Could he join them at their 3:45 appointment at the
embassy that afternoon? Of course! Consul General Keith
Moss introduced them to Dominic McCluskey, an attorney with the Paris law firm Klein Goddard, which was on
the list of approved firms for Britons in need of help. He
was the legal counsel to the Ambassador. The theme of
the meeting was quickly revealed: Trevor needed to get
himself a French lawyer, and McCluskey was there to
offer Klein Goddard's services, and, specifically, those of
his senior partner, one Theo Klein. That name again.

Politely pitching his law firm, McCluskey explained
all the reasons Trevor might need a lawyer. 'In the investigation, Trevor could be three things: a victim, a witness,
or an accused.'

Accused! No one, ever, anywhere, had suggested
Trevor might be held responsible. The French police
interview would be coming up just as soon as Trevor was
physically ready. It could be as early as next week,
though Trevor could not yet speak. Did this mean he
might, now, be questioned as a suspect? 'It filled us with

Trevor leads Diana down the aircraft steps at Le Bourget on their arrival in Paris, 30 August 1997.

BIG PICTURES

BIG PICTURES

At Le Bourget, Trevor and Kez (in checked shirt) supervise Diana's departure while Fayed driver Philippe Dourneau (right) looks on.

Trevor, Dodi and Diana in Pari

Dodi and the driver he trusted,
Henri Paul. Trevor can be seen
reflected in the door window.

Prelude to tragedy: Henri Paul (le
Diana and Dodi caught by the Ritz's secur
cameras just minutes before the cras

00:19:23   97 12HR

odi leaves the Ritz; Trevor is on the
ght, with his back to the camera.

Diana gets into the car,
with Trevor and Kez in attendance.

One of the last photos of the couple before the cras

The tunnel under the Place de l'Alma.

The wrecked car.

Overhead view of the wrec
as police prepare for its remov

POPPERFOTO/REUTERS

The Mercedes is taken away, to be examined in minute detail. This investigation would reveal was in fact in perfect working order.

AP

One of the paparazzi motorbikes which chased the car into the tunnel.

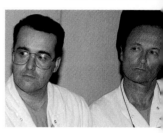

Bernard Riou (left) and Philippe Pavie
La Pitié-Salpêtrière hospital in Paris, th
doctors who tried in vain to resuscitate th
Princess after the accider

The photographers, whose relentless pursuit
of the Mercedes made them public enemy
number one until Henri Paul's drunkenness
was revealed.

Diana's coffin arrives at RAF Northo
1 September. Her funeral would take plac
five days late

BIG PICTURES

horror because the thought had simply not crossed our minds,' says Crawford, who had just assured the parents, a few hours earlier, that it could not happen. Jill and Ernie were trying to stay calm, Crawford saw, but, clearly, they had been badly shaken. 'It was very, very worrying,' Ernie admits.

They had avoided the papers and not seen the fatuous growing impatience as 'independent experts' had been quick to hurl criticism at the bodyguards' security practices. 'Had that been my assignment, I would expect to be sued,' said Ivor Haring, a VIP close-protection executive, in the *Herald Tribune*. There was the seat-belt. M. Boyer, the fireman who had helped Trevor, seeing the seat-belt pulled out and trapped against his body, had apparently assumed Trevor had been wearing it at the time of the crash. Gourmelon's report would state that 'the right front passenger had it on' – the only one of the four to be wearing a seat-belt.

It was in that single, inadvertent misreading of evidence that the myth of Trevor's seat-belt was born. It would grow, bringing him accolades as a model of seat-belt safety on one hand, but also vicious attacks ranging from unprofessionalism to being part of an assassination conspiracy on the other. *The Times* reported: '"The only person inside the car wearing a seat-belt was the bodyguard, who survived," a senior police source said.' Why was he the only one wearing a seat-belt, when the bodyguards' rules require that you stay unbelted to protect your clients? The accusing question was soon asked. An unidentified informer would report to British intelligence that 'Trevor knew about the plot and accepted he was part of it. It is the reason why he tried to fasten his seatbelt.' As the rumours spread, medical experts speculated, in print, that Trevor might never remember these details of the crash – that a trauma of this kind could leave him with permanent blanks.

They needed a drink.

'Could we have something cool to drink, please?' Jill asked, her cheeks flushed. Suddenly, thirst was all they could think of. A bizarre scene unfolded. They sat in one of Britain's most prestigious diplomatic outposts, looking out on an exquisitely manicured tennis court, as Keith Moss and several others rummaged through pockets and purses to get enough money together for the Coke machine, and sent a vice-consul off to find some soft drinks. Parched with thirst, now, the rest of them waited for his return, at last, with cans of Coca-Cola and orange. Trevor's 'total and complete recovery' was toasted, this day, with Coke.

The word 'accused' rang in their heads as they left the embassy. 'We were absolutely horrified, and felt that, up to that moment, we may have been living in a fool's paradise. We needed help and we needed it quickly, and especially now, because Trevor could be accused,' says Ernie. All were in agreement. Trevor must have his own French lawyer. Crawford would pursue it. 'We left the embassy feeling cold and scared. We did not sleep that night,' says Jill.

*

Nor did Fayed's lawyers. Late the night before, 9 September, the Paris prosecutor's office released the third report on Henri Paul's alcohol level. It confirmed the previous two: not only had his blood held three times the legal limit for driving, but it held, too, traces of prescription drugs that might have compromised his performance. The news had hit the morning press. 'THIRD TEST CONFIRMS CRASH DRIVER HAD DRUNK HEAVILY', declared *The Times*. Fayed's lawyers maintained the attack on the photographers.

Lawyer Dartevelle announced that Fayed had filed a lawsuit for violation of privacy against the helicopters buzzing the villa in St-Tropez, and asked the judge to extend the investigation of the crash to violation of privacy by the paparazzi. It looked like a smokescreen.

But some evidence Fayed could not avoid. He had finally been forced to publicly concede Paul's alcohol levels, and, through Michael Cole, he righteously condemned drink-driving. 'Mohamed wants the truth and if anyone is culpable I will personally spit on his grave.' But he did not relinquish his defence that no one knew Paul was drunk – that his staff were not culpable. Trevor could not speak. It was time to call on Kez.

Kez took the call from Paul Handley-Greaves on his mobile in Kilkenny. He'd just bought a horse, and was having a rousing good time. He still had more than a week's leave to go. 'We want you to do an interview for American TV.' No way, thought Kez. 'The last thing I want is to always be known as part of this.' And he'd heard the news the day after he got back from Paris about Paul being drunk. 'Christ, he can't have been. He looked normal!' was his shocked response. But every television show would be asking, 'Didn't you know?' Kez told Handley-Greaves, 'No, I'm not interested in doing it. I'm on holiday, for God's sake.' Handley-Greaves rang back from London. 'Look, the Boss says can't you find it in your heart to do it?' 'How could I refuse?' Kez was on the ferry next morning, was picked up at the dock and driven straight to Park Lane. He changed into a suit and, in minutes, was before ABC cameras being interviewed by Cynthia McFadden for a network show he believed would be seen only in America. 'Before the cameras actually started rolling, John Macnamara said to me, "Think about what you say" – which I took to mean that if I gave away any information that could be used against Fayed, my career would be finished – and then he sat in the room.'

'If you can just pop in here now, we're going to meet a guy from the *Mail on Sunday*,' said Macnamara afterwards. 'He's doing a piece for next Sunday.' 'For God's sake,' Kez exclaimed, as Macnamara guided him in to meet Chester Stern. The interview was short, and mainly confirmed that Dodi and Diana had only spent a little time at the Villa Windsor on the day of the crash.

Kez had been in bed about an hour when he got a shaking. 'You've got to get up, Kez, you're going on *Panorama* tonight.' 'I got up, had a shower, got my kit on, and did the *Panorama* interview. He could hear himself saying, on camera, 'Dodi's plan was a good one. It worked.' 'I was still trying to spare Mr Fayed's feelings. I didn't want to say, "This is crap." And Macnamara was sitting a few feet away from me to . . . what's the word? . . . Mind me?'

The *Daily Mail* headline the next morning, 11 September, was the Ritz's worst nightmare. 'FAYED'S MEN FACE CHARGES'. It went on: 'Paris Ritz may be prosecuted over drugged driver . . . Top executives at the Paris Ritz Hotel may face manslaughter charges over the death of Princess Diana.'

Frank Klein at the Ritz had called a meeting with Jill, Ernie and David Crawford, who carried a copy of the *Daily Mail* in his hand. He showed it to Frank Klein as he met him, and saw the man who ran the Ritz dissolve, under threat, into a terrified, agitated mess. Crawford couldn't believe the man's state. Klein had called the meeting largely – again – to urge on Trevor a French lawyer, of Fayed's choosing. His panic only intensified Crawford's determination to find a lawyer independent of Fayed. Every day, as Trevor came closer to his memories, the need for protection grew more urgent, Crawford sensed.

Ernie, at least, had had one fear set to rest regarding Trevor. Since being informed that Trevor might be an accused as well as a victim and witness, Ernie had been very concerned, and had searched out Dr Puybussent to ask for a straight answer to the question: was Trevor's blood test clear of alcohol, or anything else that could incriminate him? Dr Puybussent confirmed what Jill and Ernie had always believed: the samples were totally normal. It was a great relief, as Ernie had worried about the possible repercussions of a contaminated blood sample.

'We must tell Trevor today that he is the only survivor,' Jill was resolved as they entered the hospital on the morning of the Ritz's nightmare. They would try to listen to the rhythm of his responses. They had rung the hospital earlier to check on his readiness. It was good news. Trevor had been breathing on his own for six hours. But they dreaded what was ahead – dreaded what the shock might do to him, or what they might learn about his battered brain. Jill had dreaded it since she flew to Paris.

Jill started, as she always did, with her mantra: 'There's been a car accident . . . you're going to be all right . . .' Then she took his good hand and told him, gently, 'Trevor, you are the only survivor of the accident.' Inside, Trevor had understood. His thoughts moved slowly. But he was able to absorb his mother's words, and feel shock, and disbelief. He must confirm it. With his right hand, he pointed to the chart. Spelled out 'Dodi'.

'He is dead.'

Trevor pointed again, spelled out 'Diana'.

'Yes, she's dead, too. Henri Paul is dead.' Jill said it again. 'Trevor, you are the sole survivor.'

'I think it was then I realized what had actually happened. I think I was shocked more than anything,' Trevor recalls. His first recollections may have come the day before. But that moment is not as clear as learning of the deaths, even though 'I think I was still drugged up to the eyeballs'. He cannot describe the emotion – it's confused in his memory. But his family, a team of miracle-workers in a French hospital – and his own extraordinary strength – had pulled him back into the world.

'That was when the tears came,' says Jill. It was terrible for his mother to watch. She could sense the feeling he was trying to get out – the frustration of wanting to moan, or cry out in rage or grief. But, with no breath reaching his vocal cords, he was mute. Incapable of sound. He could not sob, or open his mouth. She tried to comfort him, but the truth had hit home. All that could be seen of his terrible need to show his feelings was a few tears that trailed down over the puffed and sutured terrain of his cheeks.

They asked him one more vital question that day. 'Do you remember the crash?'

'No.'

Trevor could not speak, but his grandmother could. Early on, Jill learned, the media found Trevor's grandmother, his Nain, in her Welsh village. She had refused to leave her home to live with a daughter, who could have protected her. The morning after Trevor learned of the deaths, Jill's sister-in-law was on the phone, distressed, as Nain was quoted again, in the *Daily Mail*. Sarah Ann Rees was eighty-five, not all that strong, Welsh-speaking, and unused to excitement. Unable to get to Trevor or his parents, reporters invaded her home. They sat at her table, and drank her tea, as she proudly told them about her beloved grandson, how he and the family were faring in Paris, and what she thought about the new blood test. 'This is dreadful news . . . It's outrageous to think all this could have been avoided if this man had just been a bit more responsible.'

This manipulation of a trusting old woman had breached the family sanctity Jill and Ernie had so jealously protected. Their faces, hers and Ernie's, had not yet appeared. The press had got only one photo of their backs running up some stairs. But not a single quote. When Jill saw Nain's picture on the front page of a tabloid on the Champs-Élysées, she nearly fainted with shock. As the larger story shrank the media's guilt, Jill's feelings against them deepened.

As his Nain became the media darling, Trevor sat up in a chair. He was conscious of the triumph, felt so proud of himself, but frustrated that he could not say it to Jill and Ernie. They were desperate to discover better ways of communicating. They must know the state of his brain. That day, they brought him a white wipe-off chart and encouraged him to hold it on his lap and try to scratch out words on the board with a marker pen.

Next day, when they arrived at his room, he was sitting in his chair, and had written something on the board. They could tell he was eager to have them read it. It was crudely printed. But, to Jill and Ernie, it was greater than any Iliad. 'Hello, Mum and Ernie. Glad you are here. Thanks for everything. Love, Trev.'

This first message released a cascade of relief. He had found a way to communicate. He had set to rest their worst fear, that his brain might be damaged. And, in his helplessness and vulnerability, he had shown the soft side of himself, 'the caring chap' his mother knew, but that he so rarely revealed. Ernie was moved to tears by Trevor's words. He had done the best he could to bridge the gap between himself and Trevor. The lack of real closeness that was natural, for Trevor was already a young man when Ernie came into their lives, hadn't stopped him for a minute from doing everything he humanly could to share this ordeal with Jill and Trevor – he felt like his father. Now, this scribbled message. It meant everything.

For the first time since the crash, Jill collapsed into tears of joy.

9

'I Don't Remember'

'It was not, in any way, Trevor's fault.' Jill and Ernie seized on that one short phrase as they sat spellbound listening to Kez as he told them all he knew. '*It was not, in any way, Trevor's fault.*' Their relief was boundless.

Kez had just arrived from London, where a scene had occurred that he chose not to share with Jill and Ernie. Paul Handley-Greaves had summoned him to his office. 'We want you to go to Paris and try to see Trevor,' said Handley-Greaves. 'And if you get in, you make sure you tell him to say to anybody who questions him that he can't remember anything about it.'

The clock was ticking. In a few days, Trevor would have to talk to the judge – next week was the rumour. Handley-Greaves and Macnamara had both tried, and failed, to get in to see Trevor. Now Trevor himself had opened the door. He had asked to see Kez, Ben Murrell reported. They had their Trojan horse, someone who could insinuate himself into Trevor's room and give him the Boss's orders.

'Why?' Kez asked, as 'a little alarm bell began ringing inside me, saying, "Hold on a minute. What does he want me to say that for?"' But Handley-Greaves dismissed the question with, 'Oh, it's going to be best, because of this drink thing. Tell him it's going to be all right.' Handley-Greaves added, 'The Boss is going to sort everything out. And tell Trevor that he's going to be looked after.'

'Yeah, I'll say that then,' Kez responded. 'If I didn't agree, there wouldn't be much chance of getting in to see Trevor,' he knew. But as he flew to Paris on Saturday, 13 September, to go on 'stand-by' for permission to see Trevor, he had no intention of fulfilling the orders.

How far did they expect him to go to help out with the Boss's grief? Or to prove his loyalty? Was he being asked to fight Fayed's battle?

Kez was happy to be in Paris, eager to escape the press coverage he knew would break in England and America over the next two days. With the French police releasing nothing and the prime target, Trevor, inaccessible, the other bodyguard's report was bound to be given huge play, Kez feared. He was right. Kez's appearance on the American ABC network was widely quoted in British newspapers. Chester Stern's story appeared in the *Mail on Sunday* on 14 September, and on Monday, the BBC would air its hour-long *Panorama* show, 'Diana: Her Last Day', which was full of Kez. Kez would hear himself helping the Boss build his case against the photographers and diverting blame from Henri Paul and the Ritz, and feel less than proud of what he had felt obligated to say with Macnamara sitting at his elbow.

'Nothing suggested Paul was drunk; he was just a nice guy,' said Kez to the *Panorama* cameras. He believed that to be true. But the candour of his other comments was mired in murk and ambiguity as he tried to please the Boss without lying. Yes, Dodi had come up with a new plan with Henri Paul driving, 'and it was a good plan . . . and it did work', he affirmed, a statement that would make him cringe many times. Most helpful to Fayed was that Kez did not repeat Dodi and Henri Paul's claim that Fayed had approved the plan. Kez's silence allowed the Boss to distance himself from any part in the fatal decisions at the Ritz; Fayed would righteously tell the French judge that he had known nothing about the decision to ask Henri Paul to drive – he was adamant that he had not been consulted.

Painting a vivid picture of escalating paparazzi harassment, Kez wound up his *Panorama* interview with a ringing indictment: 'If anyone is blamed, it should be who was hounding the car. It had been building, and came to a head that night.'

Jill and Ernie were so glad to have Kez turn up that weekend, just a day after Gareth and Chris had arrived bearing an enormous chunk of cheddar cheese from home. Having family and friends around eased their load.

Physical survival had been the easy part for Trevor. But now that he was awake he was exposed to the reality of events and to the enormity of the struggles that lay ahead if he was to return to anything resembling the health he'd known. They sensed that his recovery had moved into a new phase. The risk was no longer from his injuries, but from forces beyond his room – media pressure, the police investigation – and from the demons of thought and memory filtered through a head thudding with headache, and clouded by painkillers.

Trevor's moods were becoming volatile as he grappled with his condition and his helplessness. His sense of humour would surface from time to time. On Saturday, as Gareth explained how Helen, three months pregnant, was suffering from sickness, he wrote on his board, 'I must be pregnant too.' But his still formidable strength, combined with frustration, could make him a hazard to himself. He'd wanted to know about his injuries – and again scribbled on his board, 'What's wrong with me? Did I nearly die?' He flailed about, feeling hot.

More memories were coming. He'd struggled to write the words, 'I'll get the sack' and 'It's not my fault.' He was trying, but failing, to remember anything after he got in the car with Dodi and Diana. For the first time, he was also looking ahead – a fine sign for the state of his mind. But it was taking the form of worry, about his job – was he going to be sacked? About the Boss, and about the state of his marriage. Jill and Ernie asked, 'Do you want to see Sue?' and he scribbled on his pad, 'What's the point?' He didn't ask the most painful question: 'Will I ever work as a bodyguard, or play rugby again?' Jill refused to use the word depressed – 'it's over-used' – but he was clearly 'down'. He wanted to talk to Kez.

It would hearten him, Jill and Ernie thought. They had been so hungry to hear from Kez what had happened that night, and had listened silently at the apartment as Kez told them the story – the events leading up to the crash. Henri Paul driving to the apartments. Trying to shake off the paparazzi. The details of Dodi's plan. 'It was not, in any way, Trevor's fault.' Kez would be able to put some of Trevor's anguish to rest as well.

But on Sunday, Trevor was so agitated he banged his hand on the table. He didn't want to see Kez. Yet he wanted contact with Lara, the wonderful Irish girl Jill felt was his best friend; they arrived to find that he'd scratched out a letter to her. If only Lara were here now, Jill wished. And Trevor wanted to know what was going on. Jill and Ernie told him what the papers were saying about Henri Paul being drunk. 'He only had two drinks,' Trevor wrote, sending fear into his parents' hearts. The Trevor they knew would never, never let anyone who'd been drinking take the wheel. Later, Kez calmed their fears, explaining that both of them had thought the drinks were just pineapple juice. They were still worried, though.

On the morning of Monday, the 15th, the ticking of the clock accelerated. As Jill and Ernie met the two doctors, Chikhani and Professor Jean-Jacques Rouby, head of

Réanimation, before seeing Trevor, they were excited to be told that two major events in his recovery had occurred. The wires had been removed from his mouth – his jaws released from the elaborate construction that had held his teeth and jawbones rigid while they knitted together. They were still locked shut, but, with exercise, he could now begin to regain movement. And, matching that triumph, Trevor had been fitted with a new tracheal tube that would enable him to make sounds – to speak. 'Wonderful!' Jill and Ernie exclaimed in unison. They couldn't wait to see him.

'When we walked into the room, he was sitting in the chair. He'd taken a few steps around the room. He was trying to talk, and obviously thought he was speaking clearly – he appeared so proud of himself,' Jill saw, wishing, wishing she could help him in his great effort. 'He was desperately trying to form words, but until we became used to it, it was barely comprehensible. It sounded like someone trying to speak in the dentist's chair when your throat is full of water, and your mouth is full of metalwork.' 'It was a gurgling sound, almost like someone trying to speak underwater,' Ernie agrees. But it was clear, from Trevor's enthusiasm for the project, that 'from now on he'd try to speak more and use the board less'. Soon, they realised, he would be speaking well enough to see the judge. With this morning's leap forward, his interview was set for that Friday, 19 September.

Now, flushed with his new powers, Trevor wanted to see Kez. Kez still had no official permission. 'But no one had told us any reason why Trevor couldn't see anybody at that time,' says Jill, who planned, as soon as she and Ernie had had their private visit, to simply walk Kez and David Crawford through the gauntlet of security. Crawford, still in Paris hunting for a suitable French lawyer for Trevor, was surprised to see Kez. 'But I thought that, with Fayed's infinite resources to spend, this was just a kind gesture to have Trevor see a friend and colleague.'

Kez had been told what to expect. 'But I walked in, and I couldn't believe it. He had this massive swollen head. You could see it was Trev, but he looked just like a pumpkin, as if someone had inflated his head. He was half sitting up, drooling from the mouth. His eyes were sad-looking, and what was disturbing to me was how close he'd come to losing an eye – the cut, and the eye all droopy.' The old piss-taking humour got them through the next bit. 'We just sort of shook hands, and held hands for a minute. I was thinking, "Hold on Trevo, lad, I think you want to get engaged." But I turn him down – "No way, Trev, not looking like that."

'He couldn't open his jaws, so he had a small tablet he used to write on. He was trying to write something, but he was getting frustrated because he couldn't write properly, so he was trying to say it. And it was difficult for him to talk.' Finally, he got it down and showed it to Kez.

'That was some OT.' OT was overtime. Kez got it instantly, and burst out laughing. In just four words, Trevor had summed up the irony that had brought them to this hospital room.

'Well, it serves you right, you money-grabbing bastard,' Kez snapped back.

'It was touching, really, because he was trying to laugh, but he couldn't, and I was wiping all this mess that was coming out of his mouth. When he started laughing, though, I knew his brain was okay. It was still Trev in there. He's going to mend. He's okay. That was fantastic.' Kez hoped he'd been disguising his shock at the face. But then Trevor wrote down, 'How do I look?'

Kez was glad Jill and Ernie weren't there to hear his answer – they were waiting outside with Crawford. With a soldier's sense of humour, he said, 'Well, to be honest, you look like a vegetable and you stink of piss.' Trevor was heaving with laughter he couldn't express. 'And he kept trying to talk, getting quite emotional as well. Next, he just said on his board, "They're all dead."'

'Ah, now, don't you worry about it. You should concentrate on getting yourself better and back to the UK. You're going to be fine.' Trevor, getting a bit drowsy, kept saying, 'They're all dead.' Then he wrote, 'They've said he was drunk.'

'No, he wasn't drunk. Don't worry about it. You'll be back on the job before you know it,' said Kez.

'Do you think they'll still want me?' Then he drifted off.

'See you soon,' Kez said as he left. He'd spent no more than five or ten minutes with Trevor. He had not given him a word of Handley-Greaves's message. The shock of his mate's condition had made it easy.

'Did you get the message across?' Handley-Greaves asked him as soon as he got back to London that afternoon.

'Yeah, yeah,' said Kez.

As Kez left, Jill walked David Crawford past the two officers of the Brigade Criminelle sitting outside Trevor's door, and ushered him into Trevor's room. Crawford was struck by the heat. It reminded him of the pervasive, mind-maddening heat Camus wrote about in *L'Étranger*. 'It must have been terrible for Trevor.' His visit proved to be a 'non-meeting. I'd barely had time to introduce myself to Trevor and say, "I knew your late father," when I was asked by a nurse, since I had no written authority to be there, to leave at once.' He'd only had time to register shock at the sight of Trevor. Muffled sounds came from 'that grossly swollen head', sounds which only Jill and Ernie could begin to translate.

As they watched David 'thrown out on his ear', Jill and Ernie were distressed. Still haunted by the word 'accused' they had heard at the embassy, they could not help but be 'very, very worried about the aggressive security. We began to question whether he was actually being kept under wraps by the police as an accused rather than being protected as a witness,' says Jill. 'Why did everyone have to submit their passport to the security policeman on duty? He was a victim and a witness. This was totally wrong.' 'Since none of this was explained to us, we were very suspicious . . . and uncomfortable,' says

Ernie. He was so angry that he phoned the police, who assured him that they were there only to protect Trevor from the paparazzi – nothing more sinister.

But they felt growing pressure to find Trevor a French lawyer. That urgency had increased exponentially that morning, as the date of the judge's interview was set for the Friday. With the excitement of the speaking tube and the parade in and out of Trevor's room, Crawford had had no chance to report his progress, and now he seized a moment with Jill and Ernie. Crawford had found the right lawyer, he believed. With Jill and Ernie's approval, he had placed a call to an old friend, François D., who had lived in Crawford's home twenty years earlier as an exchange student and was now an associate in a Paris law firm.

By phone, Crawford had outlined his five criteria for a suitable lawyer to represent Trevor: 'He must speak English fluently. Be experienced in criminal law. Be sufficiently rich not to be concerned about payment. He must *not* be someone who milks the situation for publicity, putting himself in front of the television cameras every five minutes. And, of course, he must be completely independent of the Fayed organization.'

Over a fine Sunday lunch the day before, the 14th, at the home of François's parents in south Paris – a festive reunion of family and friends, really – François had produced the name of Christian Curtil. Just three years out of law school, he had dazzling credentials – a Master of Law from New York University, a top-ranked doctorate of laws from the Sorbonne, and a letterhead which boasted discreetly that he was a *Secrétaire de la Conférence*, selected in a highly prestigious competition which, each year, chose twelve young *avocats* to travel to twenty foreign cities representing the French bar. One of the rewards of the *Conférence* was being assigned some interesting criminal cases. And he and two lawyer friends were currently representing the bulk of the plaintiff cases in what promised to be one of France's higher-profile trials: the tainted-blood cases, in which many thousands of people were infected with the HIV virus and hepatitis, a monumental scandal for France.

They must meet him instantly, Jill and Ernie felt. Crawford was leaving Paris the next morning. He would call Curtil that afternoon, as soon as they left the hospital.

Curtil, at that moment, was driving back from the Fleury-Mérogis prison, the largest prison in Europe and home to several of his clients. He took a call on his mobile from a lawyer friend acting as an intermediary for François and carrying a provocative message. 'There was a car crash in Paris a few weeks ago. Maybe you have heard of that.' Curtil said, 'Yes,' although he'd been in Montreal for the first week with his eleven fellow *Secrétaires* and had scarcely followed the story. 'I found it a shame, but wasn't really that interested.'

'There is somebody related to the car crash who would like to speak to you,' said his friend, instantly firing Curtil's interest. 'I was, of course, intrigued.' Within the hour, he received a call on his mobile phone from Crawford, who explained his predicament. 'I'm due to leave Paris tomorrow at ten o'clock.' Curtil suggested a meeting with Jill and Ernie that night, eight o'clock, at his office.

As the three entered the apartment on Avenue de Friedland, Crawford's first thought was that Christian was remarkably young. 'The impact was great of this very young man guiding us into this imposing living room, a tableau of antique furniture, paintings, and collections of silver and porcelain gleaming from lit alcoves. It looked like a room lifted out of the Musée d'Orsay.' Curtil and his father, Michel, ran their law practice from offices across the hall from the salon. The father, a distinguished lawyer who had written a large portion of French copyright law, had, here, achieved his dream of living and working in the same place.

Christian was a modernist, but as a backdrop to his profession, the apartment was incomparable. He seated the three around the conference table. 'We're here,' Crawford explained, 'because the judge expects to interview Trevor this Friday, and we are concerned because we do not know whether he will be interviewed as a witness or a suspect.'

'I see no way he could be interviewed as a suspect,' Curtil speculated, 'but I know Hervé Stéphan, the *Juge d'Instruction*, personally, and will call on him tomorrow to enquire.' As he continued to listen attentively to Crawford and the couple, he was struck by 'the parents'

sense of desolation, of desperation, almost, to find someone suitable to act for their son, who could not speak or
take any steps on his own behalf'.

Curtil had not yet been instructed to represent Trevor.
But in their conversation, he proposed an option that
Trevor might become a *partie civile*. It was a status, non-
existent in Britain or America, which let direct victims,
relatives of the victim, or anyone who had, say, a moral
interest in the victim's issues, become full parties to the
case. As a *partie civile*, Trevor would have access to every
document – every interview and scrap of evidence – in
the judge's investigation. He would have the right to a
lawyer in interviews. Trevor's family was clearly eager to
get him home and get on with their lives – they were
deeply private people, he could see. But he had planted
a seed. If it sprouted, Trevor would be inextricably
involved.

As Crawford tested Curtil against his five criteria, the
young lawyer passed with flying colours. On the matter of
money, Crawford cautioned, 'M. Curtil, I see no way that
we could promise you any payment for your contact with
the judge, or for work that might arise from it.' The Rees-
Jones family did not have the funds to mount a legal
presence in Paris.

'I would be happy to do it free of charge, and look at
the position as it unfolds,' Curtil offered.

To Ernie and Jill, he seemed a dream come true. 'We
were very impressed with him,' says Jill. As they left the
meeting, Crawford felt 'that I could safely leave Paris

having placed the matter in the hands of someone far more competent than I to take it further'. A year later, he would say, 'I consider the best single move I made in this matter was to find Christian Curtil to be Trevor's French lawyer.'

Late that night, after an incredibly eventful day, Ernie took a call from Paul Handley-Greaves in London. 'He told us that when Kez arrived back in London, Mr Fayed had wanted to see him straight away. Kez, he said, told Mr Fayed that Trev was very depressed and worried about his job, at which Mr Fayed broke down and was very upset.' He had never seen him like this before, reported Handley-Greaves. Fayed was sobbing, exclaiming, 'He's like my son, he can have anything he wants.' Then Handley-Greaves delivered the Boss's message to Ernie: 'Trevor should not worry. He has a job for life.'

'Will you put that in writing?' Ernie asked him, not out of distrust but feeling that, if they could read Trevor a letter from Mr Fayed, it would do him a world of good, put his mind at rest. 'Paul told us, "Of course, no problem,"' says Jill, 'but no letter was ever received.'

Curtil strode briskly through the Palais de Justice, with its vast halls of marble columns and magisterial statues. Grandeur vanished as he climbed several narrow flights of stairs to a hallway with the plain, low-ceilinged look of an attic. He opened a door off the hallway into a rabbit warren of small offices, and entered Room 58, a drab room largely unadorned except for the wall-hung metal file case which held Hervé Stéphan's current case files.

Curtil had arranged to drop by and chat with the *Juge d'Instruction*, the judge running the case, the day after his meeting with Trevor's family. This was something of a coup for Curtil. 'Normally, if you are not involved in a case, a judge would not speak to you. But I had a good contact with this judge; I had known him from other cases. So he was confident that I would not tell him any lies.' This was the first illustration, for the English lawyers, of the French way. Conversations between judges and lawyers which would be impossible in Britain.

As investigating magistrate, Hervé Stéphan had virtually limitless powers to name those he wanted criminally prosecuted, to subpoena, interrogate and jail. When he deemed the investigation complete, he would forward his findings – the cause of the crash, the guilty parties, as he saw it – to the prosecutor, Maud Coujard, a woman scarcely older than Curtil; she would decide who, if anyone, was to be tried. Stéphan's report would carry the heaviest possible weight in that decision. Stéphan was building what would become a 10,000-page file – 'Fatal Road Accident, 31 August 1997, 00:30' – in absolute secrecy, forcing the media to rely on leaks. He shared the investigation with a strong-willed and stylish colleague, Marie-Christine Dévidal, who, as the examining magistrate on duty the night of the crash, might well, in a routine case, have been assigned to lead the investigation. But Stéphan was one of a handful of Paris judges assigned to the most sensitive *affaires délicates* – which, indeed, this was. The case was his.

Curtil had the subtle job of trying to get Stéphan, somehow, without betraying confidences, to tell him whether or not Trevor was facing any charge. As Curtil let the judge know that he might be involved later in the case, Stéphan told him, 'There is very little risk that he faces any charge, and for the moment nothing of that sort is planned.' Trevor was not, nor was he likely to be, an accused. 'I called Trevor's parents on their mobile phone, and reassured them. "He will not be accused of anything, for the moment. At least the judge will not accuse him. Maybe other parties, but not the judge."'

It was the second round of reassurance Jill and Ernie had had that day. They, too, had been summoned to the Palais de Justice, to the famous old building in which the *Maigret* detective series was shot, to meet Mme Martine Monteil, Divisional Commissioner and Chief of the Criminal Brigade. She had called them in 'to reinforce', to Jill's infinite relief, what the police had told Ernie – 'that Trevor was being protected for his own good. He was a witness. There were no charges against him.' This day had been good. But it paled before events at the hospital.

'Wait for five minutes, please,' the policeman told Jill and Ernie when they arrived to see Trevor. Their first instinct was alarm. But then, as the ward door was unlocked and they were allowed in, they saw a big shape in a dressing-gown shuffling towards them. It was Trevor, walking down the hallway to meet them. Jill could hardly contain her pride. 'Sixteen days after the accident and all the surgery and here he is, tall as he ever was, being helped to walk some twenty metres to us and back.' Ernie was thinking, 'I can't believe it. Only Trevor could do this.' 'Four nurses around him, like tugs around this big liner,' Jill thought, laughing, marvelling at the sight. All the nurses from the side wards were coming out to see the great event. *'Il est grand! Il est grand!'* they were exclaiming, clapping, laughing.

Trevor has only faint memories of people sticking their heads out of various rooms, smiling at him. 'I think perhaps they couldn't believe it could happen so quickly – sixteen days after the crash, and you're up and walking.' He clearly remembers 'Mum and Ernie coming in and me thinking, "Don't make a big issue of it, Mum. Don't go over the top." And she didn't, to be fair . . . I just walked the length of the corridor and back, but I was very definitely pleased with myself. That's another step forward, isn't it, to getting back on my feet, I thought. I felt I could have done more at that stage, but in less than forty yards I was knackered.'

Back in the room, Trevor seemed strong enough for Ernie to read him a negative clipping from a Sunday newspaper that, like others from the earliest days after the crash, criticized the bodyguards' professionalism.

Trevor seemed to 'just take it in and think about it, and did not seem upset'. But he was boiling inside, thinking, 'Bloody bastards, they weren't there. *I* was there.' Though

Ernie had been following the advice of Dr Puybussent that 'you must bring Trevor back into the real world', he asked Trevor, 'Should I have read that to you?' Trevor responded – still speaking indistinctly, but understandable to Jill and Ernie, if not to anyone else, 'I'm glad you did.' And he was. 'I could have been lying there thinking, "Great, I've survived. Everyone thinks I'm fantastic." I'd never have thought, "I'm a hero," but you could have that picture painted for you, by all the praise and attention. You need reality, don't you. Ernie did right.' But the criticism ate at him. 'Because I was positive it wasn't my fault.'

The next day, 17 September, says Jill, 'I think the full impact had probably hit him. He was very sad.' He'd stewed about the critical story. 'I'd started worrying, "God, is that what everyone thinks of me – that it's my fault?" It was pretty self-centred,' Trevor admits. Trying to buck him up, Jill and Ernie pointed out to Trevor that this was only one newspaper.

'I did get a bit upset,' Trevor admits. 'Then it was all talked about and brushed under the carpet, and we carried on with the normal routine of their visit.' They read him some of the thousands of cards and letters that were still pouring in from all over the world. Trevor could never get over this, 'people I've never met writing to me'. More were from America than from any other country. Why would Americans care about him? He was especially cheered by a scrapbook his friends at Aldershot, where he'd been stationed, had put together.

*

Trevor's voice was still muffled, but what he blurted out as Jill and Ernie entered his room for their late-afternoon visit was unmistakable.

'Why is it always me?'

Trevor was echoing the very words his mother had said when she first saw him in the hospital. Trev and his mates might have their humour, but this was the shorthand of mother and son.

She knew 'Why is it always me?' had not come out of thin air. Trevor's mind had been racing since their noon visit. 'I knew I'd nearly died. It wasn't fear I felt. All I could think of was ghosts in the closet – what I would have left behind if I had died. You'd like to leave behind a nice clean desk, if you like. But I had things tucked away back home, things that might cause embarrassment to your family, or whatever.' Introspection about the family was a new thing for Trevor.

'Gareth and John went the usual route of university, degree, good job, whereas I did my A-levels, then joined the army. Though joining the ranks is not really what your parents would have wanted – they'd have wanted you to join as an officer, but I didn't do that. I've always been independent.

'My two brothers had never been in any trouble at all, not compared to me. I was the one who had a divorce coming through, the one who'd been done for drink-driving when I was younger, the one to get into various scuffles and scrapes. Looking back, I was, in some ways, the black sheep of the family. I didn't think it nastily about myself. I just thought, bloody hell, the trouble I've got into. I've caused my mother and father a lot more trouble than the other two did.'

'He's quite a peace-loving chap, really,' Jill would reflect later. 'It's just that things happen to him. Whenever anything happened, it always seemed that Trevor was in the middle of it, but always for the best possible reasons.' There had been fights in pubs in Oswestry on occasion. 'But it's fair to say that Trevor would not stand around and see somebody knocked about. He's always the guy that would stand up for the underdog,' says Ernie. 'He would sort it out as best he could.' As he would have tried to sort out things in Paris the best he could, they knew.

As Trevor had seen Jill enter his room for the second visit of the day, the 'scrapes and scuffles' of a lifetime flooded in, and all he could think was, 'Good grief, it's me again. What else can happen? And my mum's here again for me.'

As he greeted them, a story flashed through Jill's mind. The family's classic Trevor story, it summed up all the qualities in Trevor that both made being his mother so difficult and explained why she loved him so much.

'There was a crash outside our house and he found this chap who he knew bleeding rather profusely – he was actually a diabetic. Trevor's older brother Gareth is diabetic, so he knew that he needed some sort of special medical attention. He brought this chap in and he bled all over the hall carpet, and all over the lounge carpet.'

The same story was still vivid in Trevor's mind. 'I ended up driving this guy to hospital because his mates were drunk and wouldn't drive. I knew him vaguely. He'd cut his finger quite badly, so me and my brothers bandaged that up. Since he was diabetic, we gave him some glucose. I wanted to get him to hospital, so I drove . . . and then there was blood in the car as well. It was frosty, quite slippery, and I clipped the headlight and the side of his mate's car. In the casualty room, I could hear the doctor ask him, "Are you still carrying hepatitis?" – he was a hepatitis carrier! – and I'm sitting outside, covered in this guy's blood, thinking, "Well, thanks for telling me, you bastard." Then I phoned his mother for him and she said, "Can you bring him back?" It was the middle of the night, and they wanted me to wait there till he was all stitched up, and take him home. I must admit I said to his mother, "You can come down and get him yourself." And then his mates tried to bill me for the damage to their car. I drove home and, next day, told Mum and Dad what had happened.'

'Trevor worried like mad about what his father would say because of all this blood over the carpet,' Jill recalls. 'Usually, if blood was all over the carpet, it was because Trevor had done something again.' 'Dad would clip me across the ear most of the time.' But not this time. 'This time, it was, "Well done, Trevor,"' says Jill.

As Jill and Ernie left his room that night, Trevor said it again, 'Mum, it's always me,' and added, 'I'm sorry.' Sorry not just for this monumental mess, but for all the messes of the past.

'Trevor, this time it's not your fault,' Jill said, searching for some way to soften his suffering. There wasn't much of Trevor you could hug right now. But in an intense whisper, she told him, 'We started out with you on this disaster and we intend to look after you. We'll be there with you until you tell us you're well enough to go back to living on your own.' Ernie finished the thought: 'We started this as three, and we'll stay as three throughout.'

The next day Trevor was served his first lunch. Bright pink meatball burgers surrounded by green 'splodge', as Jill called it. 'Well, it looks all right,' said Ernie, optimistically. 'It's shit,' said Trevor, 'and you don't have to eat it.' It had to be pushed in with a syringe through a mouth still clamped shut even after the wires had gone, but it was another step forward.

'Where are the scars on my face?' he asked, abruptly. 'There were no mirrors,' Jill said. 'He wasn't allowed to see his face. He was in such a mess, he wouldn't have been able to take it . . . And he had no feeling in his face. All the nerves had been disrupted when they pulled his face off.' 'It feels like I've got someone else's face on,' he said to them. 'It feels like sort of a mask.' So Jill and Ernie stood in front of Trevor and pointed to their own faces to show him where the scars were. Jill ran her fingers along the path of the deep scar that marked the flapping gash that had so shocked doctors at the crash site; it ran from the top of the left of his upper lip horizontally across the cheek down to the jawbone – six inches long. Chikhani's reconstruction could not

remove this surface scar – perhaps plastic surgery some
day.

They couldn't bear to show him, or tell him, how lop-
sided his face still was. As Jill said, 'He was never vain
about his looks. He had a pretty battered face from rugby
anyway. It wasn't a pristine face. But it was better than
the face he had now.' Trevor needed to learn about his
face. It was part of the process of grasping his new reality,
Jill realized.

The full force of the discomfort and the work ahead
was coming home. Trevor's room was steaming hot. He
could not escape it. 'You could have an itch on your face
but you couldn't scratch it because you couldn't feel what
you were doing. You were numb, and it would just stay
there,' Trevor recalls. One eye was bandaged over.
Eating, now that the feeding tube was out, required mas-
tering the feat of squeezing the 'bloody abysmal' mush
into his mouth through the syringe, without making too
much of a mess.

Then there was the indignity of bedpans. 'Naughty,
naughty,' the nurses would say, shaking their fingers at
him, as he struggled not to make another mess of himself.
'I hadn't done it on purpose. You don't shit on your own
doorstep, do you,' he'd think, annoyed at the nurses.
When the catheter came out, he made a series of disas-
trous tries at peeing neatly into a bottle, not knowing
how to make the bed go up and down to make it easier.
After being lectured again and again, 'that's bad, that's
bad', he manoeuvred on to his knees, hoping to do it

fastidiously, without pulling out the tubes in his arms. The nurses discovered him, thought he was trying to jump off the bed, and gave him another verbal boxing.

After these experiences, he welcomed the bed baths. 'It was so hot. I wasn't embarrassed. I found it easier, to be honest, if women were doing that than a bloke. You don't want a bloke washing your bollocks.'

He would struggle to move around in the bed, with a sore head and drips in his arms. 'One morning, I heard something clicking. I'd yawned and must have broken the wires in my jaw, but it felt a lot better. The worst thing was the trachea tube. It used to get full and blocked up. I used to struggle to breathe. Mum was always cleaning out the gunge. But sometimes when I was alone, I'd start gagging, and the nurse would come and stick a little tube in and get it out. It was such a relief . . . I remember actually coughing out the tracheal tube, and the nurses found it somewhere down at the end of the bed. It was bad for infection because there was a hole there, but the breathing was much easier.

'I've never been a good sleeper, and this was even worse now. Most nights, I was half awake, half asleep, burning hot. The nurses would come in and wash you down just as you were getting the best half-hour's kip you'd had all night. I just wanted to be knocked out at night-time.

'I was a bit pissed off at times, but, honestly, they were absolutely brilliant. The nurses and the doctors were outstanding.' And he found that, rather than exploding at

every frustration, 'you get this amazing feeling of acceptance . . . It's amazing what you accept as normal at the
time – accepting people turning you over, giving you a
bed bath, and a shave.' Far more of his time was spent
passively than lashing out at his frustrations. Whether it
was bedpans, or a criticism in the newspaper, 'you
become like a sponge and absorb these things. You get
institutionalized. It's a terrible thing to say – no one
enjoys being ill – but suddenly that's your life, and you're
almost enjoying it.

'I never felt real, sharp pain, throughout the whole
stay in hospital; I was sedated . . . The frustration I had
the first few weeks, more than the injuries or anything
else, was not being able to communicate – not being able
to talk when Mum and Ernie and the lads came to see
me. The chart was better than nothing, but that takes for
ever, doesn't it?' When he started to speak, 'I thought I
was speaking quite clearly. I knew in my mind what I was
saying, and to me it was clear as anything, but obviously
people on the outside couldn't understand it. After I'd
said it three times and people still couldn't understand, I
used to get frustrated.' Listening acutely, Jill and Ernie
had begun to be able to translate his garbled efforts, but,
to others, Trevor was still speaking a foreign language. As
he was still on pain medication, his thoughts were not
always clear, and sometimes he would give a whole
speech in his mind, but blurt out only a single sentence
of it – then wonder why people seemed confused.

The Princes were on his mind. He feared that William

and Harry would remember him only for the crash that killed their mother. He'd like to see them, to say, 'I'm sorry. There was nothing more I could have done.' He dictated, and Jill wrote, a letter to the Princes, and one to Mr Fayed, to whom they were all still 'very, very grateful'. Trevor got an immediate note of thanks from Prince Charles's private secretary, Stephen Lamport, but no response from Fayed. Trevor wanted to see Dodi and Diana's graves.

Facing him, the next day, was the police interview. 'I can't see the point of it. I still can't remember anything,' Trevor told Jill and Ernie as they left.

On Friday, 19 September, Jill and Ernie met Judge Stéphan – their first meeting with the investigating magistrate – at the same police headquarters where they had met Mme Monteil. As they drove off in convoy to the hospital for Trevor's interview, they laughed at yet another of the ludicrous ironies of their new life – the judge in front in a very small car, and them following in one of Mr Fayed's limos. The hospital entrance was surrounded – there were a hundred journalists and a sea of satellite dishes, 'the biggest concentration of reporters we'd ever seen'. The most important witness to the crash, and to its preamble, was about to speak. As the convoy pulled in, the paparazzi jumped in front of Jill and Ernie's car, separating them from the judge, their cameras flashing at the couple. 'We knew we'd experienced just a small taste of the pressure Diana must have felt.'

Because Trevor's speech was still so indistinct and only Jill and Ernie could understand what he was saying, they were permitted to be with him, with Ernie assigned as special interpreter. 'Jill stood behind Trevor, holding his shoulders. He was in a chair, and I leaned down as close to Trevor as I could to hear his every word,' Ernie recalls. Professor Jean-Jacques Rouby, chief of *Réanimation*, was at hand to halt the interview if Trevor seemed unwell. It had been agreed: only twenty questions would be asked, although, in fact, the judge asked more. But it took almost an hour, as the questions were lobbed back and forth in slow motion from judge to interpreter to Trevor to Ernie to interpreter and back to the judge. At the end of the interview, Trevor was drained.

He had remembered very little. But these fragments of memory are as untainted as any he would have, Trevor believes, and – given a memory still recovering from the amnesia of violent trauma – true. 'I felt quite positive about what I said. I would definitely stand by that.' His answer to the judge's first question set the tone of the interview:

Q: 'Does he remember what happened after the departure from the Ritz?'
A: 'I remember getting into this car, and I do not remember anything else.'

He remembered that 'it was Dodi who changed the plan. It was not me.' And it was Dodi who had called

Henri Paul so he could drive them from the back of the hotel. He vaguely remembered the Mercedes being followed from the Ritz by a motorcycle and two cars – one a white car with a boot that opened at the back, a hatchback.

As he waited for the taped interview to be painstakingly hand-transcribed, he hung his head in his hands. Only after he had signed each sheet of paper could he go back to bed.

Within a day, this most secret of interviews had been published, word for word, in the *Guardian* and the *Mirror*. How could this happen? Ernie, enraged, called the police, and told them, 'Your security is like a colander – full of holes!' It was not us who leaked, the police explained. It could be people working in the prosecutor's office . . . it could be the photographers. As *parties civiles*, the photographers had access to the interview.

While the interview was going on at the hospital, Christian Curtil was writing his first letter to David Crawford, stressing that 'I really think we should not wait too long until becoming a *partie civile*'. Trevor should not have seen the judge that day – with his memories so vital to the investigation – without a lawyer present, Curtil felt. 'But so long as he was just a witness, he could have no lawyer – he had virtually no rights at all,' Curtil explains. The only way to protect Trevor from the mischief others could do to him was to get him inside the investigation.

That night, Jill and Ernie flew home to Oswestry for

the weekend, swapping house and car keys with Chris and John in the lounge at Manchester airport as they, and Sue's parents, Ieuan and Mary Jones, flew to Paris to cover for them. 'We arrived home to find the neighbours had come in and left a wonderful meal – salad, baked potatoes, a pudding, lovely bottle of wine, and welcome-home cards.' They watched the BBC *Panorama* programme a friend had taped for them. 'We had been told the impact of Diana's death on the world, but we didn't really realize it until we saw *Panorama*. It brought home to us, somehow, how isolated we had been,' Jill reflects. 'The only news we got was from our telephone calls with the boys, from cuttings the embassy kept for us, most of which we couldn't face, and tidbits from people at the Ritz.'

Now all they wanted was to breathe the air of normality, and to hear the birdsong. They took Sooty for a good long walk at the racecourse on the hills behind town, on the Welsh border. Jill had a haircut, and on Saturday night, Ernie had a decent pint of beer at The Oak, where they toasted Trevor's total and complete recovery with a crowd of the rugby lads who came in. In the garden, they planted the handful of chestnut conkers they'd picked up in the Tuileries gardens in the centre of Paris. 'We decided we wanted something positive to be growing from all this.'

Jill arranged Trevor's medical care for when he came home. They prepared his room, put up his army pictures and the bronze statuette of a paratrooper he had been given when he left. 'All we need now is Trevor,' Jill noted.

They visited Nain in her Welsh village. She was in tears, and so glad to see them. In all the interviews, she had sounded so excited about her wonderful grandson. 'She seemed to think at the beginning that it was grand, and thrived on it for a while,' Ernie observed. 'But as she told us about the press harassment, we began to realize just how hunted she really was.' The photo of the entire family published around the world had been 'borrowed' by a sly photographer who talked Welsh to Nain, and then sold the picture. 'Nain was exhausted, but still would not go and stay with her daughter, or have her phone number changed.'

That Sunday, there was a special service for Trevor at Whittington, in the old brick church where he had got married. The church was packed. Jill and Ernie did not go, but took a tape of the service back for Trevor. As they got daily phone reports from the family in Paris, 'we felt almost as if we'd deserted him'. They could not wait to get back.

In their absence, though, Trevor was anything but abandoned. Sue's mother, Mary, had opened a whole new culinary vista for the young man she still loved as a son-in-law. She had brought over some food from home, one of her famous Welsh farmer's stews, as well as a baby-food mincer, a small white plastic manual gadget. Grinding up some of the stew, she gave Trevor his first minced meal, fed through the gap between his still-clenched jaws with a small plastic spoon. But the thing he really relished was the minced fresh peaches. The hospital's pink and green 'splodge' now had some competition.

On Saturday morning Chris, John, Ieuan and Mary had found Trevor sitting up when they arrived. 'He's quite perked up today, quite okay,' they'd said. But the weekend was to be terrible for Trevor, as he endured a new round of tests, including an MRI scan Dr Chikhani had requested as he continued to evaluate the success of the surgery. By Saturday night, Trevor would need comfort food as never before.

'I'd had loads of tests before, but I was unconscious.' The MRI was only the climax to a battery of tests that gave Trevor the most unrelieved discomfort and distress since he'd woken up – a lumbar puncture in his lower back to draw spinal fluid. Electrode pins stuck to his head while a current jolted through him 'that didn't half make me jump'. Zapping him with what he remembers as an enlarged drumstick, they put a shock through his back to make the muscles jump, and then another and another, on his legs, all over his body. 'Is someone doing this for a laugh – a joke,' he groaned to himself. 'It made you so tired, all these muscles just drained. I felt like a lump of meat at this stage. Then they scraped loads of dried blood from my ear with a little hook thing, and did hearing tests.'

Trevor was stuck in the MRI machine for thirty or forty minutes, hating the heat and all the weird noises. 'You're enclosed in this tube. It didn't make me feel claustrophobic, but I felt too hot and uncomfortable. They'd roll me out, now and then, then push me back in again, and I'd think, "How long is this going to go on?" It seemed a hell of a long time. They give you this button to press if you panic and want to come out. At one stage, I thought, "I'm going to press it." Then I thought, "What a complete wimp. It's only noise. So get on with it." I'd walked to the tests, but I got a wheelchair back because I felt that drained after it.' When the family came back that Saturday evening, 'they saw me just lying there, barely able to say a word'. 'The difference was unbelievable,' Ieuan would tell Trevor later.

The MRI had given him a discouraging view of his new existence. 'Your world shrinks into what you've got. You don't look into the larger things. You just see what's there.' The outside world in which he'd functioned so capably had shrunk to Room 107, and to this clicking, buzzing capsule in which he was trapped. It was as far as he could see.

Desperate to do anything she could to liven his days, Jill had even asked the delicate question, before they went home for the weekend, 'Do you want Sue to come over . . . as a friend only?', and the man who'd responded to Sue's voice even when he was unconscious – and who had responded apathetically, 'What's the point?' when the question was first asked – now said, 'No, I want Sue as a wife, not as a friend.'

While they were at home, Jill and Ernie called Lara, Trevor's close friend from Ireland, asking her to come to

Paris. Lara promised she would. They all needed her spirit. And now Jill and Ernie were on their way back to Trevor and Paris, surrounded by businessmen on the Manchester flight.

'We were definitely the odd ones out,' says Jill. 'We've got no laptop computers and no mobile phones. On the plane, the man sitting opposite us had two seats – one for himself and one for his computer.' 'It's life, Jill, but not as we know it,' said Ernie. Passing their departing family at Charles de Gaulle airport, 'we gave each other such huge hugs it must've looked like a rugby scrum'.

'No birds sing in Paris,' they suddenly noticed. But they were glad to see their favourite tramp again, the smartly dressed, cigar-smoking 'upper-class tramp' they saw each morning on the Champs-Élysées on their way to the supermarket. They had missed their daily exchange of '*Bonjour*'.

Trevor could eat. It was wonderful. Although he could hardly open his mouth, he was now trying to feed himself. But the hospital food they were serving Trevor was still 'diabolical. More green and yellow slime. We're working through the colours of the rainbow,' Ernie noted. Jill hunted down Mary's baby-food mincer and put it to work grinding up the best food the Ritz had to offer. 'It's a strange way to serve up gourmet food,' Jill smiled, as they shovelled the Ritz's finest cuisine into the mincer. 'Wonderful steaks, lovely cooked salmon, chicken, potatoes, baby carrots, pâtés . . .' But nothing seemed able to raise Trevor's spirits. Lara was arriving today, thank heaven.

She was a welcome sight, that Wednesday, this tall, athletic girl with shoulder-length sandy-coloured hair and a big loose yellow jumper. She and Trevor looked like brother and sister. Jill and Ernie took her to the hospital and Room 107. Another shock. Trevor had vanished.

'We arrived at *Réanimation* as usual only to find no Trevor, and initially no clue as to where he had gone.' Alarmed, they were quickly reassured by a nurse that he'd been transferred to Dr Chikhani's maxillofacial unit. The nurse offered to accompany them to it, since it was roughly a quarter of an hour's walk across the grounds to a much newer part of the hospital. 'It was our first chance to experience – to appreciate – how large the place was. The hospital itself is like a small town. It has a church, a large area where *boules* is played, and gardens where patients and visitors can sit. It had so many buildings, old and new, it extended, it appeared to us, as far as the eye could see,' says Jill.

'As we entered the unit, we were directed to the first floor, where we were led to the end of a long corridor. The sight we beheld was unbelievable,' says Ernie. 'In his room were four detectives, two doctors and a nurse. And Trevor. But the most worrying thing to us was that he was *locked up*,' says Jill. 'The guard was sitting in a little observation room where he could see in but you couldn't see him, and the door locked as it closed. You had to knock on the window to get out.' Trevor's new crowd of keepers viewed Jill and Ernie with suspicion, and checked Lara's passport. 'I'd like a strip search, please,' she said, eyeing the dishy policemen, lightening things with laughter, as she always did. As Jill saw the two friends' emotional greeting, the 'hugs, and kisses and tears', she breathed with relief. They settled into the kind of easy talk about everything that Trevor had always been able to have with Lara. A physiotherapist, Lara was a healer in so many ways. That night Jill and Ernie would celebrate Lara's being there by doing their only touristy thing. They went up the Eiffel Tower.

Jill and Ernie looked around the room. It was a lot more luxurious than 107, they could see. A large room, toilet facilities, lounge chairs. This was the high-security room built and used for prisoners, the staff explained. It was also used by Dr Chikhani, which is why Trevor had been brought here. They'd been concerned with the tight security in the other ward, but this prison gave them a chill. Was it for his protection? And, if so, what from? Or was he being guarded as a prisoner? Even if he were not a prisoner, the guard opening and closing this door could have a bad psychological effect on Trevor, they feared.

But Trevor was clearly revelling in the new room. 'The police were fantastic. They'd pop in and chat.' Rather than making him feeling captive, the move 'was a massive step forward for me'. The more alert he had become, the more bored and isolated he had felt in the other room. He had had no television. 'I couldn't read. I didn't have any music. There was absolutely nothing to do. Jill and Ernie's visits were the highlight of my day.' In the new room, 'I was allowed out of bed. I was allowed to walk around myself, I had a TV. I still couldn't read, but I could listen to tapes on my Walkman – some Irish music, the tapes the rugby lads and Lara had sent over.' He had a bathroom, with a mirror. 'I could wash my own face. I could see myself.'

Alone that morning, he had looked in his mirror for the first time. 'I wasn't horrified. I didn't run back to bed and cry my eyes out. But I was taken aback a fair bit. There was the swelling. The eyes looked dark. The hair all matted with blood around the cuts. I thought, "Whew, God, you don't look good." The worst was the teeth, all smashed at the front – one smashed in half, the bottom ones all jagged. It didn't look nice.'

'Although we'd been dreading Trevor looking in the mirror, I thought he'd cope – because he'd suffered so many cuts, bruises and bumps from rugby,' says Jill. 'But it upset me when he said that, though he was looking forward to seeing his young nephews and niece, he was worried that the sight of his face would frighten them.' Trevor said little, but revealed his feelings as his mother heard him say, 'Who'd ever be interested in someone so ugly?'

They could all see that his face was not yet right. It was out of line, sunk on the left-hand side. 'The only time Chikhani expressed anything less than total optimism was when he decided that the left part of my face needed fixing.' He must pull the eye socket forward, and fix the lopsidedness. Chikhani would tell Trevor next morning that surgery was scheduled for Friday.

On Thursday, Frank Klein turned up at the apartment before Jill, Ernie and Lara left for the hospital. 'We weren't sure why. He just arrived,' says Jill. 'It was the first time he suggested that the accident was not just an accident, but a bungled assassination attempt. It was a shock. It had never occurred to us.' It was the first they had heard of the assassination theory that had raged, from day one, in the Arab world, on the Internet, and, increasingly, in Mohamed Al Fayed's mind. This same day, Philippe Dourneau delivered to them a letter sent anonymously to the Ritz. It suggested that it was the French and British Secret Services that had tried to assassinate Diana and Dodi – and, of course, Trevor – and that, because Trevor had survived, his life might now be at risk. 'We began to wonder . . . Is this why the police have placed him under guard in a secure ward – to protect him from an attempt on his life? It seemed more like a James Bond plot than real life.'

The idea of conspiracy was now in the air. There was media speculation about a mystery car which Fayed claimed, at first, was carrying photographers but which, he now seemed to believe, could have been part of an assassination plot. The police had begun a nationwide search for the car that had brushed by the Mercedes seconds before the crash; they would question 3,000 owners of Fiat Unos, and turn up nothing, adding to the enigma of a car with sinister motives.

And yet the immediate threat to Trevor seemed to be the same as it had been for Diana: the paparazzi. In the past week, two photographers had been caught by police inside the *Réanimation* ward and ejected. One, police reported, bragged that he had a plan of the hospital – even the cellars – and had lurked inside since eight o'clock that morning. He would, he had said, 'use any means to get a picture of Rees-Jones because he had been offered an enormous amount of money – he spoke of two million dollars'.

They were so grateful Lara was there. Trevor was 'really, really down. Chikhani had just told him he'd have surgery the following morning. We left Lara with him to try and cheer him up. She'd done us all such a lot of good.' She left next day, as Trevor went into surgery again. That afternoon, Jill and Ernie were at the hospital, waiting for him to wake up.

While Jill and Ernie waited, David Crawford presented himself, for the second time, at the Klein Goddard law offices for a meeting with Theo Klein, two of his colleagues, and M. Brizay, who, although representing Henri Paul's family, was apparently there on behalf of Mohamed Al Fayed. Crawford had been called over to Paris, he thought, to discuss compensation for Trevor's injuries – they must want to offer Trevor a settlement. In a French industrial accident there was usually an obligation on the part of the employer to compensate; the state social security system paid out to the victim directly and then sued the responsible party for recompense. What Crawford later learned was that that obligation only arose if the employer was based in France. As Trevor was employed by an English company, he could not get compensation in this way. They might bring a civil or criminal action in France against Fayed's French empire – or perhaps even against Fayed himself – but there would be no industrial accident claim in France.

But compensation was not what the French lawyers had in mind. 'When I got there, I found we were talking – again – about an attempt to have Trevor represented by a lawyer of Fayed's choosing, with a promise of payment of his fees.' This was the fourth meeting where this agenda had been pushed. Crawford thought it had been put to rest at his last meeting here, when he had asked Theo Klein outright, 'Have you ever acted for Mohamed Al Fayed?', and Klein had said, candidly, 'Yes, I've done so, and, if instructed, would do so again.' Klein had seen the potential for conflict of interest and told Crawford that, if Trevor were to claim damages against Fayed in a separate civil claim – distinct from employment law – he'd limit his role to one of negotiating only.

'This is not on,' Crawford thought. 'They seemed not to see my concern. Their bearing was dignified, but they were trying to take me for a fool. Clearly, their brief was to get Trevor as a client at any price. Well, so far as I was concerned, I wasn't for sale. Nor was my client, Trevor.' They had Christian Curtil in the wings. In the first major test of wills, a country lawyer from Oswestry was holding the line against the daunting Fayed organization.

Trying to redeem from the meeting some control over

Trevor, the Fayed team finally agreed that, if approved, Fayed would pay the legal costs of the lawyer of Trevor's choice. But that concession came with strings: the agreement would last only so long as Trevor did not sue Fayed, did not speak to the press, and only if Trevor was not, in any way, responsible for the accident. It stripped Trevor of his freedom of action. It would be, they proposed, a secret agreement which Theo Klein would fax to Crawford.

The meeting took a bizarre turn as the sun was setting, when Theo Klein rushed home for the Sabbath, and Crawford found himself alone with Brizay, Henri Paul's lawyer. Brizay said to Crawford, 'If there is a conspiracy, your client's life is in danger.' Brizay's confessions went on. 'The car should have been driven by a competent driver or an employee of the car owner.' This man was being imprudent, at best, revealing that he knew, at this stage, that Henri Paul being unlicensed to drive and not being an employee of Étoile Limousine were significant points. 'Maybe he felt that we were on the same side, but he was letting the cat out of the bag,' Crawford mused.

That evening was Trevor's lowest point. He hadn't expected, or wanted, to face surgery again. As he was wheeled into the anaesthetist's room, he thought, 'Leave it. Just leave it.' The surgery took five hours rather than the marathon eleven of the first session, but as Trevor woke up in the recovery room, still groggy, 'I was frightened. I couldn't breathe. I started panicking, my legs started kicking and my arms were flying.' He was lying down, and the tracheal tube had blocked. Nurses rushed, sat him up, cleared the line. But he felt 'absolutely and utterly worn out. I just felt I couldn't take it . . . couldn't take much more of that. If there'd been an on/off button, I'd have pressed it then.'

He said to Jill and Ernie as they came in, 'I've had enough.'

Chikhani came in and could sense that Trevor's will was close to shattered. Trying to stir the spirit he knew was still there, he told them, as they recall, 'We're kicking Trevor out by next weekend.' Trev was coming home! 'But there was no excitement in Trevor, not a sparkle, nothing,' the parents observed, distressed. 'We were beginning to be more worried now about Trevor's mental state than anything else.'

They were both down when they left the hospital to meet David back at the apartment. Things didn't improve when he told them his meeting with Theo Klein and the other lawyers had been a disaster. They had invited David to stay with them for the two days he was in Paris. David found the apartment absolutely luxurious, and admired the exquisite detail. 'But the washing machine didn't work. We were in the middle of this super-luxury affluence yet things which would work in a normal household didn't. It was dysfunctional luxury' – a metaphor, he felt, for the Fayed organization, as he was coming to know it.

He told Jill and Ernie about the proposed agreement if Fayed were to pay for Trevor's choice of lawyer. As they heard it, Fayed's lawyers wanted Trevor to sign away any rights to contact the press at any time in exchange for job security and little else. The agreement would be secret – and Jill and Ernie must sign it, too. 'Blackmail,' Ernie commented, his first expression of anything other than gratitude to Mr Fayed. 'It effectively signed Trevor up for life to Fayed.'

Their gratefulness, and their tight focus on Trevor, had kept Jill and Ernie in a state of naïvety. Finally, the bits and pieces of evidence that had been accumulating over the past twenty-six days had gathered into suspicion. 'It seemed to us that Fayed wanted to take over Trevor's future welfare, which we felt we had control of for the moment.' Ernie now thought that Fayed was trying to manipulate and control Trevor, through Klein and his legal minions.

In the last fortnight, as their network of contacts grew so large and complex they could hardly keep it sorted out in their heads, Jill had drawn a chart showing all the players and their links to the Rees-Joneses and to each other – they called it their 'Spider'. Jill had drawn Trevor and the family in the centre, with arms going off to other names – from the embassy, lawyers, the Ritz, the hospital, and so on. Now, their Spider told the same story of control that they were struggling with. Looking at it, Jill saw that she had put Fayed at the top, and that a majority of the lines also had branches connecting directly or indirectly to Fayed. This piece of paper graphically identified his power over many of the people they dealt with and, indirectly, over themselves. If the family was the Spider's heart, Fayed was its controlling head.

They still felt grateful. But, by the end of this long and complex day, their uncritical appreciation of the man's generosity was gone. 'David and I talked on late into the night,' Ernie recorded, 'and we've come up with the decision that has got to be made by Trevor. He is either going to stick with the Fayed lawyers or be independent.' Trevor must accept, or reject, the agreement.

On Sunday, the 28th, David returned to England by the Channel Tunnel, and, for some reason, was stopped by the police, who asked him to open the boot of the car. David had offered to take Trevor's belongings, including a big red bag generally full of sweaty rugby gear, back to Oswestry. 'What's all this?' the guards asked, to which Crawford replied, 'I really don't know. I'm the solicitor for Trevor Rees-Jones, and I'm taking his belongings back to England.' They asked for no evidence, and waved him on his way with a respectful salute. Good God, Crawford thought, 'The whole world knows now who Trevor Rees-Jones is.' The last man in the world who would want it had become a celebrity.

Like a miracle, the next day was the best of days. Trevor's bandaged head looked like a giant puffball, with two drains from either side of his head like two large red earrings. But Chikhani had talked to Trevor again and now he was thrilled that he'd be going home at the weekend. And the finest news of all: he would play rugby, and work again as a bodyguard! 'It was the first time in twenty-seven days that we'd seen Trevor laugh,' says Jill.

'It was wonderful. After the depression and exhaustion of yesterday Trevor's spirit was back.' Now that he was excited and he could talk, he wanted to talk to everybody and share the news. Jill pulled out the mobile phone. 'He chatted with Nain. Talked to his sister-in-law, Helen.' He was going to come home a whole man!

The nurse in Jill seized the moment. '"Trevor, keep smiling. It's a good exercise." I think I was becoming a bit of a nag, but he must do his face and jaw exercises, otherwise the scar tissue could make the face effectively paralysed' – his jaw permanently locked.

Then, next day, Trevor's spirits crashed again, his emotional rollercoaster taking him for another ride. His mood was not helped by a team of two doctors appointed by the Brigade Criminelle to give an independent evaluation of him before he was released – a requirement. The appearance and behaviour of the pair astounded Jill and Ernie. The man, 'who has red-framed glasses to match his complexion', draws a face on a piece of paper and tries to draw the scars Trevor sustained in the accident. But, oblivious of his mistakes, he's actually drawing the scars from Trevor's rugby incidents. As the woman doctor hounds Trevor about the state of his mind, 'she reminds us of Rosa Klebb in the James Bond movie. She's really only short of spikes coming out of her shoes. She's a very cold fish,' Jill adds, chuckling at the memory. As the two poke and prod, Trevor keeps saying,

'Why don't you ask my doctor for the information?',
while Chikhani stands by 'totally embarrassed by the
whole episode', Jill and Ernie observe. 'They should
have been pensioned off long ago.'

As the medical examination ended, a physiotherapist
arrived, and 'tried to dislocate my jaw', an unhappy
Trevor reported when Jill and Ernie returned from lunch.

Trevor's release was on the understanding that he
would get proper medical care after he left, as advised by
Chikhani and his other French doctors. They accepted
the plan Jill so carefully organized. He would be taken
direct to Oswestry, where a team of four specialists,
standing by to care for him, would assess him – and hos-
pitalize him if necessary.

Trevor was in no mood to discuss the agreement and
the lawyers when Jill and Ernie tried to raise it with him
later. He just kept saying, 'I don't want to upset the
Boss . . . I don't want to upset the Boss.' Keeping the job
was, clearly, paramount in his mind. A few days later, the
black mood descended even deeper. He talked of the
crash, agonized over the seat-belt, tried to reassure himself, 'If I'd put the seat-belt on, I'd have told the
passengers to do the same.' He was going through the hell
of what Jill saw as classic survivor guilt. 'He broke down
and sobbed.' Then he apologized, over and over. Would
he ever let his feelings out without apologizing? Jill
wondered.

'I suppose I was a bit embarrassed at the time, you
don't ever want to break down, do you, and the show of

emotion didn't do me any good whatsoever, to be honest,'
Trevor said later.

The strategy for Trevor's exit from Paris was under way.
He would be leaving on Friday, 3 October. To keep the
media away, Jill and Ernie, through an embassy press
release, put it out that he was staying at the hospital for
a few more weeks. Frank Klein notified them that a
Harrods helicopter would be on hand on Friday to fly
them all back to England.

Crawford was setting things up at home. He contacted
an amateur pilot friend, who arranged to halt all flights
into a small landing strip near Oswestry for the weekend.
As an alternative, a friend who instructed Army Air
Corps helicopter pilots offered to clear a base, RAF
Shawbury, twenty miles from Oswestry, if needed; a helicopter could land there unobtrusively. Crawford liaised
with Oswestry police and the Royal Protection Unit for
West Mercia, who'd heard the conspiracy threats and
wanted to protect the family as discreetly as possible.

On Thursday, the day before he left, Trevor had his
second police interview. This time, he painted a detailed
picture of events before the Mercedes left the Ritz. For
the first time, he told the bodyguards' story of the final
hours: of Dodi's change in plans, of Henri Paul drinking
something yellow – Trevor didn't know what – of Dodi
deciding Paul would drive the car. He gave the first
insights into the frustrating dynamics of his job with
Dodi, describing how the bodyguards basically had to

follow their employer's lead, even if it meant they were unhappy with the arrangements. Trevor pointed out that Dodi was the boss, and that even though he often failed to tell them about his plans there wasn't much they could do about it.

Trevor's memory of the trip itself had not improved. He remembered the light-coloured car as they set off, but after that, everything was a blank. The police then asked him what his honest opinion was of Dodi – a question Trevor answered only after warning them that if they recorded it, he'd pull the plug on their computer – and then gave him the chance to make any final points or observations. The only thing Trevor could think of was to say that he had a headache.

Jill and Ernie had their final meeting at the embassy, and were warned to be very careful about what they said. Jill had been quoted in an 'exclusive' interview that was totally faked, and the embassy clearly feared that, on their own, they'd be exploited. Fayed's name was not mentioned, but his presence was more than hovering. It had become intrusive.

Frank Klein had called two days before departure. The organization wanted to take Trevor to London to a private hospital for two days of medical assessment, and to meet Mr Fayed. Ernie and Jill would stay at Park Lane. 'This came as a bit of a blow. Everything was set. An airport closed for his arrival.' They'd arranged a family party at home on Sunday.

'If that's what the Boss wants, I'll go for two days, and

then I want to go home,' Trevor stated, when they told him about it. Unhappily – and only on the basis of a hospital stay – Jill and Ernie felt forced to agree to the London detour.

Since the day of the crash, they'd faced every situation, entered every meeting, with a sense of control because 'we used to do a lot of forward planning'. They'd managed to avoid the media, keeping them out of their own and Trevor's lives. Now, things were being changed hourly, and they felt they were not being consulted. Next day, Frank Klein informed Jill and Ernie that they were not to go to the hospital on the day of departure. Word of Trevor's release had leaked, the hospital was under siege by the media and would be effectively sealed off. They should send a bag of Trevor's clothes to the hospital with Philippe. Right. They could understand that. 'But the departure was the first time that Fayed had interrupted our planning. It was now us having to follow him.'

'The whole experience has been like a giant snake. We never move in a straight line . . . We sort things out only to find we have to do things in a different way,' an anguished Ernie jotted down that night. 'I'm beginning to wonder what this next day will bring . . . Everything is altered, the circumstance is beyond our control.'

It was 'the worst worry and stress we have ever experienced in our lives'. They'd regain control tomorrow, back in England. Within two days, they'd be home. They'd have Trevor home. But, though he couldn't say it out loud, Ernie suspected, 'Life will never be the same again for Jill and me.'

Trying to bolster them both as they stood on the balcony taking a last look at the Arc de Triomphe on the eve of their return, Ernie put a reassuring arm around Jill's shoulder. 'Oh, we were a good team. We were the A-Team, we were.' Nothing, no one had daunted them. They could only laugh, looking back at the meetings – at the embassy, at the Ritz – 'at the picture of us looking scruffy and dishevelled with our skimpy wardrobe of summer clothes and them all in their smart suits. But even if it had been Prince Charles, we would still have taken control of the situation.'

'We didn't feel out of our depth at all,' Jill reflects. 'I think what was driving us on was the fact that we had to look out for Trevor's interests. Whoever we saw and whoever we met and whatever we were discussing was of very secondary importance. It could be Sir Michael Jay, Professor Rouby, Mr Klein – it could be Mr Fayed. If, at the end of the day, they helped with the most important thing, which was Trevor's recovery, then wonderful.'

Several of the policemen who'd been guarding Trevor dropped by his room the night before he left. They were there, on behalf of all the police who'd looked after him, to say goodbye – to wish a respected colleague *bon voyage*. They gave him their phone numbers. They presented him with a Criminal Investigation Unit T-shirt and baseball cap. They had really come to tell him, with this gesture, that he was not accused or guilty of anything. The one who spoke the best English said, on behalf of them all, 'We see you as a victim and nothing else. Get better. Good luck.' It was a small thing, really. But it meant a great deal to Trevor. 'It was a very generous thing for them to do.' The T-shirt would go into the small bag he'd carry home next day. He had no intention of framing it. He would wear it for training in the gym until he wore it out. 'I'm not very sentimental. If a T-shirt's there, use it.'

But next morning, as he got dressed for the journey home, he turned the baseball cap inside out to disguise the police logo and put it on his head. When the police lads saw it, they would know he'd appreciated the gesture and was being careful. He put on a pair of dark sunglasses, on his doctor's orders, and was escorted by guards out of his room.

Chikhani and the medical staff had prepared a trick to deceive the paparazzi as they moved Trevor the half-mile from the maxillofacial ward to *Réanimation*, where the helicopter would pick him up. They prepared a decoy patient, a dummy, wrapped its head in bandages and stuck it in the back seat of a car, and drove slowly from the ward. As the press rushed after it, Trevor was taken out of another door and moved into an unobtrusive car.

It worked. But as he arrived at *Réanimation*, where he had begun his hospital stay a month earlier, it was a madhouse. They were all chattering away; there were policemen everywhere. Trevor felt very tired, and lay on a trolley while they waited to hear the helicopter arrive.

He was then taken up in the lift to the roof, where he saw
photographers poised on all the neighbouring rooftops.
His three doctors were standing by. As he went up to
thank them and say goodbye, 'They felt proud of me,'
says Trevor, understating in the extreme. 'Dr Chikhani
was brilliant. Always positive. Always saying, "You're
going to be fine," always confident of a complete recovery.'

For Chikhani, this had been the most difficult, the
most challenging, case of his career, and his pleasure
was nearly bursting from him. Trevor's eyes were level
now, he observed. The nose looked like a nose. He was
proudest of the mid-face. Very proud. From the right-
hand side, it was hard to see that he'd been crushed.

With the crowd, the police, and the clatter of the helicopter, he could not tell Trevor, now, what he felt. As he
shook Trevor's good hand and hugged him gently, he was
thinking, 'I feel I have lived an experience. We have
lived together more than four weeks – one, two hours
every day. I was bothering you, checking everything –
new bandages, cleaning the wounds, removing the wires,
the stitches. I was with you, explaining your therapy,
trying to pull open your mouth. You had no option – you
had to go with me. Outside were men with guns. But we
got so intimate. You taught me things. Technically, you
taught me nothing. I would do the same technique, the
same strategy again. But you taught me about the hanging on. The will. You taught me about the *will*.'

They said goodbye, and Trevor shuffled aboard, with

fifty-odd staples still holding his head together. 'You'll never be as you were before. I'm not God,' Chikhani knew. But Trevor was taking a good face home to England.

Half an hour before departure, Jill and Ernie made a final visit to the Café Tilbury, the local bistro that had given them sanctuary and sanity. Jill wrote a note to the owner on a serviette, telling him that they had enjoyed his beer and camembert, and their anonymity, and they explained why they had needed it – she told him who they were. 'The owner read it, bustled out, beaming, and shook our hand, and the two waitresses came out, and all called, *"Bonne chance"* as we raced back to the apartment.'

Mid-afternoon, Fayed's delegation – Handley-Greaves, Frank Klein, Kez and Ben Murrell – arrived at the apartment for the trip to the heliport. Police detectives arrived; one set up a radio base in the apartment – this seemed like a military operation! A police detective phoned in. 'Arrangements are complete for your exit from Paris.'

Jill and Ernie rushed to the balcony to see. 'We looked down, and didn't know, at first, that it was for us. Then, we couldn't believe it.' Parked in precise formation across the street were five gleaming police motorcycles, their dashing blue-helmeted drivers at attention beside them. Three cars had pulled up. They were being treated to the blue-light run reserved for the President or visiting heads of state. Ernie grabbed his video camera to record the sight, feeling strangely detached. Why had the French police cast them as stars in this showy display of official power? 'We'd travelled through Paris for five weeks without any of this.'

The cavalcade took off in a three-car convoy – police car in the lead, Philippe driving Jill and Ernie, and another Mercedes behind – with all sirens blaring, blue lights flashing, the motorcycles riding out alongside the cars. Racing at top speed, they halted cross-traffic and moved cars out of the way as tourists gawked and strained for a look. Jill and Ernie were both in tears. 'This is crazy. Over the top,' Jill kept repeating, in stunned disbelief. 'The emotions we ran through were quite unbelievable. It was a crystallization of the whole situation in one act.' When they arrived at the Issy-les-Moulineaux heliport, 'the media were eight thick'. They were hustled aboard Fayed's luxurious green and gold Harrods helicopter, and waited for Trevor's police heli-copter to arrive.

Jill was shocked as 'we saw Trevor shuffling his way across to us. You don't realize when you're seeing some-body in a hospital, sitting in bed, dressed in a dressing-gown, how they've changed because you're seeing them in a sick role.' The 'old Trevor' they'd cheered as he'd walked towards them in the hall two weeks earlier had, to her, looked ready for the rugby pitch. Suddenly, she was seeing Trevor in an open-necked T-shirt and tracksuit bottoms, his normal clothes, 'and it came home to us how much he'd changed'. This

Trevor 'had shrunk – lost about two stone – and was very stooped'. His left arm, still in a plaster cast, stuck out, rigid. Deep scars still showed beneath the dark glasses that hid his eyes. His head was down.

Tears welled in Jill's eyes at the sight of her son. 'Typical Trevor. Even had there been a wheelchair, he would have refused it. He wanted to walk.' Ernie was reminded that, 'If you were injured on the rugby field, if you were stretchered off the pitch, you'd incur ribbing, and a fine – a *double* fine if it's an ambulance with a blue light that's required.' Even with all this, there'd be no double fine for Trevor. He was leaving Paris on his feet. The media pack crowded in on him, their long, protruding lenses pushed through the wire fence. Jill knew his head would be pounding – he was still very ill. She suddenly knew how very far her son still had to go.

PART III

MOVING ON

10

Home

'But this isn't a hospital,' said Ernie, alarmed as the dark-windowed car that had whisked them from London's Stansted airport pulled into an underground garage on Park Lane. Though exhausted, his head splitting with pain, Trevor knew well enough where they were. Fayed's headquarters. Number 60 Park Lane. In this state, he thought only, 'This is fine. It'll be good to see the lads.' Ernie and Jill were not so sanguine. 'We thought Trevor was going direct to a hospital for forty-eight hours for a full medical examination. Then home. It's all set,' said Jill to Fayed's security chief, Paul Handley-Greaves, who had sat at Trevor's side for the trip across the channel and driven them here.

Despite its luxury and 'gold-plated everything', the helicopter flight had been 'two hours of hell' for Trevor, Jill knew. 'You could see he was suffering. He couldn't

talk – none of us could because of the noise, but he had
no desire to talk.' All he could do 'was just hold his head
and survive'. Now, he desperately needed rest and medical care.

Jill and Ernie didn't know where they were, initially.
But the atmosphere made them distinctly nervous as Paul
ushered them into the heart of the Fayed empire, past the
scrutiny of security guards, cameras, the crisp click of
doors locking behind them, and up the lift into apartment
152-A. 'It seemed like a luxurious prison,' Jill observed.
'Everything was security-minded, everything locked. It
was very discreet, but also very controlled . . . And there
was still no evidence of the hospital – of nursing or medical care.'

'The doctors will come and see him here. We thought
it would be more comfortable,' Handley-Greaves
explained, as Ernie scanned, with growing apprehension,
the same sprawling display of over-the-top opulence so
familiar to them from Fayed's apartment in Paris.

Trevor moved along slowly, slumping as they settled
him on a sofa. He must eat, and then rest. They had
gourmet food on call – Fayed spared no expense, and
they were grateful – and ordered out for Chinese. They
were just preparing to eat when Handley-Greaves
knocked at the door.

'The Boss wants to see Trevor for a few minutes,' he
said, guiding their shuffling son by his elbow out of the
door. 'Fine, it's the first chance he's had since the crash.
He's wanted to see the Boss,' thought Ernie.

Ten minutes after Trevor had been taken away, Mohamed Al Fayed himself swept in. He was a shorter man than Jill imagined, but he filled the room with his presence. 'Oh, he had *quite* a commanding presence,' says Ernie. 'He sort of brushed us aside as he entered the room. We wanted to shake his hand and say, "Thank you very much for everything you've done for us. We're sorry about your son." We weren't given the opportunity for that.'

Before they could get through the niceties and say hello, Fayed was waving his arms and billowing with words like a ship under full sail: 'It's terrible, terrible, it's not an accident. No, no, it's a plot, an assassination – it's murder!'

He half sobbed as he raved on. These beautiful young people, murdered, before they could live their lives . . . terrible! 'He was boiling up, shouting with frustration and emotion – obviously, with the loss of his son, and he'd just talked to Trevor . . .' They felt such empathy for the man, but Jill and Ernie were tremendously taken aback. There had been the anonymous letter in hospital warning Trevor of a bungled assassination attempt that would now make him its target. They'd refused to really believe it, and had felt safe in the hospital's high-security ward, under close protection by the French police. But now . . .

'Hang on. Just a minute, we can't accept this,' said Ernie. 'Because if this is so, then Trevor is obviously very much at risk, even now.' And if Trevor was at risk, so were they, because they'd been constantly in his company. 'Yes, yes, this is true, this is true!' bellowed Fayed.

'Well, in that case, we need to get the police here right now,' said Ernie, raising his voice to be heard.

'No need, no need, no need,' the Boss declared as he strode out of the room, the whole astounding scene having taken place in no more than two minutes. 'Look here, we're worried, now, about Trevor's security,' Ernie said to Paul Handley-Greaves as soon as Fayed had left.

Paul said to them, 'Don't worry. This place is a fortress. Nobody can get *in*, and nobody can get *out*.'

Trevor had braced himself to face the Boss's usual bluster. 'He's a very powerful man. You can't talk, or hold a conversation with him. He talks *at* you.' But this was a different Boss, a man in terrible distress. 'He was quite upset when he first saw me. He had tears in his eyes, and all I could do was apologize and say, "I'm sorry." He went on about having doctors there and care and so on, and I just said, "Yes, that's fine, that's fine." I felt indebted to him in a big way, and I felt sorry for him. I felt a bit of responsibility, because it was his son that had been killed.'

Handley-Greaves led him next down a corridor and into a room where 'there were three doctors waiting to see me'. Trevor was so 'completely shagged out' that he meekly sat in a chair as they told him, 'It'll just be ten or fifteen minutes,' and explained what their roles were – a psychiatrist, a psychologist and a general practitioner.

'I think they were under the assumption that I was staying in Park Lane for a couple of weeks. No one ever said they were going to see if I could remember anything. It was never said at that meeting – or any meeting. But that's what it felt like.'

They asked him questions, being quite solicitous. 'Are you okay? Do you want to stop?'

'No, I'm fine, keep going,' Trevor would say. 'I just kept nodding, yes, too tired to bother. But it just didn't feel right to me. I thought I should've gone to a hospital for another week, just for recuperation more than anything.'

Alone, Jill and Ernie looked at each other, truly frightened for the first time. 'This was a much worse situation than we'd ever been in the whole time we'd been in Paris,' Ernie says. 'It was obvious to us that you couldn't speak to Fayed as a rational person.' And Trevor had not come back. They didn't know where he was, nor could they see how the doctors could have looked after him without their help. 'He's had nothing to eat, no medication – we have all his painkillers and antibiotics.'

'I'm going to look for Trevor,' said Ernie. 'Don't worry, Trevor isn't very far away,' said the bodyguard outside the door as he discreetly pointed to a door down the corridor. This must be one of the lads Trevor knew, trying to help, they hoped. But their instinct to trust was about to be overwhelmed. In his diary, Ernie recorded: 'On entering the room, I couldn't believe my eyes. What they'd got set up there in that room was Trevor sitting on an upright chair being faced by three people that had never been introduced to us' – a GP, a psychologist and a psychiatrist, it was explained. As she followed Ernie into the room, Jill shuddered at the sight. 'All three of them were positioned around Trevor. It looked to me like an interrogation.'

'A camera and video-recording gear were in the room. Not set up at that point. But I was deeply concerned that there was more to their questioning of Trevor than they were going to suggest,' thought Ernie, his unease growing.

Where was all the equipment for doing the full medical examination? Jill wondered. There was no blood-pressure cuff, no ophthalmoscope to look in his eyes . . . no bed, Jill noted. It was clear to her that Trevor was suffering back pain in that chair. 'He should have gone to bed the moment he got here,' Jill thought. Trevor was exhausted and emotionally vulnerable.

Alarm bells had rung those last few days in Paris. But this was a huge escalation of what they'd begun to see there. 'Mr Fayed desperately wanted Trevor to remember the crash so that he has someone to blame for Dodi's death. He doesn't accept that Henri Paul was drunk,' Ernie's diary would propose. 'It was obvious to us that he wanted more of Trevor than just Trevor physically; he wanted to know exactly what information Trevor would give. He wanted his mind.'

'Are you sure you're all right with this, Trevor?' Ernie asked him, as Trevor slumped in the hard-backed chair.

He got Trevor's stock answer, 'I'm fine.' The same passive resignation he'd often shown in the hospital. 'You are totally out of order,' Ernie blazed at the doctors, as, helpless and shaking with anger, he turned on his heel and slammed the door. They waited in the apartment. Fifteen . . . twenty minutes.

There was a knock on the door. It was Handley-Greaves, and Jill blurted out, 'When can we leave?' 'He was very pleasant, never threatening in his demeanour, appeared to be helpful,' Jill noted. 'But his words were quite chilling: "*You* can leave whenever you like." The implication was that we would go and Trevor would stay.'

'We're going in to get him,' said Ernie, his gathering rage now focused. They marched down the corridor and threw open the door. 'Trevor is in no fit state for this,' snapped Jill, drawing on the courage she could always find when Trevor's safety was at stake. 'We understood Trevor was going to be in hospital for forty-eight hours. Otherwise, we'd have gone straight home, where I had all the medical care the French doctors told us we needed in our home town. He's not fit. He's just not *fit*.'

'Fine, okay, that's grand,' said the psychiatrist, showing some sympathy for the situation.

'Come on, Trev, you need to take your medication,' said Jill, her hands on his shoulders, as Trevor got up very unsteadily and moved towards the door.

'Mr Fayed is doing this for Trevor's best interests, it's all for Trevor's best interests,' said the general practitioner, her voice echoing after them as Ernie guided him back to the apartment. Trevor was too drained to care, but he wanted to believe it. 'Mr Fayed believes the most expensive, the most luxurious of anything is the best thing to do – top doctors . . . At the time, I didn't see it as trying to buy my memories through medical care. I just saw him as attempting to do his best.'

The psychologist was at the apartment door within minutes with his camera and recording equipment, keen to see Trevor again. Trevor found the strength to say, 'I'll call you in the morning,' and stumbled to the sofa. As the psychologist moved his equipment into the apartment anyway, one of the close-protection lads, Darren, whispered to Ernie, 'If you like, I'll throw him out with his equipment.' They had an ally. But how far did Darren dare go to help a mate? These were decent lads, but they were powerless, really, as long as they worked for Fayed. Ernie feared he was glimpsing Trevor's fate if they didn't get him out, and home.

Were their lives – or Trevor's – at risk? Ernie told Trevor that Fayed had suggested assassination. Trevor mumbled that Dodi would have told him if he'd known of a plot, but had said nothing. 'I don't know the truth of anything any more, because there were several theories, all sorts of crazy suggestions – some sort of laser gun,' Ernie would later scribble in his diary. 'We don't know who to believe or what to believe.'

The control they had felt slipping in Paris had become a landslide. 'In the hospital, we felt very much as though we were part of the team that was looking after him. Then suddenly, when we arrived in London and he was whisked away, it was as if we'd lost him. I can't stress enough how dreadful that was,' says Jill. 'We're not prepared to hand over our lives to another force. We like to be in control of our lives. We'd lost control.'

Now they'd met Fayed and felt his power. They had wanted to believe that, even if they disagreed with him, Fayed *was* acting in Trevor's best interests. Instead, he was now putting him under pressure. Trevor was just another servant, paid to do his bidding. And Trevor was so unshakably loyal.

At 10 P.M., they were finally eating, with Trevor seeming to enjoy the minced Chinese food. There was another knock on the door. The three doctors stood looking at them. 'Just wanted to say goodnight. We'll be back in the morning.' 'Not if we see you first,' thought Jill. 'Out, out, *out*!' Ernie ordered.

'Ernie's giving them very short change. I think Dad would have given even shorter change,' Trevor suddenly thought, remembering his father. Then he said aloud, 'I think if Dad had been around, he would have hit someone by now.' Dad had had a short fuse. 'He wouldn't have stood for it. He wouldn't have taken any bullshit off Fayed at all,' he thought to himself.

It had been a long time since his dad had died. But Trevor wondered now how he would have handled not just Fayed, but the whole thing. He knew he had been quite robust and fiery on the outside, but quite a sensitive bloke on the inside. 'He wouldn't have shown any emotion to me. He would've shown it to Mum . . . He would have made sure everything was fine.'

He hoped he hadn't hurt Ernie with what he'd said. Seeing him rise to the occasion over the past five weeks, Trevor had gained enormous respect for his stepdad's toughness. 'My dad would've done it a different way, got a lot more intense. But Ernie's brilliant,' he thought as he finished the minced food and longed for bed.

Ernie laughed, 'Let's be honest, Trevor, I think I'm getting to the point of hitting someone myself.' It was now nearly eleven. Trevor had been up since five that morning. But there was yet another knock. It was the GP. 'Is there anything Trevor wants?'

Again, Ernie shut the door. They must get out and home to Oswestry. 'Trevor, we're going home as soon as we can arrange it. We don't know how, but we're going home.' Trevor said, weakly, 'Yes, I want to go home . . . I don't mind coming back, but for now, I want to go home.' They packed what few bags they had. It was late. They put Trevor to bed with his sleeping tablets, painkillers and antibiotics. For the night, they were trapped.

Jill and Ernie were fully awake at three in the morning, finalising their plans. They daren't wake Trevor. At about nine, Ernie called David Crawford in Oswestry. Could you come and collect us? 'Yes,' said David. He'd happily do anything. He'd be there in four hours, he told Ernie, who sounded tense. David wondered if he suspected the phone was bugged. Where could they meet –

the foyer of the nearby Dorchester, perhaps? How were they going to get out? 'I'll call you back in an hour or so,' Ernie promised.

The doorbell rang at 9:30. It was the psychologist. Trevor heard him knock, and heard Ernie permitting only the most cryptic exchange.

'Is Trevor okay?' the doctor asked.

'Yes.'

'Did he sleep?'

'Yes.'

'Can I see him?'

'No, he's still asleep.'

'How is Jill? Can I see her?'

'No,' said Ernie, slamming the door.

They would not sneak out like fugitives! As Paul Handley-Greaves arrived, he faced the determination that had driven their battle in Paris to save Trevor's life. 'We want to leave by 1 P.M.' It was an ultimatum. And Handley-Greaves acquiesced.

Once the security man had agreed, he behaved graciously. 'We'll take you home and send somebody with you to make sure he's okay.' Ernie called David in Oswestry. 'They've provided a car and driver, and we'll be driving up today, estimated time of arrival 5 P.M. Low-profile entry.' The police should watch for a white Volvo estate. After all the pomp and ceremony, they'd be coming home in a normal family car.

'At ten, Trevor came through to the lounge. He looked shattered. He was holding his head in his hands. You could see the turmoil, the terrible turmoil – he doesn't want to upset the Boss, but he wants to go home,' Ernie recalled. 'I was in bits – a physical wreck,' Trevor confirms. 'I'd heard the suggestion that Mum and Ernie could go home and I'd be there in this apartment by myself. And I was thinking, I'm not overly confident about looking after myself.' Trevor slumped on the sofa; Jill brought a duvet, covered him, and he dozed again.

The single positive part of the nightmare was the visit, that morning, of a maxillofacial surgeon, apparently called in to give a straightforward medical opinion on the quality of Trevor's surgery. 'Wonderful surgery, but the dentist is going to be busy,' he told Trevor. 'He's the man that showed us how to use wooden spatulas for the physiotherapy on Trevor's jaw,' says Jill. 'Trevor could only open his jaw about one centimetre – less than half an inch. We had to push spatulas, tongue depressors, into his mouth, and try each day to increase the number. It was very painful. But if we didn't do it, the jaw would seize up and he'd never be able to open it. It would be locked for ever.' Highly motivated by this threat, Jill and Ernie eagerly took the little stack of spatulas he gave them to take home. The visit took a fairly shattering one and a half hours.

They had a nervous half-hour as Darren Wardman, the assigned bodyguard, took Trevor to go and collect some of his belongings from the staff accommodation next door. Jill stepped outside for a brief meeting with the psychologist, who gave her a tape recorder. 'Trevor might feel the need to talk into the tape,' he suggested. 'If memories come back, he should be able to voice them, talk them through.' Then he lectured her on how to watch for post-traumatic stress disorder.

Jill exploded inside: 'Yes, it is perfectly likely that he might suffer PTSD in the future. But what we have at the moment is a man recovering from a serious accident and two serious operations and what he mainly needs is physical care and TLC – that's what he needs. He does not need psychological mumbo-jumbo. What Trevor needs is *not available* at 60 Park Lane!'

Darren, on Fayed's orders, would be driving them and staying a while with Trevor to help out. For now, Jill and Ernie had suspended suspicion of Fayed's larger motives. They'd have Trevor home.

The car left at 3 P.M. As Darren drove out of the underground garage, they breathed a sigh of relief. It was a slow journey through London to the motorway, then, eventually, they saw a wonderful sight – the sign for Shropshire. 'We're going to make it now,' Ernie thought. They had escaped the forcefield of one of the most powerful men in England. They'd be in Oswestry by tea-time.

Sunday, 5 October. Five weeks to the day since the accident.

'I've got to go to church. I've got to thank somebody,' Trevor had said to Jill and Ernie as he arrived home late on Saturday.

'I wasn't a great church-goer. I used to sing in the

choir. But I felt I had to go. They'd had a service for me when I was in hospital.' Up at nine on Sunday morning, he looked terrible. 'His back is hurting, he is so thin, but still tall and upright,' Ernie noted, concerned at Trevor's ambitious plans. They bathed and fed him, and very, very slowly, Trevor dressed himself in a smart outfit – a pair of chinos and blazer, a greeny-blue shirt and tie.

They drove the two miles to Whittington, a charming small village of brick and half-timbered buildings on the edge of the Shropshire Plain, which, Jill loved to say, 'is a fairly typical Shropshire village. It's got a village green, a pub, a church, and a castle with a moat.' The bells were ringing in the church, the same bells which had rung for several family weddings – Trevor and Sue, Ernie and his first wife, Chris and Heather.

There was usually a good congregation at Whittington, and a good turn-out that morning. Jill, Ernie and Darren supported Trevor as he came, slowly, into the church. 'We walked in at the back and people looked round and there was this gasp. Everybody looked round, saw Trevor, and the gasp just went through the church. You could hear sniffs and sobs. It was amazing,' says Jill, still moved by the memory.

They got him settled into a pew, about halfway up. The sun shone through the windows, hitting Trevor's still-sensitive eyes. The church was charged with emotion as the rector moved through the service. 'Then Trevor decided to take communion. It was something he had to do. So he and I walked up to the communion rail. "He can't do it," we thought. The church went silent. It was so tense. People just moved in to help him – and he managed to kneel down, stiff as he was,' says Jill.

'Being Trevor, he stayed for the whole service,' says Ernie. 'And then, after, everybody came up and hugged him and shook his hand, hugged me and Ernie. They were just so happy to see him.' Jill adds, 'Everybody wanted us to stay and talk, and wanted to touch him.' 'He's pleased by the response,' Ernie observed.

'I wasn't that well at the time, to be honest. I can't remember a great deal about it. I know that I couldn't really walk. I had someone there to help me, as I was unsteady on my feet. And my eyesight wasn't good – terrible double vision. You'd put your foot down on the step and you didn't know where it was.' But, as Darren prepared to help him into the car for the short drive to Sue's parents' farm, Trevor said, 'I want to walk there.' The two hundred yards seemed to take for ever.

Jill and Ernie had begun their day in their garden, checking all the plants, and enjoying the ordinary peace they hadn't had for five weeks – quiet, no traffic, no feeling of restraint, just the birds. As the rector and David Crawford arrived at Ieuan and Mary's, they all settled in for a quiet cup of coffee and a chat and the peace continued. Is it possible, Jill wondered, as they drove Trevor back home, that life might return to normal?

But the media has added Oswestry to its list of targets. For his homecoming, satellite 'earth stations' had been set up in the market square in town. They were just back

from church when two *Shropshire Star* reporters were at
the door. Darren sent them away.

Interview requests were flooding into 'Harrods' – the
generic term Trevor's Oswestry team used for anything to
do with the Fayed organization. There'd already been a
flood of inaccurate reporting. The family rule held. No
interviews. Ian Lucas, the young proprietor of Crawford
Lucas solicitors, who had been low-profile so far, had
told Harrods' PR chief Michael Cole to forward all media
requests directly to him.

But, like the paparazzi, the reporters and TV crews
who poured into Oswestry cared little for protocol. They
hammered on the door. The media had missed Trevor's
visit to church. 'They were still sleeping in The Boote
across the street from the church and missed the catch of
the year,' Jill exulted. They would not let another photo
opportunity escape.

Caring for Trevor had suddenly expanded from two
hours a day at his hospital bedside to a consuming round-
the-clock job, with Trevor, at first, obstructing his own
recovery. The minute he got home from the church service, he called Nain. Then he called Gareth, John and
Chris. The doorbell rang, and 'the endless stream of visitors began'. His brothers and their wives, Ernie's son.
The rugby lads. By 2:30 they were hanging from the
rafters. The 'invasion', as Jill and Ernie called it, would
go on for weeks, the crowd starting around nine each
day, and going on non-stop through the evening.

'I think I should still have been in hospital for another

week or so at least,' says Trevor, looking back. 'I wasn't well at all. I just used to lie around on the sofa and take the pills that I was given, and that was it. I was quite happy to come home, but, obviously, I was a bit nervous. You get cosseted in hospital, don't you. I think the only reason I was at home was that Mum was a qualified nurse.' He kept his insecurities well disguised.

Trevor would tell everyone who came the entire story of the crash, with video tapes of the aftermath and Diana's funeral running in the background. As Jill heard him tell it over and over again, she thought, 'To be honest, I think it's mostly just wanting to see his friends, wanting them to see he is all right, wanting to tell them what happened. He needs to talk about it.' He trusted them to keep it confidential. But she felt, too, that 'maybe somebody who's always been big and strong, powerful, a leader – somebody people wanted to be with and to emulate – who suddenly finds himself weak, not capable of looking after himself, feels vulnerable, and frightened'. Maybe talking was his way of affirming himself, of keeping the fears away.

'Whenever the phone rang, he'd say, "Is it for me, is it for me?" Even if he was in bed, if the phone rang, a head would come round the door, "Is it for me?" It was almost as if he couldn't bear to miss anything.'

Jill took it in her stride. 'I was used to it. I had lived always with three lads who always had their friends in. I was definitely used to having a houseful of men needing feeding. I was being Mum, and I like being Mum.' Jill was feeding a dozen at a time, keeping the fridge full of food. Sue was in and out, unsettling Trevor. They knew he still loved her. Trevor would call her on the phone, and he knew he was making excuses for her. 'I remember Mum and Ernie saying to me that if she wanted to be with you, she would be here now.' Helping look after him. 'He desperately needed to reconnect with his life at that time. He needed his friends. It was necessary for him,' Jill knew.

'But we're fighting a losing battle,' she said to Ernie, as they struggled 'to try to control the flow of people so that we could get the proper food down him, get him to have adequate rest, make sure he had his physio done on time.' His scars must be massaged and softened, or they'd never fade. He must force himself to walk, each step a jarring pain. They must work relentlessly on getting his jaw open. 'We were told he ought to have physio eight times a day. There were only twenty-four hours in any day. There just wasn't the time for us to do everything.' Jill suffered for him. 'He had this excruciating backache, this terrible head pain – his whole body was wracked with pain.' The powerful painkillers Chikhani had given him had run out; the local replacements couldn't control the headaches. At half-past four one night, she heard him pacing, and found him 'in such a state, saying "I can't sleep. I can't sleep."'

His recovery was measured by spatulas, by the number they could stack in his mouth as they tried to pry open his jaws. It was agony for Trevor, and glacially slow. He couldn't do it for himself. They started with seven the first day, 'forcing his jaws open for six minutes, increasing it one spatula at a time. We got up to nine that day.' The goal was twenty-four. 'They became our milestones,' says Jill. 'When you can open your mouth nearly an inch, it's really wonderful.'

They were also chauffeuring him back and forth to doctors, oral surgeons, ophthalmologists. He still had metal staples ear to ear from the second facial surgery, and an infected scar. There was more eye, and wrist, surgery ahead and his teeth to be rebuilt. Jill was on indefinite compassionate leave; on her first, tearful visit to see her friends at the surgery, they'd told her, 'We don't expect to see you until the new year' – they would keep her job open. 'Our day was totally wrapped up with what Trevor required. It was a total commitment to getting him better,' says Jill, recalling, 'the nervous *energy* one expends'. When she got on the scales, she had lost two stone – twenty-eight pounds – the same as Trevor!

Darren, and then Kez, helped with Trevor for the first two weeks, each staying for a week. Their brief from Handley-Greaves, as Kez heard it, was to 'ensure that he was not hassled by the press – at the time, the press were desperate to speak to him or any of his family – and to assist in any way we could to take the load off Jill and Ernie'. Their experience with the paparazzi was paying off. 'Kez and Darren fended off the national press on the phone, at the door, and were very adept at avoiding direct contact with the local press, who always seemed to get wind of when Trevor was due to visit his physios, specialists or dentists. They also managed to keep him out of view of most of the TV crews,' an appreciative Jill recalls. They vetted the dozens of calls coming in each day, sorting out friends from reporters.

As Fayed bodyguards, the two lads were also good at the humbler tasks, like shopping for groceries. 'To be honest, I felt a little awkward at first,' says Kez, 'but they just took me in and treated me like a family member.' Kez spoke to the Ops Room at Park Lane daily, 'nothing heavy, just reporting in to keep the lads posted on Trev's recovery, in all its gory details. In particular, Trevor's mealtimes were a source of great hilarity, as I regaled the team with the full horror of watching Trev splutter and suck his way through one of Jill's beautiful meals that had to be chopped almost to a mince because of the state of his mouth and jaw!

'Mostly, Trev and I would just talk, and have a short walk daily.' Watching him from the window on his walks, Jill saw 'a very young old man. Twenty-nine going on seventy. It wasn't so obvious when he was lying on the settee, but as soon as he was doing something he would normally do, like walk down the road, it suddenly hit you.' To Kez, 'he looked like a spat-out pastie bimbling along and slavering'. The piss-taking never stopped. But even Kez was touched when he took Trevor walking up at the racecourse. 'He was walking maybe two hundred metres maximum, but he was starting his training. That's character.' Kez said to him, 'This time next year you're

going to be running.' And he was. He was running in
less than a year.

They were making physical progress. The eleventh of
October, the Saturday following his return, was a day of
triumph for Trevor's recovery. Three days earlier, they'd
worked up to thirteen spatulas. But they'd had a disaster
when the entire stack sprang out of Trevor's mouth, and
sent both mother and son into tears – Trevor from pain,
Jill from feeling responsible. Today, they successfully
inserted fourteen spatulas.

It was also a day of triumph for recovering his life. He
returned to the rugby club for the first time. He was
greeted by a film crew, but once in the covered viewing
platform at the pitch, watching the game, he was protected. 'He was still fairly wobbly and he felt the cold
terribly. Halfway through, he went and sat in a car with a
drink of tea,' says Jill. 'Then he went into the club afterwards.' This was the moment Jill had prayed for, but
dreaded. At home, entertaining the town, he was the
wounded hero. But here, in the club where his athleti-
cism and personality had earned him his place, how
would he feel? How would the lads feel?

'Hey, the crash-test dummy just walked in,' said one of
the lads, as he entered and sat close to the heater – 'hug-
ging the heater', his mother says. The piss-taking had
begun. 'I was just in the door, and it was "jigsaw", or "I
see you've got a Mercedes badge stamped on your head".
You can't get away with anything down there.' Trevor
could see that 'some of them were quite shocked at my

appearance and didn't know what to say'. A little girl
came up, fascinated, and said, 'Why have you got lines
all over your face?' 'Because I've had lots of operations,'
said Trevor. She was fine with it. He didn't want to
frighten the kids.

Trevor stood up and shuffled to the bar. 'He didn't
stay there very long, but to see him standing up at the bar
with his friends was a big moment for me,' says Jill. 'It
was just the most terrific atmosphere. He's supported the
rugby club for years. He's done the usual things like
painting the clubhouse, been down the drains – he's lived
and breathed rugby, quite honestly. And they gave him an
absolutely overwhelming welcome.'

Trevor had his first half-pint of beer that day. 'And I
must say, he never had to pay for a drink,' Ernie laughs.
'I was quite jealous of that.'

His team had lost. But Trevor had won back an important part of his life.

For Ernie, Trevor's progress was coming at too high a
price. 'Things are getting a bit too heavy for me,' he confided to his diary after a week of the invasion. 'I think
Trev is very demanding, and seems to have forgotten how
to say please and thank you. He's holding court in the
lounge. He tends to take over the settee and he's talking,
which is good for him, but he's now got a houseful –
something like eight people. Brett, Mike Owen, Terry
Roberts, Derek, Jane, Sally, Betty, you name it, they're
here. Gareth arrived and asked if I was all right, and I

said, "I'm not sure. I think I'm going quietly mad, but it's okay because I know a good shrink." Trevor explains who I mean, and the evening carries on without me.'

'I think I was *very* protective of Trevor,' says Ernie, reflecting on the exhausting week, 'and I found it was becoming increasingly difficult to control the situation – to be able to look after him properly, as we both had in Paris. He wasn't resting enough, taking time to eat, or getting enough physio. Trevor's priorities were not *mine* at this time.'

When he wasn't helping Trevor, Ernie tried to busy himself with his hobbies, took up his upholstery class again, doing the dining-room chairs in rose brocade. He played badminton with his son Chris each Tuesday night, and found refuge in his small den, 'the only bit of sanity in a house that's gone mad'.

Jill and Ernie needed as badly as Trevor did to reconnect with their friends. Their first night out was to visit their bridge-playing friends. 'We used to play about once a month, and having been out of circulation for so long, were really looking forward to another step back to our normal life,' says Jill. 'They welcomed us warmly but didn't press us for information, other than "How's Trevor?" and "How are you coping?" It was so comfortable to know we didn't need to be guarded, and we relaxed. We enjoyed a gin and tonic, our bridge-playing drink, and sat down at the card table. We played atrociously! We couldn't make a single contract. We couldn't concentrate on our play, but it didn't matter at all. We were home and enjoying our normal social scene.'

Pressures were continuing to build within the family, though, as Trevor's care came into conflict with the crowd that surrounded him. 'Jill can handle it better than me. I see it as a total invasion. The strain of living like this is terrible,' Ernie agonized to himself. 'I feel as if I'm not in control of anything. The house is full of aliens, visitors, phone calls.' Ernie felt more and more isolated. Hiding in his den, he drew a picture of himself – a little stick man under a glass dome, with his hands up in a gesture of futility, while four arrows pressed in on him: 'Trev, Press, Friends, Visitors.' Jill and Ernie were becoming concerned that their occasional happy hours with a bottle of Chilean red wine were becoming a daily escape. 'We like a glass of wine in the evening, but I think we were a bit worried that we were drinking too much.' To Ernie, since their family orbit had intersected with Fayed's, their life had become 'a serpent with a thrashing tail. You never knew which way the tail was going to thrash, next time round.'

Early Sunday evening, 12 October, he finally blew. 'I just took off.' It was set off by a little thing. Sooty refused to go for a walk, 'so I set off for a pint at The Oak. Everyone asked me about Trevor, but no one asked about *me*. Two pints later and I'm no happier!' Discovering him gone without a word, Jill leaped into the car and went hunting for him, frantic. She found him walking back home, and Ernie climbed into the car. 'When Jill came desperately trying to find me in Oswestry, it forced me back into reality. But, at the time, I wasn't sure that I was coming back.'

It wasn't just 'the invasion'. Fayed's pressure, too, had followed them home from London, Ernie felt. He was becoming obsessed with getting Fayed, as well as 'the invasion', out of their lives. Word came from Trevor that 'Mr Fayed wanted to buy Trevor a flat in town', and install an expensive security system in it as well. It even crossed Jill and Ernie's minds that Kez and Darren, decent blokes though they seemed, might be on a secret mission to report Trevor's memories to Fayed. There was no evidence. 'But because of our London experience, we'd begun to see shadows where there were none,' says Jill. And Ben Murrell had told them, in Paris, that he'd been told to report back.

Fayed had also sent more money with Darren when he came up to help the first week Trevor was home – a float of £1,000. Trevor guessed Fayed had sent it, generously, 'to help cover the costs of Jill and Ernie feeding and looking after two extra bodies', but Jill was happy to feed them as friends.

'We don't want his money. Don't want him in our home, in our lives. We don't need money to look after Trevor because we love him,' said Ernie. 'There is a life outside this organization,' he kept trying to persuade Trevor. 'There is a life *after* Fayed just as there was life *before* Fayed.' But Trevor wanted to get back to work, and did not want to offend the Boss by seeming unappreciative.

He didn't feel as Jill and Ernie did, that Fayed's bungs were manipulative, and when Fayed gave him £3,000 for a desperately needed holiday before Christmas he struggled briefly with how it might look on the Park Lane video tapes, then accepted it with a clear conscience. It was gracious that Fayed had paid for a private medical consultant and a physio not covered by the British health service. But Jill and Ernie hated being beholden at all. 'There's no way I could ever take this money directly back to Fayed,' Trevor told them. So Jill and Ernie came up with an idea: 'Give it back to the hospital.' Ernie made the decision. They would send the money to La Pitié-Salpêtrière in Paris. Trevor would take it over when he next went to Paris to see Dr Chikhani.

In Paris, events were about to pull them even more deeply into the abnormal world that still swirled around Diana's death. Christian Curtil had finally been named Trevor's lawyer, and after the weeks of struggle to impose his own counsel on Trevor, Fayed had agreed to pay his and the British lawyers' fees. Christian reported to David Crawford in a 13 October letter that he would be signing the fees covenant in Brizay's office in Paris two days later, that Wednesday, at 2:30 – a triumph for Trevor's lawyers. They had achieved for Trevor total legal independence while keeping a good relationship with Fayed. 'Christian and I were quite prepared to act for Trevor without the agreement, but it gave us some small additional comfort with regard to costs,' said David, very pleased.

Trevor had approved the agreement, and had also agreed to become a *partie civile*. Christian was preparing the documents for filing on 16 October. As Christian had explained to Jill and Ernie in Paris, becoming a *partie* was the only way Trevor could gain access to the judge's file, intrude his own interests actively into the investigation, protect himself, and, not incidentally, work to claim damages within the French justice system.

There was one other thing about becoming a *partie civile* which Christian did not dare mention to Trevor, given his loyalty to the Boss. 'The act of Trevor becoming a *partie civile* is already an attack, in a way, against Fayed.' It gave Trevor the power to open Pandora's Box on the acts and decisions that had so nearly killed him, and to cast light on areas that might embarrass or implicate Fayed's Paris empire.

As a *partie civile*, Trevor would be in interesting company: the ten photographers; the parents of Henri Paul, represented by Jean-Pierre Brizay; Diana's mother, Frances Shand Kydd, her sister Lady Sarah McCorquodale and her husband, represented by M. Toucas; and Mohamed Al Fayed, represented by Bernard Dartevelle and Georges Kiejman. Christian reminded David Crawford by letter, 'As I told you, I know Mr Kiejman very well, who in particular is a very close friend of my father, since his office and ours are quite specialized in copyright.' Christian wondered if perhaps these personal bonds with Kiejman had helped persuade the Fayed camp to approve him, Christian, as Trevor's lawyer.

On 16 October, as Trevor became a *partie civile*, Christian went immediately to the Palais de Justice to start reading the file. He put his other cases on the back-burner, and for three weeks spent his days engrossed in the study of the growing stack of documents. Under the watchful eyes of a court *gendarme* standing nearby, he sat out in the hall, at a table. No document was permitted outside of this area. For fear of having the seized crash photos stolen – photos so disturbing Christian could never bear to see them again – the file was actually kept in a safe for the first three months. Here, the illusion of absolute secrecy was maintained.

In fact, there had been rampant leaks from day one, as the media hunted ferociously for anyone who might give information. 'Everything had been said,' as Christian put it. Trevor's was the only important, untold story. 'And suddenly there is a new move. A new voice. A new chance for the media.' And – in one of the great ironies of the French system – he, the only living witness, was free to speak.

Parties themselves were the only ones not bound by confidentiality; as long as they did not show any documents from the judge's file, they could tell anyone anything. Now Trevor was a *partie*. And as his surrogate, Christian became the instant darling of the press. Letters, calls, faxes poured in; reporters camped on his doorstep. 'I had been involved in French media interest because of other cases, but certainly not in international media. This was completely new. They never quit.'

The French system had come as a shock to the foreign press. The deep secrecy and absolute control of the investigation by the French courts was frustrating for reporters who were used to doing their own aggressive investigating. 'In France the press only reports what the court is doing,' Christian explains. And the court said nothing, issued no statements.

For lawyers, the French system held one massive limiting factor. Once the prosecutor had named the focus of the criminal investigation – the paparazzi, in this case – the pursuit and testing of their guilt was the *only* line of investigation the judge could follow. The trick was to subtly try to expand the case by looking for anything the judge had not yet targeted for investigation, and make a compelling request that it be explored. It was the way French lawyers moved a case forward. The basic instruments of dynamic advocacy English and American lawyers enjoyed – discovery, depositions, aggressive investigation – were not available. Christian must comb every piece of paper as it entered the file, looking for contradictions, surprises, anything that might push the investigation in the direction of his client's interests.

His search was driven by a single question: who is responsible for the damage done to my client? He must find, first, where culpability lay; the world, as well as Trevor, wanted and needed to know who or what had caused the crash. Then, he must assess compensation for Trevor. He had been severely injured, and might never work as a bodyguard again. His memory, health and appearance might be for ever compromised. If Trevor deserved compensation, who should pay? The French courts paid notoriously low damages – civil far less than criminal. But if the investigation were to point fingers of guilt – at the Ritz, who knew? – the courts could be a source of at least some help for Trevor. Or . . . Fayed could well afford a settlement – might he offer one?

'From the first, I didn't think there was a case against the photographers.' Witnesses showed confusion in their testimony, told conflicting stories of what the paparazzi did and where they were. No alcohol had been found in the photographers. Henri Paul's drunkenness overwhelmed all other evidence, and seemed to cast the photographers as no more than a secondary cause. But you couldn't sue a dead man – Trevor had no case against Henri Paul.

Christian noted that several photographers described Trevor being friendly to them, especially Romuald Rat, David Oderkerken and Stéphane Darmon. He had smiled, shaken their hands. This was the technique Trevor and Kez had successfully used to defuse the explosive situation on the day of the crash – trying to disarm the paparazzi into co-operation.

But might Trevor's friendliness be seen as *encouraging* the paparazzi?

Christian hungrily read Trevor's first interviews with the judge in hospital on 19 September and 2 October – the first official words of the client he had not yet met. Dodi Fayed's pivotal role in pre-crash planning leaped out from Trevor's testimony, as Trevor described the difficulties of working for someone who didn't always tell him what was going on, and sometimes made decisions about security arrangements without consulting him. It was Dodi, he saw from Trevor's statements, who had taken the decision to use a third car, and asked Henri Paul to drive.

Quickly, Christian filed a request with the judge asking for a report on the inside of the motor car, his first step in expanding the case. The car was being rigorously examined by the Institut de Recherche Criminelle de la Gendarmerie Nationale (IRCGN) as well as by other experts, and full reports would take time. In the meantime, he searched the Mercedes repair invoices. Early reports on the airbags. There was no question that they had inflated; in all the photos, you could see the white skin of Henri Paul's and Trevor's deflated airbags in the tangled debris of the crashed car. But when had Trevor's deployed? At the major impact on the thirteenth pillar? Or could it have inflated earlier – perhaps on contact with the widely hunted Fiat Uno – and left Trevor unprotected for the lethal impact seconds later?

The seat-belt issue caught his eye. Christian noted that Trevor had told the judge that he never wore a seat-belt in a city unless the car drove too fast. And yet the earliest police reports of the scene had him wearing one. Trevor had already been attacked in the press for being the only passenger with a seat-belt on – a vulnerable area for him.

With these unknowns, the media must be kept as a friend. As blue files full of documents stacked up on his office floor, he saw that 'the file' gave him formidable control in a high-profile case like this one. The media needed him. And he could set the rules.

Christian and Ian Lucas, who'd never met, discussed by phone how to co-ordinate media for the Rees-Joneses. They established a policy. Use us, his lawyers in Oswestry and Paris, as your contact and we'll keep you informed. If there is any news, we'll release it equally to everyone. There will be no favours. But start bothering the family, and you'll get nothing. From the beginning, 'Christian probably felt we should be giving out more snippets of news,' Ian noted. 'They'll write something anyway – let's control it,' was Christian's argument. But the family wanted nothing released. Nothing.

'They didn't just want Trevor's story, they wanted ours. We were in the phone book. CNN kept phoning, and ABC, NBC,' said Jill, as the new media pressure in Paris translated directly to Oswestry, and to their privacy. Her son Gareth's dental office in Birmingham was 'absolutely besieged. We actually had to run up the road – we felt so annoyed. We were back home and yet we seemed trapped again. It was an invasion here. In Paris, we could accept it because it was part of the big picture, but here, no, we couldn't accept it, it was totally out of order.' Jill and Ernie Scotch-taped to the door a handwritten sign on a piece of paper: 'No press. No comment. Please respect our privacy.'

'Let's go to the office,' Jill would often suggest to Ernie, early in the morning. It was the nickname they had given their favourite walk through the sheep and cattle farms, hills and woods to the grassy green oval of the abandoned racecourse. Taking the dog, 'the office' became the one place they could talk, unwatched and private.

To protect the family, Oswestry had closed ranks. In the pubs, in the shops, in Jill's surgery, the town sent reporters away empty-handed. A man arrived, one day, at The George, one of Trevor's favourite pubs, and said, 'I'm looking for Trevor Rees-Jones. Do you know where he lives?' 'Who?' said the landlord, as somebody made a quick call to Trevor and asked, 'Do you know him, Trev?' As Trevor said, 'Oh, sure, he's an old friend of mine from the army,' the landlord told the man, 'It's okay, Trevor's coming down.'

'What you've got to understand is that the whole of Oswestry knew Trevor before this event. He was a local character. He'd been to school here . . . Trevor was always in the front of anything that was going on – if there was a party, if there was something going on in town, he would always be there. He liked to be in the front, part of a group. He would never miss a sportsmen's night anywhere in Oswestry,' says Jill.

'Oswestry has been fantastic. They've really looked after me and rallied round,' says Trevor of a town and a life that had been largely bounded by a territory so small that it could be seen in its entirety from one of the hot-air balloons that rises from the Shropshire Plain. A place whose rural pace and social balances had never been shaken by the pressures that played on Birmingham or Liverpool, nor disturbed by tourists. The intrusion of this historic story was testing the integrity and balance of both place and people.

On 1 November Trevor was to leave Oswestry for Paris to see Dr Chikhani and go to London en route. His first trip back to 60 Park Lane, Trevor felt it would be 'nice to give Mum a break. I'd just go down to London for four days or so, to see the psychiatrist, see the company doctor, and perhaps see Fayed. They gave me one of the guest apartments, which was very plush. I really was looked after well. The fridge was full of food, a couple of beers. But I'd have preferred to have slept down in the security accommodation.' On 3 November, he had his first session with the psychiatrist Fayed had hired – the psychiatrist he'd met briefly at Park Lane on his return from Paris.

'We should feel really good about this and we don't,' Jill and Ernie confided to each other. 'This was the first time in eight weeks that Trevor had not been with us. It was the strangest feeling. We felt bereft.' With their first free day stretching ahead, however, they spoiled themselves, did things they wanted to do. Watched an old film and read papers in the pub. 'Jill had this wonderful smile on her face all day,' Ernie noted.

At 7:30 P.M., Trevor called, very unhappy. He'd rung Sue, and they'd had a good old row. Shall we come down to London? Jill asked. No, I'll be okay, thanks, he said.

Jill had to face it. 'He's nowhere near made it yet, nowhere near.'

On 6 November, Trevor went across to Paris by train, staying with Ben Murrell at the Villa Windsor. When he met Dr Chikhani, the surgeon seemed well pleased with his handiwork. Trevor gave him a bottle of Scotch and a silk bow-tie – Jill couldn't find a wooden one. And he gave the hospital Fayed's 'float' of £1,000. Christian met his client for the first time. He went through the file with him, already several thousand pages, and showed Trevor the photos taken at the crash site. How could the photographers not have assisted those in the car, but stood back and taken photos? He couldn't believe it. Trevor wanted to see the site. He asked the Ritz driver to take him on the crash route, from the Ritz through the Alma tunnel. He was interested, more than anything. He didn't expect it to trigger memories. And it did not.

On 8 November, Trevor was home from Paris. At the rugby club, he stood up at the bar while he had a few beers. Ernie and Jill sat back at the tables, watching him be just one of the lads again. 'It was all quite normal.' Very, very poignant. At home later that evening, 'he was sitting on the settee, everything seemed fine, and he suddenly just completely broke down. It was horrible,' Jill recalls.

'I think he appears to put on a great show for his friends, but when he's back with us, he doesn't feel he has to put on an act,' Ernie thought. Jill had other thoughts. 'Standing at the bar, he probably compared what he was now to what he had been before. Since he'd come back, he'd almost always sat down at the club, and sitting down, perhaps he could put himself in the sick role. But being able to stand and meet people eye to eye, I think maybe it all hit him – all the changes in his life.'

Paris, and then the rugby club, had been a ruthless reality check. With Chikhani, and in the terrible photos, he had faced the truly shattering damage the crash had done to him, physically. Perhaps, standing at the bar, still in pain, he'd faced how far he still had to go to be back on the pitch with the lads – and found it intolerable. Minutes after the outburst, Trevor had got himself together, the old Trevor they knew, and, as always, apologized. 'Trevor, you're not to apologize, ever,' they both told him.

But they wouldn't mind if he started boiling an egg. Back from walking the dog one morning, Jill and Ernie found Trevor sitting on the settee waiting for his breakfast, 'like a bird in the nest waiting to be fed', as Jill saw it. He'd come in the night before from having a drink and woken them up. Jill's instinct, with Trevor, was always 'to rush to his defence and say that this is a man who's been so severely ill that you can't expect him to really concentrate on anything but his own recovery . . . But I'd just had enough. I blew my top – just blew up and told Trevor he was a selfish little devil.' It honestly hadn't occurred to him. He was sorry. Jill recognized, then, that Trevor was ready to move out.

Ernie had been obsessed for some time with Trevor

moving to his own place. It was too soon for Trevor, Jill
had feared. Worried about Trevor's readiness to be on his
own, torn by 'the extra conflict of Ernie not being able to
cope', Jill felt herself to be 'right in the middle of it'.
They'd do his laundry, bring him food, be there every
day. But he seemed so insecure about moving out. 'It's
very hard for a mother to let go, to stop looking after a
child, even a 29-year-old one. But I felt Ernie's tremendous conflict – his contradiction in emotions. He was
feeling so depressed and out of control of his own environment, but it didn't stop him from being enormously
concerned and caring of Trevor. I just didn't have any
room or energy for anything but Trevor, and it probably
wasn't a good thing. Perhaps I should have stepped back
a bit.'

Before the summer, Trevor had been ready to move
into a small red-brick bungalow, the newly converted
'old cider press' in an alley off Willow Street, just a mile
from Jill and Ernie's. The owner, a friend, had held on to
it for him when he heard about the accident. It was time
for Trevor to become independent, and for Jill and Ernie
to reclaim their lives. They began equipping the house.
He could move in at the end of November. If he was able.

On 11 November, they all visited the little house he
planned to rent. The same day, 'he actually got up and
cooked an egg'. Ernie exulted. He was writing dozens of
appreciative letters to people who had wished him well.
'Things are looking up.' On Friday, 28 November, Trevor

spent his first night in his new home. He jokingly said, 'Well, I've been thrown out of my home twice.' Jill guessed he meant Sue, and now his family home. 'Emotionally, it was a huge tug for me. I know it's an illogical response, but, as a mother, I felt, "Oh, gosh, is my little boy going to be all right?" He was so alone.' 'And he's got nothing, absolutely nothing,' Ernie saw. 'That night, we had a celebratory meal. We need a lot more of these,' Ernie recorded.

After all Jill's worry, Trevor was just fine. 'When it was first suggested, I was a bit shocked, I suppose, and nervous as well at going out on my own. I suppose I even felt a bit hard done by, at that stage. After a couple of days there, I realized what idiotic feelings I was having. In fact, it was the best thing I ever did. I had no reason to be nervous.'

Oswestry's warmth became almost overwhelming as Trevor walked the streets on his own now, and found himself a celebrity. 'Suddenly, everyone knows your name, and it's "Oh, hello Trevor, how's it going?" If they see I've had another eye operation, it'll be "How's that gone?" People you've only had acquaintance with before want to be your best friend. It's nice more than anything. It's great. But sometimes, if you just want to pop into the shops or walk into Boots for tape for the wrist or something, it will take you about half an hour longer than it would as people stop and talk to you. I never want to be rude, but sometimes if you're in a rush, you've just got to keep your head down. Sometimes I smile to myself, almost seeing myself in that Princess Diana pose of keeping your eyes on the pavement.'

He'd begun to dread the phone as invitations poured in. 'I'd be spending every single spare moment travelling around the country visiting friends who want to see me. It's fantastic. And I appreciate every single one of them. Sometimes people think I'm rude because I keep putting them off on the phone. It's not a question of being rude. It's a question of having a routine back in my life, to get back to normality.'

With Trevor's move to the 'old cider press' the media also became more controllable. 'It was when Trevor moved into his place that Ian took up the reins of being his agent, if you like, in respect of the media,' Ernie recalls. Ian handled the local media invasion, as well as the Harrods calls, playing the same role for the family as the embassy had played in Paris.

'I'm very lucky,' thought Trevor. 'If anyone phones me up or turns up at my doorstep, I just say, "Go to my solicitors" and I give them the phone number or tell them where it is. Ian and David have been very strong with people, saying that if you go directly to Trevor, then if anything does happen, you're not going to be part of it. It's kept them quiet, waiting to see if anything will happen.' 'It did sort of ease off when Ian took over,' says a grateful Jill.

Jill finally felt able to return to work and, on 1 December, went back to her job at the surgery in Oswestry. 'I was so happy to be back.' She treasured the control she had there, in her work, as much as she valued control of her private life. Behind the door with the sign 'Sister Rees-Jones', she worked from two self-contained rooms. Her computer held the week's schedule and list of appointments, including the diabetic patients who attended her clinics. Her eldest son, being a diabetic, had motivated her to make it her special interest. It was wonderful to be surrounded again by the familiar tools of the trade, to be back to normality. Progress was being made. She, like Trevor, was beginning to reclaim her life.

Before Trevor left for Paris again for his 19 December interview with the judge, his first since leaving hospital, Fayed had called him in for a brief session. 'Every time he talked about the crash, he got quite passionate and upset. He waved his arms a fair bit – went on about conspiracies, and told me that he had his own investigation going.' This time, 'I was really surprised by his approach. It seemed that he wanted me to ask the judge about the Fiat Uno, and various things . . . Obviously, he's not stupid enough to say, "You're going to ask the judge this." It was done indirectly.

'I didn't just say no. I said, "Okay, no problem."' But he did not intend to mention them to the judge.

Trevor was 'thirsty, and conscious that I had a bit of a hangover' when he met the judge the morning of 19 December 1997. He'd gone over to Paris on the Eurostar with Kez the night before, and met up with Ben at the Villa Windsor. They'd gone into Paris for 'a bit of a night'.

Christian was distressed. He felt the Ritz had taken control of Trevor. He'd had a total of five minutes with his client before seeing the judge. They'd driven him to the courts. There, they had faced a media mob he'd never experienced before. This chaotic experience taught Christian, in a stroke, the full implications of Trevor having become a *partie civile*. Trevor had, indeed, given the Diana story new life. Trevor had no illusions about the source of his celebrity. 'The only reason people are interested in me is because of her.' But interested they were. And Trevor still would not speak.

Ian and David now agreed with Christian that Trevor must give at least scraps of 'minor information, or the press will lose sympathy with you . . . They are inventing things which are completely untrue.' The media, Christian had said many times, 'can be your best friend or your worst enemy'.

'When I first got home, my idea was to say nothing at all, and not to speak to anyone. I've always looked at other people who've given stories and done things and thought, "Oh, yes, it's the old cashing-in thing." But as it's gone along, I've seen that saying nothing is not really a viable way of doing things because they'll write something anyway.' The media furore of 19 December showed Trevor that total silence only sharpened their hunger, and he reluctantly agreed that – so long as they cleared it with him – Ian and Christian could appease the press, when needed, with brief comments.

Jill and Ernie watched Trevor's arrival at the Palais de

Justice on TV, horrified. The media were all over him. 'They look like a pack of hounds,' Jill cried out, wanting to protect him. 'He looked so frail. It came as a shock. He'd been gaining weight, and making good progress. But to see him on film, he looked almost like he did at the beginning.' His left eye sagged, and the scars in his cheek were so deep. Jill had kept her spirits high, being strong for both Trevor and Ernie. But now she felt they were 'all being buffeted by the media and by Fayed'. Jill's 'down time' began here.

11

Trial by Tabloid

By 1 February 1998, Trevor was well enough to be back at work. 'Good on you, Trev, you've done quite well here,' he thought to himself as he walked into 60 Park Lane for his first day of work. Just five months after the crash, Trevor had achieved one of his major goals from the moment he was conscious. It was part-time; 'just working on the Ops desk at 60 Park Lane, basically logging phone calls and radio messages'. But he was back and felt, 'I could've carried on with a twelve-hour shift if I'd been left alone.'

On 2 February, he had his second session with the psychiatrist. He also talked to Fayed again, the first of many conversations after his return to work. 'I talked to the Boss quite often – I saw him twice, even three times a week during this period. And he would say various things like what do you think about this, about that, do you remember this, do you remember that? There was a flash, there was a Fiat Uno. He'd give his side of things. Every time he saw me, he would start getting tears in his eyes. He was distraught, so I'm not going to say to him, "You're talking a load of bollocks." I would say, "Yes, that's a possibility, of course it's a possibility.'"

He called home every two or three days. He'd hear his mother's anxiety, asking how it was going. 'The *work's* been okay,' he'd say. But they could tell. Trevor was shattered.

When Ernie picked him up from the train on 6 February, their worries about Trevor increased. The *Sun* was coming to Oswestry soon to do a photo story, arranged by Harrods, Trevor told them. He seemed unworried, and seemed to think the *Sun* would be okay. 'It had been quiet in town at that point, because Trevor was back at work,' but Ernie could suddenly feel the pressure closing in on them again. Jill was very upset. Of course they couldn't control what happened to Trevor when he was in London. But even when he was back in Oswestry, now, she felt him being pulled away by 'outside influences', and felt helpless to pull him back. As he became physically stronger, Trevor's emotional state worried her more. In addition to Fayed and the media, she suspected an old army friend, David Liddle, was trying to join the bandwagon by telling his story to the press as well.

Still at home in Oswestry, Trevor rang up on Tuesday, 10 February, to tell Ernie that the *Sun* photo shoot had been in town that day. 'Next day, I picked up a paper, fearing the worst, and Trevor was all over the inside pages of the *Sun*.' After the *Sun* story, Trevor said to them, 'Wouldn't it be nice just to disappear, see my mates in New Zealand, and get away.'

Jill could see the damage media pressures could do. Nain was weakening after all the hounding. She was eighty-five now, and not well. Jill herself found it increasingly hard to focus on her work, even though she was there only three days a week. The 'down time' that had started when she saw Trevor on TV in Paris was deepening into an unshakable gloom, a state so unlike her usual self. 'I felt I was being pulled down with Trevor.'

'It never ends. On Thursday, February 12, it starts again,' Ernie confided wearily to his diary. 'The *Mirror* newspaper has the first five pages devoted to Trevor's boss, Al Fayed, who makes ridiculous claims about Dodi and Diana, and also about Trevor – about what he can remember. Trevor has no memory of the crash, and could not have said these things.'

Fayed had given *Mirror* editor Piers Morgan what was touted as the first newspaper interview he had granted since the accident, a sensationalized three-part story that ran on 12, 13 and 14 February. In it, Fayed unleashed his frustration and grief, and his suspicions. 'I believe in my heart 99.9 per cent that it was not an accident. There was a conspiracy and I will . . . find the person who caused this accident. I will not sleep. I will not rest until I have done so.' In Paris, his lawyer, Georges Kiejman, was

prodding the judge to investigate a specific Fiat Uno that
Fayed's own investigative team had turned up, its candidate for the assassin's vehicle.

But Fayed's *Mirror* interview bristled with other
claims. Trevor and Kez knew most of them to be inaccurate – if not outright fantasies.

Fayed revealed Diana's 'last words', given to him, he
said, by a nurse outside the operating theatre where
Diana had died; Kez knew that Fayed had never left the
hospital steps, and had two security lads as witnesses.

The emerald and diamond ring that Fayed claimed he
had paid for and that would have sealed their engagement that very night had been chosen by the couple in
Monte Carlo a week before the crash, he said; Trevor and
Kez were sure it had not. The Monte Carlo walk on 23
August had absolutely not included a stop at Repossi
jewellers. When, later, Fayed's website stated unequivocally that 'the Princess helped choose it on the evening
of August 22 in Monte Carlo', that claim, too, was
backed by nothing but bravado, the bodyguards
believed, no more reliable than the twisted labyrinth of
conflicting stories Fayed and others had told about the
ring.

Fayed told Piers Morgan, 'I last spoke to Dodi fifteen
minutes before the accident and said to him, "Now look,
don't do any tricks when you leave the hotel. Go out the
front door and say hello, talk to the paparazzi."' But Kez
had been told by both Dodi and Henri Paul that the plan
for Paul to drive from the back of the hotel had been

approved by Fayed himself. Had they been telling the truth? Fayed denied all knowledge of the plan.

The fantasies continued to build. Fayed had, in fact, not learned of Diana's death at the hospital, as the story claimed; Kez had told him as he arrived at Le Bourget. A small point, perhaps.

But not a small point was Fayed's claim that Trevor had heard Diana's voice, and her words, in the crashed car. 'Trevor remembers her saying, "Where is Dodi? Where is Dodi?"' Fayed boasted. 'Trevor has been seeing two psychiatrists . . . and he remembers more every time.' Yes, Trevor had had a sort of dream, heard a voice. He might have mentioned it to a few blokes in the hierarchy. The Boss was so hungry for memories, and he wanted to help. But it was only a single word, 'Dodi', and Trevor didn't trust it to be a true memory. Now, in print for all England to read, the Boss had distorted their half-dozen agitated exchanges over the past few weeks into this! For Jill and Ernie, it conjured the fears they had felt in London that Fayed was trying to influence Trevor's memories.

Fayed was not done with Trevor. He put him in the story, too, to defend Henri Paul. 'Trevor is one of my top guys and if he had spotted anything untoward about Henri Paul, he would not have allowed him to drive that car.'

As long as Trevor worked for Fayed and served his purposes, he was safe, Christian suspected, as he searched the files in Paris. But this praise for Trevor could be reversed very quickly, he feared, if Fayed ever felt the need for another scapegoat – if the trails of guilt he was pursuing went cold. Christian could see them cooling, though this wasn't the time to mention his alarm to Trevor.

For tedious months, Christian had scrutinized hundreds of matter-of-fact reports: police, medical, airport weather, Paris traffic patterns, anonymous witnesses, loyal Ritz staff, lists of photos, indignant statements by the photographers – and, again and again, updates on the exhaustive village-by-village search for the mystery Fiat. But, early in 1998, Christian sensed a fresh undercurrent bubbling up through the files. On 26 January, as he studied the most recent three volumes, he had found – almost lost among the testimonials to Henri Paul's fine and sober character – the statement of the barman, Alain Willaumez, who had been on hand as Paul was served his two glasses of Ricard *pastis*. He claimed to have seen Paul staggering. This was at odds with Trevor's – and other witnesses' – statements. But worth noting.

Willaumez's statement caught Christian's attention with an even more striking claim: that Frank Klein, the powerful president of the Ritz, had ordered all staff, in their statements to police, to stick to Kez's statement that Henri Paul had been drinking fruit juice that evening. And there was something else. Willaumez also testified that he'd learned from one of the barmen that François Tendil, the night-security man, told him that he had tried to stop Henri Paul from driving. Willaumez had stated that he had learned from Bruno Bavoine, the first barman, that Tendil had told Willaumez he had tried to persuade Paul not to drive, but in vain. Willaumez felt it was obvious that Tendil, a security officer, was not senior enough to prevent Paul from driving. But *why* had Tendil tried to stop him, Christian wondered. Did Tendil know about the drinking, or perhaps worry that Paul was not a proper chauffeur? The answer lay in the rest of Willaumez's statement to the judge, when he said that he had mentioned to François Tendil that Paul had been drunk when he left the bar, and Tendil replied that he *knew*.

Christian wondered what other acts and decisions at the Ritz that night had still to emerge. What secrets were being held within Étoile Limousine, as well?

On 23 February, Trevor was sent upstairs for his third meeting with the psychiatrist, near the Boss's office. 'I'd dreamed things perhaps three times. I must have mentioned to the doctor having these vague recollections or dream-type things, and said to him, "Sometimes I think they're true, sometimes I think they're suspect. I don't really believe them."' These post-trauma memories were likely to be unreliable, the psychiatrist confirmed.

'This guy *never* pressed for memories. He was a spot-on man, a smashing bloke,' in Trevor's view. 'We'd sit down and have a cup of coffee and a talk, and he'd ask if anything was worrying me. After the first time, when I told him there was absolutely nothing worrying me, I kept seeing him, I suppose, as a favour to Fayed. Ops would tell me, "We've lined up another meeting for you to see the doctor," and I'd say, "I don't really think I need to, but I'll play ball.'"

Frustrating though it may be for Fayed, the psychiatrist's belief that Trevor's post-trauma memories are unlikely to be reliable is the common expert view. Though conclusive proof of true or false memories still eludes the scientists, there is wide consensus that the kind of amnesia and memory disturbances that Trevor experiences are extremely common. 'This kind of retrograde amnesia – forgetting events that happened in the seconds or minutes just before a head trauma, and having a patchy memory for events prior to that – is totally expected in even minor crashes,' says Daniel L. Schacter, Professor and Chair of Harvard University's Department of Psychology and a world expert on memory distortion. 'In this case – with massive swelling on the brain and prolonged unconsciousness – it would be stunning if it *didn't* happen.' The reasons *why* he has a three-minute memory gap are less well understood, 'but most of us see it as a failure of the last three minutes to consolidate in the brain's long-term memory', Schacter adds – the process interrupted by the violent assault to the head and, possibly, by subtle brain damage that may not even show on scans. If the memories were coming back, 'spontaneous recovery would have occurred relatively soon after the event. As time goes on, the likelihood increases that they will not. Memory loss for the few minutes before the trauma is almost always permanent.'

After his latest session with the psychiatrist, Trevor went back to his quarters, and within ten minutes the doctor and Paul Handley-Greaves were at the door. The doctor had been called in to see Fayed right after his session with Trevor. 'I've just seen Mr Fayed, and he's upset,' he told Trevor, as he sat down with him. 'He thinks you remember things, and I told him you don't. I'm confused – do you, or don't you?'

'No, I don't,' said Trevor. Fayed wanted to see them. The three of them now marched up to the Boss's office for a chat.

'His main thing then was to prove that this wasn't an accident. So far as I was concerned, it was just a crash.' But the Boss wanted more, and bombarded Trevor: 'Trevor, do you remember a Fiat Uno? We *know* who was following you during the trip – do you remember a flash?'

Trevor quickly saw that all the times he'd said to the Boss, 'That's a possibility' in response to Fayed's cock-eyed theories were coming back to haunt him. 'When I'm saying "Maybe, it's a possibility," he's taking it as "Yes, I agree with you."'

Handley-Greaves chimed in, 'I was there, Trevor, and I thought you said you remembered things,' showing himself to be the Boss's man, Trevor thought.

'I said before that anything's a possibility. I never said I *remembered*. I don't remember anything but getting in the car back at the Ritz,' Trevor insisted to the Boss. 'I won't swear on any memory apart from what I've said to the judge.'

'I can't understand why your memory's not come back. You're getting better now,' Fayed barked at Trevor. His frustration turning to fury, he stormed at the doctor: 'What's *wrong* with him?'

The medical man spoke up for his patient. 'He's probably not going to remember any more.' The Boss finally gave up, turned solicitous, and cautioned Trevor, 'You be *sure* you get back to the doctor.'

But the Boss was not about to be cheated of the cornerstone of his strategy. He needed it, now, to divert the press. A new scandal had broken over his head. He was in trouble over the breaking-into of Tiny Rowland's safety-deposit box at Harrods in December 1995, and was about to be humiliated by being forced to present himself at Kennington police station on 2 March for questioning on the matter. He was caught, also, in noisy litigation with *Vanity Fair* over a story which had charged him with racist employment policies and sexual harassment at Harrods, allegations which he denied.

Paul Handley-Greaves had good reason to collaborate in creating a diversion. He, too, would be submitting himself with Fayed at the police station for his alleged role in the break-in. And in the *Vanity Fair* case he had been involved in an elaborate entrapment scheme in which he falsely claimed that he had for sale a compromising video of his employer.

Two nights after Trevor's brouhaha with Fayed and the

psychiatrist, Handley-Greaves was on another assignment for the Boss. Out for a few drinks with Trevor, he
suggested, Trevor recalls, 'that, obviously, the Boss was
under fire, feeling victimized, and would I be prepared to
do something for him. You know, do an interview and
mention these memories.'

'These memories' were something Trevor wished he'd
kept to himself, and, frankly, wished the Boss had kept to
himself when he'd talked to the *Mirror*. 'I've always said
I was unsure of this woman's voice saying, "Dodi".
Looking back, it can't be true, and as soon as I said it, I
totally regretted it.' Now, the Harrods people were running with it.

The two of them went over to Handley-Greaves's
place, and the security man continued to press his case.

Trevor stalled. 'I'm seeing the judge again in March to
give more testimony. Look, I'm prepared to do something,
but not until after I've seen the judge and after I've talked
to my solicitors about it.' Handley-Greaves ignored this.

'I'll phone you in the morning up at Park Lane and get
your decision.'

'Well, I can't give you a decision – give me a couple of
weeks,' said Trevor.

'No,' Handley-Greaves told him. 'You've got to make
the decision tomorrow.'

They'd had a few drinks by now, and Trevor 'was feeling disappointed that Paul was so far in the Boss's back
pocket', pushing this interview thing so hard, and he said
straight to his face, 'I don't trust you as far as I can spit.'

Handley-Greaves laughed and said, 'I can't believe you're sitting in my house, drinking my beer, telling me this.'

'I'm telling you you're the Boss's man.'

'Yes, I am,' Handley-Greaves said.

Trevor called a cab to go back to the quarters at Park Lane, and said to Paul as he left, 'Okay, ring me in the morning.'

'I sat down and thought, to be honest, what harm is it going to do? I'm not sure if these are true memories or not. I won't lie about anything. But what harm would be done? I'm not going to say anything that's outrageous to upset the Princess's family – I'm not saying I saw them getting an engagement ring, or saw them jumping into bed together, which I never would anyway.' Trevor's instinct said 'I don't want to do this', 'but I felt well by then, I wanted to help the Boss. I hoped it wouldn't hurt anyone.'

'Yes, I'll do this interview,' Trevor told Handley-Greaves when he rang the next morning, Thursday, 26 February.

'I accepted it. I accepted a lot of things at that time because I felt a need to help Fayed. And I wanted to stay in his employment. I was happy to be back in the job. I enjoyed working with the lads there, and my main aim, even when I first woke up in hospital, was to go back to work as quickly as possible. If I was of the attitude I am now, I would have told Paul to get stuffed. I would have said "sod it" . . . My big mistake was that I didn't talk to solicitors until afterwards. But I wasn't on such close terms with Ian and David as I am now. It was a lot earlier. All I wanted was to stay at work.'

Mid-morning, Trevor got a call. 'The Boss wants to see you at Harrods.'

'I went across to Harrods, first into the Ops Room, and saw this Piers Morgan, who I recognized as the *Mirror* bloke – he's been on TV a lot. I was directed into a small meeting room, and I said to Paul, "What's he doing here?" and he said – I'm not lying, this is word for word – "Don't worry, it's nothing to do with you. He's here for another matter to see the Boss. Basically, you're the bait to get him here and all you have to do is say hello to him, and that perhaps we'll do something in the future. We'll just go into the board room to meet Piers Morgan."

'Then Piers Morgan walked in with a photographer. Mr Fayed and the director of security, John Macnamara, walked in. I still thought it was just to see how I was getting on. So I sat there and said hello. The next thing, he'd set up a tape recorder and started asking questions.

'Everyone's got a choice. Although I was completely thrown I had a choice to stand up and say, "I'm not doing this," but the decision I made at that time was, "Right, I'll do it. In for a penny, in for a pound. Let's get on with it."'

From the start, 'the main thing Piers Morgan wanted to aim at was the so-called memory of Diana's voice. That was the thing he wanted. At that stage, even though I was desperate to remember something, I told him I was not very certain myself. He kept coming back to it, wanting more and more details. I was quite annoyed, really, that that was all he was zeroing in on. Looking back, I definitely felt that Piers Morgan had been primed – prompted, I think – to ask certain things.

'Then he tried to ask about Sue, and I wasn't keen to answer. That's when the interview wound up . . . Fayed had been there at the beginning, then he left. Paul Handley-Greaves and John Macnamara were present throughout. Fayed walked in probably five minutes before the end and said, "Let's call it a day."

'I hope this isn't going to come out until I've seen the judge. Legally, I've got to tell him these things first,' Trevor said. 'The interview was not much longer than half an hour, to be honest. It was the end of my shift, so I was due to go home. The minute I'd done it, I regretted it.'

He called David Crawford, remorseful, and told him what had happened. 'Oh, my God, what have you done!' was the tone of David's response, as Trevor heard it. They won't publish until I've seen the judge – I've told them, Trevor explained.

Crawford called Ian Lucas. It was outrageous, both lawyers agreed. 'We'd been trying to keep control. We had it until Trevor went back to work,' says Lucas. In hindsight, he saw, 'There had been signs the moment he went back – the *Sun* photographer that Harrods sent up to Oswestry a week earlier – and when I say Harrods, I mean *Fayed*.' When Ian had got wind of the *Sun* piece, he'd tried to reach Michael Cole, then faxed him: 'This is a clear breach of our request that all media enquiries will be forwarded to me in Oswestry.' The *Sun* had published anyway.

Now Harrods had set up the *Mirror*, the *Sun*'s main rival. Their client, Trevor, 'was, clearly, just a pawn in the game'. Whatever the game was. 'It was delicate. Trevor still wanted his job. But we were losing control of the situation.' He and Crawford did nothing on Thursday or Friday. They still had time to sort it out. Trevor had told the *Mirror* not to publish until after his appearance before the judge. Fayed was scheduled to testify on 12 March, Trevor on 16 March.

On Friday, 27 February, the day after the interview with Piers Morgan, Trevor took the train home, and, sensing trouble from his voice on the phone, Jill and Ernie rushed over to his place during Jill's lunch break. They were shaken by what they found. 'He looked as if he was at the end of his tether,' says Ernie. 'He was pacing and pacing, and clicking his fingers the way he does when he's anxious, trying to ease the tension in his body,' Jill saw. He paced the floor, sat down, then stood up and went for a walk. Then he told them the whole story. 'They wanted me to do it, they were very happy that I did it. And I was desperate to try to remember something.' Trevor also reported that he'd just heard from Paul Handley-Greaves that Sue was trying to sell her story. He couldn't believe it. Sue!

'That didn't help Trev. He no longer trusted anyone.

He felt as if he was surrounded by people with hidden agendas, all motivated by money or self-promotion,' was Ernie's opinion of it.

When Sue's story ran in the *News of the World* a few weeks later, on 15 March, her version of his snapped mouth wires evoked a rueful laugh from Trevor. 'According to Sue Rees-Jones, when the bodyguard's parents broke the news that Princess Diana and Dodi Fayed had been killed in the crash, her husband's mouth dropped open at the shock, requiring the delicate wiring to be rebuilt,' was how a later book described her statements. 'When I read Sue's quote in the paper about breaking the wires in my jaw, and that the reason it happened was that I was so upset about the deaths of everyone, I had to laugh to myself,' says Trevor, 'because the truth is so much more boring. I yawned one morning, there was a bit of a click, and I found I could actually move my jaw a little bit, and speak, which was great at the time.'

Jill's laughs were now few. She was so upset she couldn't concentrate on anything at work that afternoon. The 'down time' for Jill had spiralled into depression. 'Although I dislike the term "depression", I suppose it could be said that I was suffering a form of "reactive depression" brought on by the constant media hassle and so-called expert criticism of Trevor.'

'No matter what I said to Jill, I couldn't get through to her,' says Ernie. 'It was seeing Trevor so emotionally traumatized. You know that there's nothing you can do about it. You're just sitting there watching somebody crumbling in front of your eyes, somebody you'd worked so hard to get well . . . He'd done so much physically, and now you see him crumbling emotionally.'

'Trevor knew he should never have agreed. But what could he do? It wasn't his choice; he'd been coerced into it. It's the inability to do anything! If you can at least try to sort it out, you don't feel so impotent,' said Jill. Thank God he was confiding in them. Who else could he talk to? 'There is life after Fayed. Consider your options,' Ernie kept telling him. Jill didn't. 'I felt he had to make his own decision. And I know Trevor only too well. You can't make him do anything.'

Trevor had helped Fayed again, that day, when he'd had a call from Harrods saying that the pictures of him in a suit with Piers Morgan hadn't come out, and would he mind if they sent another photographer up to Oswestry. 'How can I say no, when I've said yes to everything else?' Trevor thought. But they arrived with a TV crew as well, and he refused to talk on camera. They finally settled for taking a video of him walking across Cae Glas Park.

That night, his walk was splashed across Sky TV, with a promo for his story in the *Mirror*, launching the next day.

On Saturday, 28 February, Trevor's face, scars and all, duly filled the front page of the *Mirror*. 'I SURVIVED', the headline screamed. The subhead proclaimed 'Exclusive: Diana's bodyguard Trevor Rees-Jones tells his own story'. Inside were two pages pitching the three-part series that would begin on Monday with 'the year's most astonishing interview'.

For Trevor, 'this leader in the *Mirror* is when I began to lose faith in the Boss. I was absolutely flabbergasted. I'd told them no publication until I'd seen the judge. It was *never* exclusive.' And there, inside, was the worst – a very presentable half-page photograph of Piers Morgan and himself in a suit sitting at an elegant desk at Harrods with a tape recorder between them – the very photograph they'd told him *yesterday* had not turned out and had to be re-taken. He'd been completely conned. Harrods had treated him like a fool.

'From that point on, I felt cheated,' says Trevor. 'That's where my relationship with work started deteriorating.'

He called Handley-Greaves and declared that he, Trevor, was now at liberty to talk to whoever he wished. He called David, who urged him to get down to the office.

Ian Lucas was picking up his usual morning paper at the newsagent's on his way to the office on Saturday morning when he saw the *Mirror*. Trevor's face filled the front page. David joined him at the office. 'We were furious,' says Ian. 'It implied they'd *bought* Trevor's story,' and that Trevor remembered most of what happened that night. The media had assumed, from a *Mirror* press release the night before – a press release that they, Trevor's lawyers, knew nothing about – that Trevor had sold his story as a 'worldwide exclusive'. Now they were on the doorstep demanding a story, too. 'The wolves were at the door. We got Trevor in, and we got under way.'

As England waited for the sensational series to begin on Monday, an urgent, secret drama was unfolding by phone and fax between London and Oswestry. It would be the turning point in the battle to persuade Trevor to take control of his own future. Ian, who'd had a rather minor role in Trevor's case so far, handling media, and had met him only once or twice, was now on the front lines.

Could they stop the series – get an injunction against the *Mirror*? No, David guessed. There was no contract. They were free to publish. And Trevor was free to talk to anyone he wished. 'Also, Trevor wouldn't let us kill the story. He said he didn't want to criticize, or get into a battle with, Fayed. Two things were of great concern to Trevor,' Ian explains. 'First was the perception that he was going to be profiting from the crash.' You had to admire that. Even Sue, his ex-wife, was apparently selling her story, Trevor had just told them. 'The second thing was that he still wanted to maintain his relationship with Fayed.' Trevor was the client, their boss, they had to respect his wishes. But several points had to be made public, fast: 'That the story was *not* exclusive. That Trevor had been told there would be nothing published before he saw the judge or without his lawyers' approval. And that he hadn't been paid a penny.' A press release was called for.

At 1:26 P.M., Ian faxed a tough and candid press release to Fayed's press office. Michael Cole had gone. A press officer, on holiday, called in from his car, insisting that Mr Fayed must personally approve it. Paul Handley-Greaves called on his mobile phone, aggressive about what he claimed was an error – no, Fayed was *not* in the room through the whole interview, as the statement claimed. 'Is he right?' Ian asked Trevor. He crossed it out with his pencil when Trevor confirmed it.

Fayed's chief London lawyer, Stuart Benson, got in on the act, calling and faxing to correct 'untruths' about the psychiatrist: no, no, no, Trevor had *not* seen a psychiatrist at Fayed's request 'in an attempt to remember more of the events of 31 August', as the release said, but solely for his *own good*. That, too, was softened, the offending lines struck out by Trevor.

All afternoon, they negotiated, calls and faxes flying – with dozens of media calls coming in as a counterpoint to the crisis. The *Mirror* story had attracted a new breed, for Ian: female American TV journalists, pitching interviews for the major network news programmes. Saturday afternoon brought to their door the most tenacious of all, Jackie Jabara of CBS News. Her earlier letters were in Ian's file. But now, here she was in Oswestry, at the Wynnstay Hotel, two minutes' walk from the Crawford Lucas office.

Jabara had called before coming over. How best to approach Trevor? she had asked. Late afternoon, she turned up at the office – David met her – to deliver a handwritten letter to Trevor. 'I write to you on behalf of CBS News and Dan Rather to invite you to be

Trevor's mother Jill and stepfather Ernie (behind, in striped shirt) arrive at la Pitié-Salpêtrière hospital to visit Trevor, September 1997.

PA

Jill sitting in Fayed's opulent apartment off the Champs-Élysées. Although grateful for Fayed's hospitality, towards the end of their stay they began to feel uncomfortable as they felt control of Trevor's destiny slipping away from them.

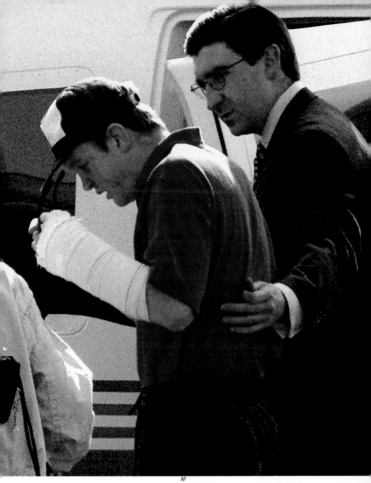

Fayed's chief of personal security,
Paul Handley-Greaves, shepherds a
still clearly unwell Trevor aboard the
helicopter for the return to Britain,
Friday, 3 October 1997.

The church at Whittington near
Trevor's home in Oswestry, where he
went two days later to give thanks for
his recovery and to the community
that had given so much support.

Trevor begins to enjoy life again at a friend's wedding about a month after his return. His face, however, clearly shows the extent of his injuries, and he was yet to regain his full strength.

The legal battle begins. Trevor, flanked by Kez and Ben Murrell, arrives at the Palais de Justice for his first interview with the judge, 19 December.

Trevor's team:
lawyers David Crawford (top),
Ian Lucas (middle)
and Christian Curtil.

Two shots of Trevor at the Palais de Justice on 3 March 1998. Six months after the crash, his face and left eye still bear witness to his ordeal.

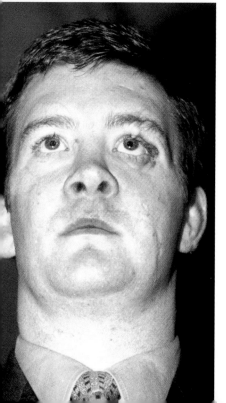

Trevor's grandmother, Nain, who was so proud of her grandson she was delighted to talk to the press – although they perhaps had less honourable motives.

Trevor and Ernie during the impromptu cricket game in the grounds of Sweeney Hall on the first anniversary of the crash.

In the thick of it: Trevor (in striped jersey, tackling) back playing the game he loves during the 1998/99 season, barely a year after the crash that nearly killed him.

Rooting for the team:
Trevor in characteristic pose at
a rugby match.

Trevor with Dr Luc Chikhani,
the surgeon who performed such miracles in
reconstructing Trevor's face.

Moving c
Trevor, Jill and Ernie in Oswest
February 200

interviewed by our network,' her letter began. As Ian
would soon see for himself, Jabara was 'a very attractive,
beautifully dressed American journalist who was there to
get the interview. She was polite in the way American
people are, very accommodating – in contrast to British
journalists, who are much more assertive and up-front –
but very dogged as well.' He and Christian would later
joke, as these women became daily fixtures, that the
American networks always assigned beautiful, sexy
women to get the interviews. They were also mannerly
and smart. To Ian, Jabara's classiness spoke of the very
deep pockets and power he perceived the American networks to have.

'Who's Dan Rather?' Ian wondered to himself as he
scanned her letter. The name was no more familiar to
him than the others who were calling in – Barbara
Walters, Katie Couric. Jabara's 'big sales pitch was for *60
Minutes*, *48 Hours* and *Public Eye* with Bryant Gumbel'.
When Jabara followed up with a call a few hours later,
Ian told her, as he had told ABC, NBC, the BBC and the
rest, 'The *Mirror* is not an exclusive interview. The out-
come is not entirely clear at this stage, but should
become clearer during the course of the day. Ring back
around four or five.' The office was a madhouse, and they
had to get the press release out.

As Trevor blue-pencilled, the statement was progressively diluted. 'Trevor wouldn't let us be as tough as we
wanted to be,' Ian fretted. But he saw that they had a
little leverage to exploit. 'Harrods were trying to keep us

on-side because they knew that Trevor was in Oswestry now – physically with us. We had physical control of him. If he'd been in London, they would have manipulated him, and the story would have just come out.' Stuart Benson even wrote a flattering rider at the end of the press release, in Trevor's voice: 'I have been very concerned to read previous articles in the press suggesting that I did not, on the night in question, conduct myself professionally . . . These allegations are wholly spurious.'

The Fayed team may not have known how little control his lawyers actually had over Trevor. 'We were urging him to resign. We wanted him to leave that very weekend. We were spinning round, out of control, because this *Mirror* thing had happened. If he'd just said, "I resign" we could have recovered the situation. The headline "BODYGUARD RESIGNS" would have completely discredited the interview. Nobody would have taken the contents of the articles seriously. We wouldn't have needed to say anything.' But Trevor refused. 'He wanted to keep in with Fayed.'

Ian had no idea that, as he pushed Trevor to resign, Trevor was getting just as much if not more pressure from Jill and Ernie as well. Ian had not even met them yet.

The fallback was a leave of absence, which Ian – on one of his many calls to Stuart Benson that day – presented as a *'fait accompli'*. He didn't have to negotiate. 'The Fayed camp was in a very exposed position. I think they feared that if they'd refused a leave of absence,

Trevor would have resigned on the spot.' Now, if only
Trevor would agree to take it.

'Eventually, after a few drafts and quite a few ani-
mated discussions, we got a press release out around
tea-time on Saturday.' It was sent to the Press Association
for release at 6:20 P.M.

'I wish to explain how the interview with Mr Piers
Morgan took place and make absolutely clear that I have
received no payment from the interview and, indeed,
have never received any payment from the press,' it
began. Trevor chided Piers Morgan. 'I understand that
the *Mirror* contacted other press outlets last night claiming rights over an "exclusive" article . . . without
contacting me or my solicitors. The result has been to
make my life hell for the last twenty-four hours. I have
felt forced to go into hiding.'

Trevor left to see his parents and his friend, Helen, his
physiotherapist, as soon as the release was finished. The
lawyers didn't want him at the office when the press mob
arrived. The first media calls, with offers to buy Trevor's
story, started within the hour. At 8:30 on Saturday night,
Piers Morgan phoned. Ian had been waiting for his call.
Morgan had read the press release; even watered down, it
had the desired effect. Ian could hear his children in the
background as the editor of the powerful tabloid offered
concessions. 'He was happy to give us a statement
making it clear that it was not exclusive, that Trevor had
not been paid, and to send us every word that was going
to be published so that we could check it first.' He agreed

to pay legal costs in connection with the articles – later
agreed at £10,000. 'He knew he was in a very difficult
position. He'd been thinking he had the greatest scoop in
the world, and it was about to collapse around his ears.
We could get anything we wanted.'

Morgan also let a few things slip. When Ian told him
that Trevor was very upset because he'd not been shown
the content of the interview, Morgan professed amaze-
ment. 'I sent every word of the piece through to Mr Fayed
for his approval, I kept in close liaison with Handley-
Greaves. I *thought* that Trevor had approved it.' Morgan
would fax his statement and the first instalment of the
series to Ian early next morning.

When Ian and David finally dragged themselves down
the stairs and on to the dark street at 10:30 that evening,
they had to elbow through a 'scrum' of cameras and
reporters. An even larger scrum would greet them next
day.

For Ian, 'the shit really hit the fan the next morning',
Sunday, 1 March. 'The press release made it clear that
there was no exclusive deal and the press assumed that
Trevor was up for grabs.' It triggered a bidding war. The
Sun, England's biggest-selling newspaper, opened with
£50,000, and quickly moved up to £200,000, with other
papers and networks coming in with competing bids. The
lawyers were not about to turn them down lightly.
'Trevor's the pauper here,' Ian was thinking. Lots of other
people had sold their story. They had to represent

Trevor's interests responsibly. The lawyers had their own interests, too. The one and only payment of legal fees they'd received had come from Fayed on Friday, under terrific *Mirror* pressure, even though they had a costs contract signed by Stuart Benson for Fayed. They were long since committed to going forward with Trevor on principle, regardless. But it would be nice.

While Ian fielded the bids, Trevor and David Crawford were feverishly editing the first story, faxed through by Piers Morgan and due to appear next day. 'Trevor's letting too much through in an effort to please the Boss,' Ian feared, glancing over the final product. Monday's headline would read: 'I heard Diana call out for Dodi after the crash'. The story went on: 'I have had flashes of a female voice calling out in the back of the car. First, it's a groan. Then Dodi's name is called. I don't remember if it is over and over again . . . It could only have been Princess Diana. I was conscious, and so was she.' Ian and David knew Trevor had told Piers Morgan that he doubted the memory. Why had he not insisted on adding a caveat about his doubts? He was playing into Fayed's strategy of the great romance. He was letting through a statement that a psychiatrist, the morning of the interview, had helped him remember – something even the psychiatrist felt was open to question. 'He's such a straight shooter that it was proof, to us, of the coercive atmosphere that he would let some of this stuff through.' But they could only advise.

As they worked on it a letter arrived from the

Shropshire Star. 'Good God, what's this, Trevor?' a
shocked Ian asked. 'The *Shropshire Star* – the suppos-
edly supportive local paper – was coming out with a
story and was asking us if we had any comment on
Trevor's old drink-driving conviction.' Trevor had been
twenty-one – nine years ago. He'd had a few pints, hit a
car – no driver involved – and, afraid he'd be charged
with being over the limit, had driven away from the
scene. It was a disgraceful, immature bit of behaviour.
Trevor was clearly full of remorse. But it was, legally, a
spent conviction – the press was prohibited from using
it. Ian shot off a letter to the *Star*, threatening legal
sanctions. 'But it's inevitably going to come out – it
could still be banner headlines in the *Shropshire Star*.
How can we exercise control?' he pondered. His parlia-
mentary campaign experience was coming into play. 'I
had a perfect vehicle in Piers Morgan, who was doing
everything he could to help me. I rang him up and
asked him to put in just a small sidebar on the drink-
driving story, with a statement from Trevor, along with
the larger story.' It would run on Tuesday, spiking the
local piece.

The *Sun* had set a 2 P.M. deadline for their offer to
buy Trevor's story. Late morning, Ian called Piers Morgan
'and let him know that we were having these offers and
that we were hovering. There was a pause – total silence.
He hadn't realized this at all. And he suddenly saw how
precarious his position was. If the *Sun* had come out the
next day with Trevor's story and a big criticism of the

Mirror, it could have been almost terminal to Piers Morgan's career.'

'You wouldn't do that,' Morgan said, clearly shaken.

'We have to investigate the options for our client. We'll let you know late afternoon.'

Through an intense afternoon, they toyed with what, to them, was a fortune. When you scribbled down the various offers and added them up, it came to roughly half a million pounds. The *Sun* was still the high bidder. As much as he wanted Trevor to break free of Fayed, Ian felt obliged to tell him, 'If you sell an interview to the *Sun*, spiking the *Mirror* story, it would blow Fayed's media strategy out of the water. Your relationship with Fayed would be terminated.' Trevor decided to reject all bids and stay with the *Mirror*. 'The easy decision for him at that stage was not to take the money.'

As he lifted his head and surveyed these extraordinary two days, the paradox for Ian, who had, with this crisis, just begun to know Trevor, was: 'With the overwhelming weight of influence on the scales for leaving Fayed – the pressure of three lawyers, in two countries, and his parents, all urging him to break free – why did he stay?' His bafflement was nothing compared to the conflicts Trevor faced. Money wasn't one of them.

'I turned down half a million pounds in an afternoon,' Trevor mused. 'I was happy to. I didn't want it.' Two weeks later, Trevor would, just as easily, turn down a written offer of $1 million from the American tabloid the *National Enquirer*.

Ian called Piers Morgan to tell him the good news.
'God, he was relieved.' Ian couldn't resist teasing him
about the soap opera he was about to let loose on the
world. 'Isn't this a little Mills & Boonish?' he said,
chuckling. 'I had one of my sub-editors write it,' Morgan
responded. Jokes aside, the lawyers knew that they still
faced a disaster for Trevor's credibility when this rubbish
hit the stands.

'It was around tea-time when we all retired and went
back home. We were pretty exhausted,' says Ian. But also
elated. Trevor's lawyers had scored a victory in damage
control. 'It was absolutely the turning point. It showed us
unequivocally that Trevor was being used by Fayed. And
it became obvious to Trevor that he was being used as
well,' Ian reflects. 'Fayed had thought we were country
cousins. But over that weekend, he learned that we
weren't going to be pushed around.'

'We're personalities in a tabloid newspaper,' said Jill and
Ernie, trying to laugh as they saw Jill's picture, with
Trevor's, on the front page of the *Mirror* on Tuesday, 3
March. The series had hit the streets the day before, and
the nation was devouring it. The three days of the series
were the worst of nightmares for the Rees-Joneses. 'We
had no control. We felt totally exposed.'

The opening article, on Monday 2 March, had titillated
with the headline: 'I HEARD DIANA CALL OUT FOR DODI
AFTER THE CRASH'. Here was the love confirmed, and the
memories Fayed had wanted. The stories critical of

Trevor started the same day. Trevor was distraught, and came up for lunch.

'Trevor was wound up, cracking his fingers again, not able to believe the things being said about him in the press,' Ernie noted. 'He's given one interview to the *Mirror*, and because it wasn't shared around, all the other newspapers are having a go at him.' Jill knew that Trevor had to make the choice to quit on his own, but she searched for alternatives. What about sick leave, she suggested. It would get him away from Fayed, without actually quitting. That night, Trevor and Darren went out and got drunk.

Harrods had sent Darren up on the Sunday to 'look after him' during the *Mirror* siege. The media presence was so intense in Oswestry that he and Trevor had gone to a neighbouring town, Ellesmere, for a night out. 'They had one heck of a good night in Ellesmere,' Ernie observed next day. Monday night, they escaped to Sweeney Hall, a local hotel, and Darren drove back to London the next day. Trevor's birthday.

Trevor's thirtieth birthday began with the paper blaring out: 'Mum took my hand and said: "There's no easy way of telling you this . . . Diana and Dodi are both dead."' That powerful moment turned into such maudlin trash! Photos of the whole family were inside – they'd got Ernie and Jill's wedding photo, from Nain, of course. Trevor had to face the added embarrassment of the sidebar revealing that he had been arrested for drink-driving at the age of twenty-one, which Ian had negotiated with

Piers Morgan. 'It was a very stupid thing to do, and, of course, I paid the punishment of losing my licence for a year,' Trevor was quoted as saying. 'But in a funny way it taught me a very valuable lesson. I never even thought of drinking and driving again. And my resolve was definitely hardened to those who do.'

Jill and Ernie were so preoccupied with Trevor's story, they almost missed the one just below it, 'Cops quiz Al Fayed over theft claims'. While Trevor endured the humiliation of his drink-drive story, Fayed faced another round of sleaze: 'Mr Al Fayed admitted in January that members of his staff broke into Mr Rowland's deposit box [not at Fayed's request] and that he, Fayed, was present as they copied documents.' But this scandal was overshadowed by the sensation of Trevor's series. Trevor was diverting the nation excellently.

For Jill and Ernie, six months of fighting to hold on to their privacy and to strengthen Trevor seemed shattered by these terrible few days. After all it had survived, the Rees-Jones family had slid to its lowest ebb.

Trevor's lawyers cringed as the expected critical attacks on the *Mirror* series rolled in. In the *Guardian*, Henry Porter's article 'The Bodyguard's Tale' was scathing: 'The spectacle of Al Fayed's determination to gain acceptance first for himself and now for his account of August 31st [here] assumes the proportions of a destructive monomania you find in a character from Balzac. It's an obsession that cares for little, least of all, it would seem, for Diana's two children, who are constantly assailed by Fayed-inspired speculation concerning their mother's death.' He referred, of course, to the most sensational revelation in the series. 'Rees-Jones . . . is now able to assert, with psychiatric help, that he heard Diana calling out Dodi's name after the impact . . . I don't want to be harsh on Rees-Jones, but we must ask how much has been suggested to his fragile record of that evening . . . We can take it that Al Fayed was listening to the interview . . .'

'Trevor's being perceived as being a Fayed puppet' – as little more than a mouthpiece for this paranoid man, Ian worried.

Also, he'd spilled his story before he had given these new memories to the judge's investigation; his next and final interview was the following week. It was bad form. The judge might see him as unreliable, and that could hurt the good opinion his lawyers had worked so hard to maintain.

Their negotiated compromises with the *Mirror* had been an eleventh-hour reaction, driven by desperation, not by a positive strategy. They needed one.

12

'I'm Not Going Back'

Trevor's lawyers now knew he was at war with Fayed. Watching Fayed's team at close range in Paris, Christian saw that, in fighting the Fayed empire, they faced an awesome opponent. 'They have enormous power. They buy people out, whoever they are – be it media, politicians, or anyone else. The only way to cope with it is, rather than just defend oneself, to attack.' If Trevor's credibility were to be salvaged, they must stop reacting and fight back. But how?

Brainstorming back and forth between Paris and Oswestry, the three lawyers knew that Trevor must be seen as contrite over giving the interviews before he'd seen the judge but, above all, as independent of Fayed. Christian 'did not want the press to think that Trevor was naïve enough to have granted the interview, and then complained when it did not turn out as he wanted. I

wanted the blame put on the right person.' Ian rang
Christian with an idea. 'Can Trevor go to see the judge
earlier than the appointment later this month?' Christian
thought for a moment, and responded, 'Why not? I'll
arrange it.'

Christian made an appointment with the judge,
employing again what Ian saw as 'the mysterious way
Christian has of communicating with the judge. He
apparently just pops in to see him and tells him what's
happening off the record, so to speak. It's a very personal relationship.' 'Nothing is mandatory, really,' says
Christian.

As he met him, Christian wondered if Judge Stéphan
knew that 'the struggle is really between Fayed and
Trevor. I'm not even sure the judge is aware of this battle.'
He decided he would not tell him what they were going
through 'because I did not find it very elegant'. Instead,
he put copies of the *Mirror* stories and Trevor's explana-
tory statement into his hands, whispered Trevor's
apologies, and won a meeting two days hence. Judge
Stéphan would be pleased to see Trevor on Friday at two
o'clock.

But Fayed must not know that Trevor had initiated the
meeting, they believed, or he would increase the pressure
on Trevor. They needed the media's help. If Fayed had
been surprised by the aggressive acts of the three lawyers
last weekend as they forced Piers Morgan's hand and
negotiated an independent press release, they had seen
nothing yet. With Ian and Christian fending off an army

of press hungry for even crumbs of news, the lawyers adroitly devised a cover for the Paris trip. 'We were spinning to the press that the judge was furious and was hauling Trevor across the channel to give him a real dressing-down for giving the interview,' says Ian. They slipped it quietly to the press, in snippets, and by phone.

'Meanwhile, we were also making it baldly clear to Fayed and Harrods that the judge was hopping mad and that Trevor had to go see him on Friday,' adds Ian. 'In fact the judge was unhappy, but he wasn't *that* unhappy,' says Christian with a slight smile. The tactic 'was so effective that even Trevor came to expect that he was going to get dressed down by the judge', Ian observed.

Trevor's passage to Paris had been tightly planned: David would pick him up in London and drive him to Paris via the Channel Tunnel. But the plan collapsed the night before, when Trevor cancelled. Distressed, David had called Ian from London, 'Trevor's just told me that Harrods have made arrangements for his transport to Paris. They're taking him by Eurostar.' To the lawyers this was tantamount to kidnap. 'We hadn't wanted him to see Harrods at all that week, but, because he's an up-front sort of guy who thought it was the right thing, he insisted on it,' Ian says. Now he was gone. Racing to Paris, David had tried, and failed, to intercept Trevor before he was whisked by Ritz limousine to the bodyguards' quarters at the Villa Windsor. There, David feared, he would again be trapped in 'the hermetically sealed environment' Fayed had created around him and his family from the moment of Jill and Ernie's arrival in Paris after the crash.

Trevor felt none of his lawyers' urgency. 'At the time, David had arranged to pick me up in his car in London, and we'd go to Paris together, spend the night, and go to Christian Curtil's office next morning. The suggestion came up at work that I go across with Darren and spend the night at the villa, which I was happy to do, to be honest. At the end of the day, I was happier to be travelling and having a laugh with a mate than to spend that time with my solicitors. Who wouldn't be? My lawyers were getting quite insistent, at the time, and I was getting fed up to the back teeth with them. I'd arranged a time to meet at Christian's office, and I planned to be there on time.

'On the train, Darren mentioned that the Boss wanted me *not* to use the embassy transport. My comment was that I was going to use it because it had been all arranged. Darren said, "Fine, he's going to be angry about it," but didn't push the point.'

As Trevor began to feel the pressure building from both sides, he felt like saying, 'What's the bloody fuss?'

'What do we do now? We've lost our client!' Taking the call on his mobile phone in a restaurant, Christian Curtil could hear the frustration in David Crawford's voice as his British colleague reported Trevor's actions. It was Thursday, 5 March, the night before Trevor's interview with the judge.

The three lawyers were now convinced that the on-the-ground, physical battle for control of Trevor had escalated into open warfare. The struggle had been focused, from the first days after the crash, on trying to put Trevor in the hands of a Fayed lawyer. Efforts to isolate him from his own team had now turned brazen.

When David arrived at Christian's office at ten on Friday morning, he was shocked to see the Ritz Mercedes parked right outside the door of Curtil's building, blocking the entire pavement. At least Fayed's people had delivered Trevor on time. At Christian's request, Trevor had been subpoenaed by the British Embassy to appear in Christian's office several hours before the interview with the judge.

And he would drive to court in an embassy car. Christian would not permit a repeat of the disaster of 19 December, when the Ritz people had driven himself and Trevor to court. Then, Christian had had only five minutes with Trevor before seeing the judge, and, at court, had been overwhelmed by media. Not again! He had called the British Embassy and asked for help.

'With the crowd of journalists, it's impossible to take my own car and park. We need a car and a bodyguard.'

'We are not bodyguards,' the first secretary told Christian.

'Neither am I. And, after all, he's *your* national, not mine.'

The embassy committed one vehicle – a minibus – and three people.

But Trevor had a Fayed entourage, clearly assigned to stay close. The Étoile driver François Fievet, and the now familiar bodyguards, Ben Murrell and Darren Wardman, waited in the car while Trevor went upstairs to Christian's office. 'I doubt if Trevor would physically be able to leave the premises,' Crawford worried. They didn't want Fayed's presence anywhere near Trevor. 'We had to indicate that Trevor was acting independently, and not as a puppet of the Fayed organization.' Crawford asked Trevor, 'Please go and tell them to move.' Half an hour later, Trevor went down. They didn't move. Trevor went down several times during the morning, 'but he either couldn't – or wouldn't – get them to move'.

'I refused, which I think was the right decision, because they were needed,' says Trevor. 'I told the lads to stay.'

Frank Klein, president of the Ritz, called Christian during his meeting with David and Trevor to say that Fayed was unhappy that the embassy – the British Establishment with whom Fayed had his own war – was driving Trevor to the courts. 'Well, I don't really care. Besides, I can't speak to you,' said Christian, reminding Klein that he could not speak to witnesses. 'Fayed is surrounded by idiots!' he thought. He told Klein that there must be no further interference with Trevor or with the handling of the case, or he would put a formal complaint on file.

Christian noted that 'Klein was terrified, very frightened'. He may have feared that he had overplayed his

hand. Or he may have feared that Christian was referring
to an event which had occurred early that morning at the
Villa Windsor. For in Trevor's jacket was a letter he had
refused to sign.

That morning, the sole survivor had made several moves
towards independence from Fayed. Trevor, in his own
private way, had reached a crisis of decision in his difficult struggle to do the right thing by everybody – by
Fayed, his family, and himself. The loss of trust had continued to build since the *Mirror* story. 'After the series, I
went back to work. They wanted to see me again. They
said it was all a mistake – that they'd had a go at Piers
Morgan because they didn't know it was going to be
released.' Trevor didn't believe it. 'Obviously, it was set
up to happen that day, otherwise why was Piers Morgan
there?' He blamed no one. 'It was my choice.' But events
that morning at the Villa Windsor convinced him that it
was time to act on his smouldering concerns.

There, inside the villa, he had been confronted with a
letter Frank Klein had urged him to sign. Klein handed
the letter to Trevor, who glanced over it, and was out-
raged. 'They were asking me to sign a letter which
basically said I want Christian Curtil to investigate the
crash, and David and Ian to sort out things in Britain –
they didn't want them to have contact.' With a rebel-
liousness his lawyers had not seen, 'I absolutely lost my
temper. I swore at them. "How dare you, these are my
lawyers!" I refused to sign it.' Seeing Trevor swinging

his arms, furious, Klein asked Ben to stay in the room.

'This letter was finally it. I just felt totally used by Fayed, more than anything.' As soon as they'd left the villa, he called Ian on his mobile phone to report the event. He then called Christian, and told him. 'Then Ben, Darren and myself drove to Curtil's office.'

Going through what he was going to say to the judge, Trevor had little time at the meeting with Christian and David to do more than show David the letter. 'It was clearly a very clumsy attempt to drive a wedge between us and expose differences which didn't exist,' David swiftly saw as he slipped it into his briefcase. They'd discuss it later.

The struggle to physically possess Trevor climaxed as Trevor and the two lawyers came down from Curtil's office to the pavement en route to the courts for the two o'clock interview with the judge. The minibus and the Mercedes were poised for action, the three men from each vehicle bristling with purpose. 'It was obvious to me, just before we went down, that David and Christian didn't want the lads there, but I did,' says Trevor. 'They were getting their knickers in a twist over absolutely nothing, in my view. I thought they'd be needed, at the end of the day. I knew them, was confident having them around. I didn't know the embassy blokes from Adam. I was also aware that the Boss expected me to go in one of the Ritz cars and the lawyers wanted me in the minibus, and I thought, "The way they're acting is bloody drama school."'

'We got down to the pavement, the minibus and the Mercedes behind us. There were a few photographers and scooters. You could tell that Darren and Ben wanted me to get in the car because that would make their life easier, but they weren't going to force the issue. And the lawyers wanted it the other way. I went up to the lads and told them, "I'm going in the minibus, but you follow close behind." I was pissed off – total over-reaction on everyone's part. On one side, I had faith in the lads. On the other, the lawyers were telling me it would be a good idea for me to be seen as independent. A no-win situation for me.' Pulled between his mates and his lawyers, Trevor was 'pissed off at both sides'.

The court was a mob scene worse than 19 December. 'I've never experienced anything like it in my life,' says Christian. 'Hundreds of TV crews – hundreds of cameras. Plus the radio . . . worldwide press. They filled the corridors and the entrance. You couldn't get in. You couldn't get out. And not just the court, but the whole drive, from the office to the court and back. The *gendarmes* in court had no experience of anything like this. More than seventy had been specially appointed – just for Trevor! When Robert De Niro came to the courts there wasn't this crowd.'

'I was taken aback,' says Trevor. 'There'd been crowds in St-Tropez with Dodi and the Princess – big crowds of tourists and photographers – but never this many photographers, never enclosed like this in that courthouse yard. A couple of hundred, easily. They just seemed to swarm towards the vehicle when we drove up. Then tried to get through.' 'It's too much,' he was thinking, 'This unbelievable interest in the whole thing.' Even though, this time, they'd gone in the back of the courthouse, 'there was pushing and shoving, and that's when Darren and Ben came into their own. We basically pushed our way through.'

The judge was as mild as Christian had expected. 'He was slightly annoyed that he didn't get to speak to me first,' Trevor recalls, 'but I told the judge directly that the things I'd been reported to remember, the voice, I didn't believe myself, really.' Trevor now felt that all his memories of the crash were of 'very questionable credibility', probably dreams. He had, equally, believed another 'memory' – one he'd told the *Mirror* about, 'but it obviously wasn't sensational enough for them. It was a dream I had in hospital that I believed had actually happened. I thought it was a real event.' Trevor thought he had 'been moved out of intensive care into an ambulance, into a ward of some description'. He'd asked Jill 'when I was fully conscious, if I'd been in the same room all along. Apparently I had. But if you'd have asked me, I'd have told you I'd been moved. It wasn't a memory, it was a dream. I suspect both of them were.'

As he left, a contrite Trevor reassured the judge that if he felt he had anything more to say, he would make sure he spoke to him first. Stéphan told him, basically, 'You're just a victim in this case. You can do what you want.'

After the interview, Christian went to the front

entrance and met the media. His promise that they'd get this chance had prevented even more chaos on his arrival. He spent an hour giving twenty interviews. In French, English, even in German.

Meanwhile, says Trevor, 'when I got back from court in the minibus to Christian's office, minus Christian, I got out, went into the office, discussed with David how it went, and waited for Christian to return. I knew it was time to get to the Eurostar. The Mercedes was waiting for me to come down. I thought David and Christian knew I was going back to Park Lane in the Mercedes. When the time came, I went down to join the lads and we were off.'

David left Christian at six and drove through the night, arriving back in Oswestry at five in the morning. En route, he dictated his thoughts: 'It appears to us that this whole charade turns on the fear that all Fayed's employees have of him . . . It seems a rather difficult shield to penetrate and get through to Trevor the seriousness of the predicament he finds himself in . . . He says he understands this . . . but he is clearly heavily influenced, if not pressurized, by the people he meets back in London. Quite what form this pressure takes is not clear . . .'

It was about to become very clear to Trevor. 'I got back to London on the Eurostar late that afternoon, and the Boss wanted to see me at Oxted. Paul Handley-Greaves drove me down, on his own, and then I had to deal with the Boss.'

Trevor was led to the Boss's big tent out on the lawn, and Trevor could see he wasn't happy at all.

'Why did you go with the embassy? It's MI6 trying to get to you!' Fayed exploded.

'No, it isn't,' Trevor snapped back. 'I asked our lads to come on behind in the car, and—'

Fayed turned to an attack on Ian and David. It was always a bit of a monologue when the Boss started losing his temper, Trevor knew.

'Your lawyers, they're small-town lawyers. They don't know what they're doing. They're not representing you properly.'

'I'm happy with them. I'm happy with you—'

'You *betrayed* me. You wouldn't sign the letter. You fought with Frank Klein. Took the embassy transport!'

'I don't believe you can accuse me of disloyalty,' Trevor retorted, trying to hold his temper. 'I've done nothing against you. I haven't done *anything*. The reason I took the embassy transport is my solicitors thought – *and* a lawyer at Harrods thought – it was a good idea for me to be seen to be independent.'

The Boss was fuming now, sort of chanting, implying an ultimatum – be loyal, or leave.

'I'll take this for a certain amount of time, but enough's enough,' Trevor stormed inside.

'Do you want me to make a decision *now* if I'm going to leave work or not, because I'll make a decision. I'll stand up and walk out of here.' Trevor was getting up to leave as Paul Handley-Greaves intervened, calming the Boss down. The shouting stopped, but, still blustering, Fayed said, 'No, no, don't make a decision now.'

Trevor had already made it. David and Ian had been pressing him, if he wouldn't quit straight away, to at least take a leave of absence. He'd come round to seeing their position. He didn't want to leave work, but he could see that he needed a bit of time away.

'I'm asking for a leave of absence. I need to make up my mind,' he told the Boss.

As Trevor left the tent, the Boss, still seated, called out a civil farewell, 'Fine, fine, take care of yourself,' as Handley-Greaves stayed on.

'Has our client been found?' The query came in a 9 March letter to David Crawford from Christian Curtil. 'I just had a telephone call from the embassy asking if he had arrived safely. They had apparently been waiting for him at the Eurostar in Paris, and had delayed the train for twenty minutes for him.' The embassy had planned to speed him straight on to the train, avoiding passport checks and so on. Trevor had 'had no idea of the embassy's plans to speed me through specially'. Since he'd left Christian's office three days earlier, the lawyers hadn't heard a word from Trevor. Had he spontaneously gone off on the leave of absence his lawyers had been trying to suggest? 'We wanted him back in Oswestry,' says Ian. 'He had disappeared. We'd lost him, so far as we were concerned,' David saw.

Trevor was, in fact, in Oswestry, keeping himself to

himself. After the showdown with Fayed, he had returned
quietly to begin his leave of absence on Sunday, 8 March.
On the following Wednesday he went over to Jill and
Ernie's for dinner and – at the table where they had
shared so much – he talked to them about the trip to
Paris and his interview with Judge Stéphan. As they
heard about the fight with Frank Klein over the letter at
the Villa Windsor, it confirmed to Jill and Ernie 'that
Fayed wants to own Trev, lock, stock and barrel'.

Trevor told them, upset, that Dave Liddle, his old pal
from the Paras, had told his story to the *Sun*. It had been
published on 2 March, in the middle of the *Mirror* series.
The story even ran under Trevor's byline, as if he had
written it.

'Dave Liddle,' Trevor told Jill and Ernie, 'had been in
touch two or three times by phone, chatted about rugby,
how're you getting on sort of thing. I told him nothing
about the accident at all. I hadn't heard from him for a
while, and had a message from him on the answering
machine that basically said the *Sun* had been in touch
with him, wanted to do a story about knowing me, and
would I ring him if it was okay. I didn't answer, thinking
that gave the message that it wasn't okay, and next thing
I know it's in print. He wrote things about the army
which, in general, were true. He wrote things about the
crash which I hadn't told him, and said he'd been up to
see me, which wasn't true.

'At the end of the day, I can't believe he's done it, and
find it extremely disappointing. I thought better of the

man. I appreciate that everyone needs money, but there are better ways of getting it.'

Even more disappointing, Sue's story would run in *News of the World* on 15 March, for all the world to read. As Trevor saw everyone getting in on the media bandwagon, he exploded, 'Why the hell should they be interested in me? It's nothing to do with the accident. Or with me. It's because it was the Princess of Wales. It always will be.'

Those who had not exploited him, it seemed, were angry with him. He'd had rows with Klein and Fayed. Even David had felt forced to tell Jill and Ernie that Trevor must resign or lose his lawyers – that they were being made to look like fools because they seemed to have no control over their client. 'He has upset everyone around him, including David, Ian, Fayed and the judge. He hasn't got a lot of friends. Trev seems to be in a no-win situation,' Ernie would pour out to his diary later, this quiet man's pen driven to a new intensity.

'I think they are all forgetting how Trev is still recovering from the car crash that almost killed him,' said Jill, in his defence. 'He needs time to sort out himself, and his brain.' The whole awful frenzy that began with the *Mirror* had set Trevor back, Jill feared.

'Take sick leave, Trevor, not just a leave of absence,' Jill urged him again, this time with the force of both a veteran nurse and a mother close to desperation. 'You're not fit to do the job you're employed to do because of an accident that happened while you were doing the job.'

His wrist, his shoulder, his jaw, his face, they'd all got a long way to go, with more operations to put things right. 'The sensible thing, Trevor, would be to go to the doctor and say, please put me off sick *because I am not capable of doing my job.*'

'I don't need sick leave.' He told them again, as he had so often, 'I want to keep my job.'

'He liked his job. He said it was quite well paid apart from anything else, and he enjoyed it,' Ernie noted, with frustration.

When Jill and Ernie saw the Boss on television the next day, 12 March, as he was in Paris for his interview with the judge, they were sad that the man who had been their kind benefactor now seemed so dangerous. Seeing Fayed blustering on TV, they knew that the leave of absence, even sick leave, were stop-gaps, not the solution.

The following day Christian raced to the courts to get the transcript of Fayed's testimony and dashed a report off to David. 'On Trevor, there is absolutely nothing since he did not even mention him. Instead, he talked about the excellent job he felt that Stéphan was doing and expressed his faith in the French judicial system. Then he said that he could not say anything concerning Henri Paul other than that he was a very professional employee about whom he had no complaint.'

Christian saw, in Fayed's ignoring Trevor and praising Paul, the seeds of later attack.

The three lawyers were in agreement. They could not continue to risk their own reputations by representing a man who was perceived to be in Fayed's pocket. He must resign, 'or you're on your own, mate', as Ian put it. 'We were pushing him in that direction. And when we needed to bring in the heavy artillery to back us up, we got Christian to write Trevor a letter.' On 30 March, the bad cop made his appearance on cue: Christian drafted a tough five-page letter to Trevor. Fearing his phone was bugged, he reached David in Annecy in the Alps, and asked him to return through Paris to approve the draft and deliver it to Trevor.

'Dear Trevor . . . since most probably nobody will be sentenced to imprisonment, the problem comes down to a question of compensation and legal liability . . . In other words, Mr Al Fayed is going to be forced to at least accept part of it, if only because of the liability of Henri Paul and of Mr Klein, both employees of the Ritz.' If the judge named the Ritz as responsible – with or without the photographers – Fayed could find the Ritz on trial, in a criminal court. Trevor could then claim damages within the trial. Even if there were no criminal trial, any evidence from the judge could be used to help Trevor – in an English civil claim for damages against Trevor's employer, perhaps, or in a French civil action against the Ritz. But that could take several years. And Christian had never really believed that a French claim for damages against the Ritz would succeed unless there was a criminal trial. He knew that Fayed was working to avoid a trial: 'Since he is perfectly aware of it, Mr Al Fayed's only way out is to find others, including you, partly liable for the accident . . . [he] is already building up this plan.'

Christian went on to warn Trevor that 'since the conspiracy theory no longer seems to be credible', he and David Crawford thought Fayed was trying to build a case that Trevor had failed to do his job responsibly – that he should have stopped Henri Paul from driving, not had his seat-belt fastened, not permitted such speed, and so on. What Christian saw was

> the beginning of an orchestrated campaign against you . . . Fayed praised Henri Paul in his interview with the judge, but said *absolutely nothing about you*, not wanting to appear too satisfied so that he could turn on you later – and Fayed is trying to control what you say to the press, thus controlling the investigation.
>
> As you know, for the moment, the press is your best ally . . . The press's general opinion is that you have been exemplary hitherto in your desire to be faithful to Mr Al Fayed. But since he is becoming unfair to you, it would be very hypocritical to now continue to do so and say what he tells you to . . .
>
> I am not trying to put you under pressure . . . but it is my duty to warn you that . . . I don't want to compromise my professional integrity . . . and if you choose to stay with Mr Al Fayed, I might even be forced to ask you to be represented by another lawyer.

Christian had been 'quite brutal in the letter I wrote him. But I had to be. He had to understand things. I could not continue to play alone in this courtyard.' Christian felt profoundly alone. He felt remote from Trevor, who stayed completely apart from the case. 'Sometimes I have the impression that the media thinks it was me in the car. Anything they know of him is through me. Sometimes I had to explain that it was not a battle between Fayed and myself – I was only assisting Trevor,' Christian reflected. 'I'm very lonely in the decision-making . . . I share it with David and Ian to know what they think, and then we sell it to Trevor. But I am the only one to have the file – my father doesn't know the file. The pressure is immense . . . and I don't have *that* many years of experience,' he said in droll reference to the fact that he was barely four years out of university.

The lawyers were sad that it had come to an ultimatum. From the earliest stages, Ian had always felt that Trevor was on the right side. As lawyers, 'It's good to be on the right side.' From the outset he'd felt sympathy for Trevor – the extraordinary pressures, a media target, his serious injuries, all the rest of it. 'But I didn't know if he was a nice, or a nasty, guy. My perception of him developed. Here's a young man always trying to do the right thing,' Ian believed.

He perhaps felt closer to Trevor than David did. They were closer in age, for one thing. And Christian barely knew him. 'I've always tried not to put Trevor under

pressure to make decisions because he doesn't respond
positively to it. He draws into himself and circles the
wagons,' says Ian. 'Trevor thinks very carefully before
he makes a decision – and these are really big decisions.
When he makes the right decision on something, for the
most part he sticks to it.'

Observing Trevor from a distance, Christian was sympathetic, also, to the pressures on him. He felt that
Trevor's apparent blind loyalty to Fayed was far more
complex than fear of losing his job – or fear of Fayed's
power to hurt him. 'He'd been in the military, used to
obeying orders. As a bodyguard, he was told to wait, to go
there, do this.' For the first time, Trevor was being forced
to make the kind of decisions nothing in his training had
prepared him for, Christian suspected. Suddenly, he had
to be the commanding general. 'I do not want him to
obey; I want him to *decide*.'

'You don't disobey a direct order,' said Trevor later. It
had been drummed into him. But in the Paras or in close
protection, if you were any good, you had to bring your
own judgement and independent action into it as well. 'In
security, you're told to do something. But as long as the
end product's what's asked for, then how you do it is up to
you.'

'But he's had to face this alone, when his whole life,
he's done everything with the group – the paratroops,
rugby, security. Breaking from Fayed means breaking
from the group,' Ian speculated, as he looked for an
understanding of Trevor's resistance to leaving Fayed.

Even the surveillance work in Northern Ireland he'd shared with a team of four. 'Now his situation is so singular. It's such an irony that now, he has to walk alone, sink or swim. He can share this with no one.'

But the lawyers stood together. 'The mere fact that we were prepared to walk away from it meant that we had principles and boundaries that we wouldn't cross,' said Ian. 'I already knew David had his principles and would doggedly stick to them – we'd worked together for seven years. But to find Christian, who would do the same, was great fortune, and great skill, on David's part.'

And now they had put Trevor on notice. If this was, as they believed, a struggle between David and Goliath, the underdog's slingshot had better soon find its mark.

On 31 March, Jill and Ernie were home from a good skiing holiday in Italy, another step in their return to normal life. In moments, they were back in the turmoil of Trevor's final decision. Trevor called, telling them that he'd received a worrying letter from Christian, who was pressing him to leave Fayed or lose his lawyers. David Crawford was pressing the same argument from Oswestry. They drove over to see him after work, with a gift, an old map of Shropshire sent to him by CBS's Jackie Jabara, who had been working tenaciously since the *Mirror* series to get an exclusive interview with Trevor for Dan Rather's *48 Hours*.

'I've not hurt anyone. I was just doing my job,' Trevor said several times, agitated, trying to clear his thinking.

'Trevor is in the middle,' his mother saw, distressed that 'he is being forced to make this huge decision when he is not yet well enough to do so. Nobody, including Trev, realises how far he is from being fit.' There was more surgery next week.

During these final hours and days of painful decision-making for Trevor, he had been deeply impressed by something one of the lads at work had said as they patrolled outside Harrods. 'Trev, you've been given a second chance. You should be enjoying every single day you wake up. You should be happy, enjoying life. You're not, are you?' 'No, I'm not,' said Trevor. 'Don't trust those bastards up there,' his friend had said. 'The only agenda they've got is their own. They don't care about you. If I was you, I'd never have come back.'

Trevor had never thought of the job as a trap. And yet Kez had said to him recently, 'How many times in the job have you said to a guy, "How long have you been here now?" and he says, "Bloody hell, it's eight years." Then they always add, "Oh, I'll just do another six months, get that little bit more money together, and then I'll get that other job." But, of course, that other job never comes.'

'Giving up a twenty-odd-grand job, it is a big thing,' Trevor debated in his mind, struggling with his choices.

'He's almost agreed to resign, but is unsure how Fayed will take it,' Ernie sensed. 'We did it in Paris. We can sort it out again,' they reassured him as they left and drove home.

On 6 April, Trevor had more surgery on his wrist. It

went well, but when they called, he was feeling cold and unwell, and had all the symptoms of infection or flu. His doctor put him on antibiotics, 'But he still refuses to come home to us. I'm very concerned,' said Jill. After six days of stoic misery, Trevor gave in and let Jill bring him home 'for a dose of TLC. Whether his swift recovery after that was due to the antibiotics or Mum's TLC would be hard to say,' says Ernie. Jill was still urging sick leave.

But Trevor felt well enough to go to Cardiff that Friday, 17 April, for a rugby match. Ops had told him to take his bleeper wherever he went during his leave of absence. 'On the Saturday, I had the bleep: "Call Oxted".' He called Ops. 'The Boss wants you in Scotland, on Monday,' he was told.

'I was pretty angry. First, I had not even had all my time off yet. Second, I hadn't decided if I was going back to work, and, lastly, I thought it was a really short time to give before going to Scotland. Giving one day's notice is a bit ridiculous.' And to Scotland! 'I really felt like it was a punishment posting.' Kez had been sent off to Scotland, and seemed perfectly happy there on the estates, with all the horses. 'But I had no desire to work up there even if I *was* going back.'

'I haven't decided whether I'm coming back or not. I'm watching rugby right now. I'll ring you after the weekend,' Trevor responded.

Inside, he'd made his decision. 'Since I've come out of hospital, I've tried to do the best by absolutely everyone, and ended up not always doing the best by myself. It's left me stuck in the middle, with Fayed saying I've been influenced by other people and some of the media saying I'm being influenced by Fayed, and my family and lawyers tugging at me to get mad at Fayed for exploiting me, not understanding how I could stay loyal so long . . . But I'm *not* a yes man. I take my own counsel.' He had taken it, and was finally ready to act.

'And that was it. I phoned on Monday and said, "I've decided I'm not going back."' 'Fine, good luck,' said the lad at Ops.

'So I resigned. I really feel that they forced my hand, and that if they'd done things differently, I would still be there and willing to help. I think the whole episode was handled badly in the way they constantly put pressure on me. They would always want more, and I suppose that since the *Mirror* interview they felt they could get it. After all, I'd done that one,' Trevor reflected.

Ian Lucas sent out a press release announcing Trevor's resignation:

I wish to move forward in my life after the tragic events of last August. It is for this reason that I have decided, with regret, to end my present employment. I wish to thank my employers and Mr Mohamed Al Fayed personally for the help and support they have given me through this very difficult time.

Fayed's London lawyer Stuart Benson replied that 'Mr

Fayed was very sorry to learn of Trevor's decision, and
would be delighted to re-employ him at a later date'. He
also informed the lawyers that Fayed would no longer
pay legal costs. Ian and David were mildly amused; he'd
only paid once, under pressure during the *Mirror*
episode. Months were overdue.

Trevor called Jill and Ernie around lunchtime to tell
them he'd resigned. They'd got a call to say that a man
from Special Branch was coming to Oswestry to check on
his security, then a call from David to tell them that
Christian Curtil was arriving from Paris. A *Shropshire
Star* reporter was on their doorstep, demanding, 'Why
has Trevor resigned?' 'That's Trevor's business,' they
snapped, annoyed.

But everything else paled into insignificance. Trevor
had broken free. He had done the right thing by himself,
at last.

'I started to feel better as soon as I knew that Trevor
was going to leave,' says Jill. Her 'down time' was over.
Monday 20 April was the beginning of Jill's return to the
buoyant view of life that was her natural state.

For Ernie, resignation day marked the last entry in
the diary into which he had poured his heartache and
frustrations for eight months. A chapter had been closed
on a huge part of the story. Trevor had saved his own
soul.

Ernie's last diary entry was prophetic. 'We know how
powerful Fayed is, and wonder whether Trev and Kez are
going to be set up and become fall guys. We shall see

what happens.' As Ernie closed page 264 of his diary, a new page was opening for Trevor.

'As soon as I resigned, I have to admit it felt like a huge weight had been taken off my shoulders. Even though it meant that I would no longer be getting a wage, it felt like I could distance myself from what was going on. We made a statement to the press, and it was received well by Fayed. I knew that wouldn't last, but for me it was a nice quiet period. I tried to forget everything about the crash as much as I could, and concentrate on what was going on at home.

'A bit later I got offered a job in a sports shop which had just been taken over by a couple of mates, and that was the first step towards getting a normal routine back in my life. It was only three and a half days a week. But it was miles better than sitting at home mulling things over. I wanted to move on.'

Now, with Trevor's resignation, Christian Curtil's concerns about Fayed attacking Trevor grew. 'I think Fayed's going to become very angry, and we should probably start being very careful,' he cautioned David in a 28 April letter. Perhaps they were being followed, their phones bugged. He now knew Fayed was capable of ruthless, unpredictable acts. He had seen – in Fayed's relentless efforts to force Trevor to his will, in his irrational rages when thwarted – the frightening potential of unbridled power combined with an obsessive nature. Fayed could well turn on Trevor with a violence that surpassed anything they had yet seen, Christian feared. Trevor could become the lightning-rod for Fayed's frustrations, which had to be building. For the investigation was not going in the direction Fayed was trying to force it to go. Judge Stéphan's work was giving him no fuel for the conspiracy theory that consumed him. And it was daring to shine the spotlight of suspicion on Fayed's personal empire in Paris.

Some 'very interesting leaks from the press' had informed Christian that the investigation was putting more pressure on the Ritz. That very day, Judge Stéphan had hauled the usual cast of Ritz and Étoile characters – Klein, Roulet, Musa, Dourneau – in for another round of interviews. It was an emergency effort by the judge, Christian was told, 'to trap them in inconsistencies' before they read an article breaking on Monday in *Voici* based on an interview with Frédéric Lucard, the driver who had delivered the Mercedes to the back of the Ritz.

Curtil saw opportunity in this new round of interviews – both to protect Trevor from Fayed, and to get him some well-deserved damages. They could be the source of evidence that Trevor's life had been put wrongfully at risk, the basis of a complaint – a formal request to investigate and to accuse someone other than the photographers with criminal responsibility. It would be the means of bringing out the true contributing causes of the crash, as well as giving Trevor a basis for gaining damages from the courts. 'In my opinion,' Christian told Ian, 'we could only obtain damages in France before a

criminal court.' But Trevor could use the evidence of the
inquiry to commence a civil claim against his employers
in England – if they were found to be negligent. Why
should this horribly injured victim of the crash not exercise his right to claim for damages?

The judge's late-April interviews did not give
Christian enough strong evidence to file a complaint. Yet
other events were making it even more urgent for Trevor
to act. The threat from Fayed was dramatically increased
as the lawyers got word of what was happening to Kez up
in Scotland.

Kez resigned on 2 June, after a stormy showdown with
Fayed on Monday, 25 May at Fayed's Balnagown Castle
in Scotland. For the first time, at that meeting, Fayed
had abusively, verbally accused the bodyguards of causing the crash. The outburst, laced with obscene
references, had been triggered by Kez refusing to do
another TV 'conspiracy' show for him, and by his saying
to the Boss, 'May I be frank. I don't agree at all with the
conspiracy rubbish, it was just an accident.' According to
Kez, 'Fayed exploded at this: "How the fuck could you let
this happen? You two idiots are to blame" . . . He began
to rant about Trevor and said, "That bastard has my
curse. He was supposed to be loyal and he's fucking left
me . . . I have paid for the best fucking psychiatrists in
the country and they say he's fine!"'

Fayed's ranting had gone on to conspiracy again,
blaming the British government, Prince Philip and the
security services for the crash. 'All those bastards are in

it together.' In his fury, he was bundling the bodyguards and conspiracy together into a mad package of blame. Fayed threatened Kez with doing the television programme or losing his job – and Kez resigned a week later. He subsequently took Fayed to court for the money he thought he was owed and they agreed that they remembered events differently and struck a deal. Kez confirmed that he had never been asked to lie.

Kez would explain his resignation to the judge on 3 July: 'My employer is convinced that the Princess of Wales and his son were the victims of a plot and he expected me to support this idea, which it was not possible for me to do, in all honesty.'

Kez eagerly called Trevor to share the moment, and wondered aloud to him, 'You don't think he'll go after us, do you?' Trevor had said, 'No, no,' still wanting to think the best of the Boss.

Then, on the heels of Kez's resignation, there was the confrontation between the photographers and the *parties civiles* on 5 June in Paris. Christian suspected that this would be a theatrical showpiece that would not serve Trevor's interests – Trevor had no case against the photographers. They had not pursued him. Trevor should not be represented, Christian argued to Ian and David, and he was not. All the other *parties* did attend. Fayed followed an outburst in court in which he condemned the photographers as 'vultures' with a ruthless attack on Diana's mother, in front of the press. 'She's a snob. She thinks she is the Queen of Sheba,' he raved.

'She walked out on her family and I don't give a damn about her.'

Georges Kiejman spoke for Fayed at the confrontation, and asked one question to photographer Romuald Rat that put Christian on alert as he read the transcript the following day. He wrote to David, 'One interesting question was raised by Kiejman to Rat, asking him to confirm that Trevor told the photographers that they were not bothering the couple, and that they could take pictures as long as they did not come too close. Rat confirmed that comment.' The question underlined Christian's fears, 'since it obviously protects the photographers, and suggests that Trevor encouraged them. It is as if there was a shift towards an allegation of guilt on Trevor.' He'd been waiting for this.

By 8 June, Christian had prepared Trevor's complaint, but still needed more evidence before he could file it.

On 30 June, Christian filed a request to Judge Stéphan for new interrogations of Ritz and Étoile officials and drivers, hoping to catch the men in contradictions, and have them incriminate each other – as Judge Stéphan had tried to do. His strategy was to fault their recollections and play them off against each other.

Trevor was becoming a reluctant aggressor. Christian had seen from the start that 'the act of Trevor becoming a *partie civile* was already an attack, in a way, against Fayed'. But now, with this request, Trevor had made his first overt move against his former boss. Though not physically in Paris, his presence in the investigation had just become pivotal. For Trevor was the only *partie* forcing the action that might reveal the less obvious causes of the crash. If he did not, Christian feared, only half-truths would ever come out. The Spencers were silent. Only Trevor, to protect himself, was casting the investigative net over the Ritz, over Étoile.

In late June, the file had revealed a threat to Trevor's life. Here was the statement of driver Olivier Lafaye, claiming he had been told someone was planning to kill Trevor to keep him from talking about the cause of the crash, Christian reported to Crawford. 'Apparently it would have been fake doctors introduced into the hospital to kill Trevor.' The threat might be baseless, both Christian and Crawford suspected. 'But I think, with the fear and uncertainty then, some people had it in mind that it would be best if Trevor did not survive,' he told Crawford. 'It *could* have been an attempted assassination.' Christian was alarmed, and asked that Lafaye be interviewed again.

A few days later, on 3 July, Kez gave his statement to the judge and – as Christian read his transcript next day – provided rare insight into the genesis of 'Dodi's plan', insight that implicated Fayed himself in the fatal decisions: 'At a certain moment, M. Paul left for the first-floor suite where Dodi and the Princess were. Some minutes later, he came back and announced the plan had been changed . . . Trevor and I were not in agreement with the new steps, and decided to call our superior in London, the head of security of Mohamed Al Fayed.

Henri Paul then said there's no point in calling him because Mr Fayed had given the green light to the plan . . . Henri Paul left to see about the car. Five minutes later, Dodi came to the door of the suite and asked us if we were in agreement with the plan. We told him we were not in agreement at all and he must ring his father back. Dodi told us again that there was no point *because his father was in agreement*.' Christian's evidence was building.

Nain died in June, as surely a victim of the crash as Diana, the family believed. 'We initially felt that the press were either directly or indirectly responsible for the crash so that didn't exactly put them in very good favour with us. We felt that they were responsible, in some measure, for Nain's death from the harassment she received.' Jill suspected that 'the extreme stress caused gastric problems and she developed a gastric ulcer without anybody realizing it until she had an enormous gastrointestinal bleed'. Jill was now cynical about the press. 'I was a fairly gullible sort of person and if something was written down in black and white in the papers, I tended to believe it. I don't any more.'

'Nain could never say no. She always wanted to talk, and it became too much, perhaps,' Trevor reflected. He'd continued to 'pop in and see her every couple of weeks. It's a half-hour, forty-minute drive.' He'd been keen on trying to get her into the old folks' home in the village just up the road from where she lived, 'just for the company.

Because she spent hours and hours sitting on her own. She had a lot of harsh things in her life. Her husband died at a very young age. Then my dad died. For many years, that was her main thing – her son had died. And then I had this accident. And she never had anyone with her then. She had no one, even to talk to about it. She sat on her own.' Trevor's feelings grew intense on the subject of Nain's death.

'The only people she had to talk to were the press who came knocking on the door. She thought they were these lovely people coming to see her with flowers. She hardly ever locked the door, and she'd make them tea. And they'd end up sitting down, taking photos as she talked to a reporter. They weren't doing it for her good. They weren't doing it for anyone's good, really. They used her. That is exploitation at its worst.

'The power of the media is scary. They rule the country, to a certain extent. It's a scary thought that you could pick up a newspaper that says you're accused of the murder of the Princess of Wales. That could have happened, it could well have happened.'

The family went to Nain's Welsh village, Llanfyllin, and buried her in the same graveyard where her husband and son Colin were buried. Quiet and undisturbed.

Life in Oswestry took on a veneer of normality that summer. Trevor was working at his part-time job at the Peter Richards sports shop on Willow Street. 'The shop work was not what I was used to. It's selling golf balls,

stringing rackets. Some mates pop in for a cup of tea. It's
bloody boring.' It was definitely not as challenging as
protecting the Princess of Wales. 'At least I was getting a
routine back. But I soon realized that there was no escap-
ing what had happened after all, as I had to speak to Ian
at least twice a week. I sometimes needed an hour or so
off work to visit the office. But then coming back to the
shop was like coming back to reality. I knew it wasn't
ideal for ever, but at that time it was definitely what I
needed.'

He never seemed to be through with the operations.
He'd have two wrist operations, two to remove plates from
the side and below his left eye – and a series of oral
surgeries – before he was through. Until the investigation
was over and he was fully healed, Trevor had to put his
life on hold.

But, out of sight of the town, he was working steadily
towards a major goal: to return to the rugby pitch. It
moved Jill each time she and Ernie would be walking the
racecourse and see Trevor from a distance, jogging with a
mate much fitter than himself, working so hard to be
strong enough to survive the scrum again, to be one of
them – 'asking himself', Jill imagined, '"Will I ever get
back to being as I was before?" It must have crossed his
mind, because it certainly crossed ours.'

It was less than a year since he'd been cut out of the
Mercedes, more dead than alive, when he returned to
the rugby pitch to play a game. 'It was only half a match
for Oswestry's second team, which is no great shakes.

But it was within twelve months of the accident,' says Trevor. As he entered the first scrum, he congratulated himself, 'Good on you, Trevor, you've done it. Back on the pitch within a year.'

'I had to be there, but I couldn't watch,' says Jill. 'He's got all this metalwork in his face and diving into these scrums. But he wouldn't have wanted anybody to have been careful with him, or there would have been no point in his playing. I sat on the grass and felt my chest tighten and tears gather in my eyes – whether from relief, worry, or joy, I don't really know. But I knew this was Trevor's own yardstick for recovery. To see him back on the pitch was a truly overwhelming experience.'

If only he were as emotionally strong. He was the same old Trevor on the outside, quiet about his successes, stoic about the crash. 'I think about it hardly at all – I've more thoughts about what's going to happen on Saturday in rugby,' he'd say. 'It was sad, but it was a job. It was an industrial accident, if you like. It was tragic, don't get me wrong. But it wasn't the most important thing that's happened to me in my life. Finding my dad dead was ten times worse. That was horrendous, horrible . . . I woke up, and Christ, I had some up and down days, but it's all working up here, in my head, so no problem. I've worked hard and I'm quite proud of myself for the fact that I'm back doing everything. But I didn't lose a leg, wasn't in a wheelchair, wasn't badly burned. I'm so lucky . . . I think it's been worse for Mum and Ernie.'

As he shrugged it off, his mother sensed more emotion

inside than he showed. She glimpsed it at a family barbecue that summer. Everyone was having such a fine
time, the Irish music Trevor loved was playing. Suddenly
Trevor broke down. 'All my brothers were there with
wives or girlfriends and kids, and I just felt like a complete spare part – I expect any single bloke would. I
suppose I felt it more because of what had happened. It
came down to I just didn't want to be there. So I told
Mum I was going down to a pub to have a beer with some
of the lads,' Trevor explains, making light of it.

But after, he felt embarrassed, and apologized. Jill
said, as she'd said before, 'No, Trevor, don't apologize,
ever.' She saw, with the deepest sadness, how vast the
losses to his life had been.

'Trevor has lost everything. He's lost his job. He's lost
his looks. He's lost his health. He's lost his wife. He's lost
his home. He's lost his privacy. The only thing he's
gained is this incredible amount of debt.'

The one who needed it most had no companion to talk
to – no wife or girlfriend. He confided in herself and
Ernie. But it wasn't the same, Jill knew. He was so bot-
tled up. Acting so blasé and unfeeling about the crash.
'He isn't the sort of person who normally sits and broods
over things . . . I think maybe he's trying to sort it out on
his own. The stiff upper lip is all very well, but it hides
lots of things, and if they stay deeply buried, you never
know what's going to happen.'

In late summer, she was in Trevor's room at home,
showing a friend the stacks of letters they'd stored in

boxes under the bed when, suddenly, tears flooded her eyes. 'I'm afraid he's just going to explode,' she heard herself saying.

Trevor had resigned, but he hadn't escaped. His lost memories were making Fayed an even angrier adversary. In July, the psychiatrist gave testimony to the judge, testifying to Trevor's strong personality but also to the weakness of his memories. Since nearly a year had passed since the accident, the psychiatrist felt that it was highly unlikely Trevor would remember anything else, and that even if he did, it would be of extremely doubtful credibility.

Trevor's memories were fading as a tool to serve Fayed's strategy.

Pressure was building like Paris's summer heat towards 31 August: the first anniversary of Diana's death. On the 25th, just as Christian had requested, the Ritz–Étoile team were interviewed again. Klein, Roulet, Siegel. Christian noted that they were interviewed not by Stéphan, but by the secondary judge, Marie-Christine Dévidal. 'It is a message, a symbolic way of showing that our request is to be treated in a secondary manner,' Christian suspected. The courts were a club. Once the prosecution had named the criminal suspects, it was rare that another judge would challenge that.

But as he read the transcripts of the statements at the Palais de Justice next day, Christian smiled with satisfaction. Here, in abundance, leaping from the pages,

were the contradictions and buck-passing he had suspected.

Here was Étoile director Niels Siegel confirming that,
although he was absent that night, he had *never* been
asked by the Ritz to provide a car without a driver, that
he normally would have refused, but that, in this particular case, since it was Dodi Fayed who was asking, he
might have accepted: an admission that he would have
abandoned professional policy to please Fayed's son! He
also said that at least two legally licensed drivers, Musa
and Lucard, were there and could have driven.

Here was the Ritz's assistant manager, Claude
Roulet – who, in all fairness, had gone home minutes
before the crash – backing away from any responsibility
for decisions, saying it was Dodi and the bodyguards who
took the decision that Henri Paul was to drive.

Above all, here was Frank Klein, targeting the bodyguards, a preview of Fayed's strategy, Christian felt sure.
He admitted that Henri Paul never drove clients but –
contradicting Siegel – also said that there was no spare
driver for the car. He'd asked a night-security man,
Thierry Rocher, if he had given the order, said Klein,
and Rocher had said no, it was the bodyguards who had
gone outside the hotel, *pointed their fingers at Henri
Paul, and told him he was to drive.* With a sentimentality
that struck Trevor's lawyers, Klein reported that Dodi
told him that he and Diana were to be married. And
Klein reported that Dodi had told him at least ten days
before the crash that he would be coming to Paris with

his girlfriend at the end of August – confirming Trevor's claim that Dodi never informed him of his plans.

With these interviews, the gross cause – Henri Paul's drunkenness – could no longer be seen in isolation from the contributing factors. They spread cause and guilt beyond two dead men, and absolved the photographers from narrow culpability. As Christian avidly read the interviews, the picture being painted was of broken rules and bad decisions driven by fear at every level of the chain of command, with fear of Fayed at the top. It was the same chain of power Jill and Ernie had revealed in their 'Spider'. The evidence was hardening for a complaint.

The first anniversary was almost upon them. 'The media had been pressing us for months to make a contribution to this anniversary period,' says Christian. In Paris, in Oswestry, discussion raged. Would, or should, Trevor give an interview? CBS's Jackie Jabara was still courting Christian and Ian, hoping for an exclusive.

Holding his course, Trevor made the decision: he would give no interview. A positive decision, Christian felt. 'But we now had to do something.' Christian, it was decided, would give cautious interviews on Trevor's behalf.

Pursued by the American networks, he flew to New York on a scouting mission. 'CBS called me and wanted me to guarantee to them that I only plan to see CBS people,' he told Crawford by phone. He would make no such promise. He met Barbara Walters, Larry King, Katie Couric, Dan Rather and all their bosses but 'at the end of the day decided that Dan Rather provided the best format for the interview I was to give'. Jabara won her interview with Christian, an exclusive for the US.

When Christian flew to New York for the taping, there was Jabara, sitting beside him again – as she had on an earlier trip to Manchester – taking no chances that this hard-won exclusive would slip through her fingers. 'The moment I had given the interview, she disappeared. I never heard from her again,' says Christian, smiling at the fickleness of network news. 'During the month of August, I gave something like fifty to sixty interviews to the international press.'

Ian, handling the media at home, was arranging the one thing it was agreed Trevor would do – a brief televised statement which would be released to everyone, at the same time. Ian noticed, with a chill, that Trevor intuitively moved the pictures of Ian's family away from the mantel behind his desk for their security as the TV cameras shot Trevor at Ian's desk. Ian bought a bouquet of red carnations and set them on the desk, to soften Trevor's presence a bit. Trevor made his statement:

I have at the front of my mind the fact that three people were killed in the accident last August. On this, the first occasion that I have spoken publicly, I wish to extend my sympathy to the families and friends of those killed . . . I ask you to appreciate that the next month

will be a difficult time for the relatives of those killed in
the accident last August. It will also be a difficult time
for me and my family. I ask you all to respect our privacy at this time and allow us all to deal with the
anniversary in our own way . . .

Christian had been receiving threatening calls and letters
for several months. At 8:30 A.M., a week before the
anniversary, his secretary took a call from a male voice,
saying, 'I'm a new client. I want to speak to M. Curtil.'
'He'll be arriving at any moment,' she responded. A few
minutes after nine, Christian had just crossed the inner
courtyard of his office building and was approaching the
elevator when a tall, rather fat man in a white turban
stepped out of the shadows and punched him in the face,
striking a blow on the cheek that made Christian faint
momentarily, and stumble off balance. The attacker said
nothing, made no attempt to steal his wallet, and then
vanished, leaving a bruised and rattled Christian to take
the lift up to the office. Shortly, the man called again, and
Christian took his call. 'I'll get you another time,' was all
he said. His voice had no accent. 'He acted as if it was
evident to me that I would know *why* he could get me.'
He called the police, and the Minister of the Interior, to
report the attack and the threats.

Trevor was threatened too. Five days before the
anniversary, he was working at the sports shop when a
call came in for him. A man asked for Trevor Rees-Jones,
and Trevor said, 'Speaking.' The man said, 'You keep

your mouth shut.' 'What about?' said Trevor. 'What are you on about?' The man went on about being from MI6, probably pretending. Seconds later he called again. 'Piss off,' Trevor told him, thinking, 'Oh God, how pathetic. Whoever you are, just bloody grow up.'

'You know who we are,' said the voice. The other lad in the shop took the next call, and the phone went dead. 'I telephoned Ian, and he called the police.' If it keeps happening, we'll put a trace on the line, they told him. Next time he called, the threat was stronger: 'Keep your mouth shut or we'll come round and sort you out. We'll do you.' Trevor had been taken aback at first. But by now, he was getting bloody pissed off.

'Really,' said Trevor. 'Well, you know where I am. We're here till half-past five. Feel free to pop in any time.' If it was a real threat he, personally, didn't take it too seriously. 'What I was concerned about was if this sort of thing happened to Mum.'

Three days before the anniversary and two days after the Ritz–Étoile interviews with the judge, on 27 August, Fayed launched his public attack on the bodyguards. *Time* magazine hit the news-stands in the US four days ahead of its regular Monday publication date, with a first-anniversary report on the crash. In it, Fayed was quoted: 'I am not on good terms with them [the bodyguards]. I didn't want them to leave, because the investigation is still running and I need them. But they are the people who caused the devastation and the accident through their incompetence and unprofessional practices. They had rules, and they moved away from the rules. They let me down.'

Trevor had been accused. Not by the French judge, as Jill and Ernie had feared, but by the Boss. The 'unbelievable' had happened. Just as Ernie had predicted in his diary on Trevor's resignation, Trevor and Kez had, indeed, been 'set up'. What they found so unnerving about Fayed was that his fury, his sense of hurt and betrayal, came from his own skewed sense of reality, so you could never know where or how he would explode.

Ian was on holiday when the attack came, and Crawford and Christian drafted a statement, which Trevor approved. Referring to Fayed's gallant offer at Trevor's resignation four months earlier that he 'would be delighted to re-employ him at a later date', Crawford included the ironic statement: 'These hardly seem the words of someone who holds the bodyguards wholly or partly responsible for his son's death.'

As the frontal attack the lawyers had expected finally came, Trevor was stunned, but still not capable of anger against Fayed. While Kez says, 'It annoyed the shit out of me,' Trevor could not share Kez's fury. Even if his lawyers hadn't been over-reacting over Fayed as much as he'd thought, he did not share their sense of danger. Bullies did not alarm him in the least. 'But I do find it disappointing that he changed from thinking I was the best thing since sliced bread and has suddenly turned his attack against me and Kez. Now, he says, "They've let me down," and I haven't. I've never let him down. I did my job properly and the only interview I've ever done is the *Mirror* interview that was put on by Fayed's people, and controlled by them. I think it's sad that Fayed's blaming us now, but I'm not an overly vindictive person. If I did decide to be vindictive against someone, it scares me what I could do.'

It cheered him to hear confirmed from Kez that ordinary people were taking the bodyguards' side, saying to Kez in pubs, 'Your old gaffer's losing it' or 'Don't let him bother you, mate' – even old women at the Post Office were saying, 'Chin up, love!' And dozens were asking about Trevor. 'How could you not be touched by people showing concern for two blokes they don't even know? It kept me from going insane,' says Kez.

Christian had been prepared to go into hiding with Trevor, to protect his privacy around the time of the anniversary. But when David Crawford had checked out Trevor's plans, 'He answered me with this wonderful expression, "I'm just going to sit it out."'

After months of fevered preparation a number of 'Diana shows' were unleashed on TV screens, in newspapers and magazines, as Diana's life, and death, were examined again, peaking on the night of the anniversary, 31 August. In Britain the paralysis that had gripped the nation a year earlier had gone; the compulsion to watch and cling had diminished. England, characteristically, was getting on with it. Yet thousands of people flowed past Kensington Palace, weeping, laying flowers, keeping vigil; some made the pilgrimage to Diana's grave on an island on the Spencer family estate, now that Diana's brother had opened it to the public.

Millions snatched up the tabloids, which were still exploiting her magic to sell papers. 'What readers want, even more than Leonardo DiCaprio, is Princess Diana, still number one, even in death,' said a member of the paparazzi pack, still struggling, like the rest of them, to find a substitute. Now he chases movie stars, shoots Fergie's new house, and hunts for shots of Charles and Camilla, he confessed on CNN's anniversary show.

'It's a Diana story. She's immortal, like Kennedy. In five years, there will be another Oliver Stone movie, finding new theories. It will last thirty years,' mused Christian Curtil as he hid out in Paris. In America that night, in prime time, CBS was airing his interview on its Diana special.

For the Rees-Jones family, the day was strangely quiet. Trevor's televised statement pleading for privacy seemed to have struck a chord with even the most aggressive tabloids. 'The only time I had someone on the doorstep was the day before the anniversary. When I saw them, I just walked to the corner shop, got a pint of milk and walked back again. They got boring photos of me buying another pint of milk, were quite happy with that, and drove off.'

No matter how many TV vans might have rolled into Oswestry, the Rees-Jones family had decided that it would not be driven into hiding. On 31 August, the family gathered, eleven strong, to share a very long lunch at a nearby country hotel, Sweeney Hall. Then, for two hours, they played a makeshift game of cricket on the lawn, with a stick John found in the woods as their bat. They took the bat home, ready for next year's lunch.

When Trevor heard that his mother planned to make this an annual event, he laughed and said, 'Good grief, I hope not.' Sentiment had never been his strong suit.

13

Moving On

On 23 September, Christian filed the long-planned complaint with the prosecutor, Mme Coujard, against the Ritz and Étoile for the criminal offence of 'endangering a person'. Trevor was still reluctant, still hoping he could leave everything behind with no attacks on anyone. But 'Christian had told me that the only way I could get damages for injuries was if someone was found criminally liable for the accident. And the way to do that was to file your own complaint against "X", an unknown party, for endangering life by providing an unqualified driver.'

Revealing, as he rarely does, the disturbing unknowns ahead of him, Trevor adds, 'I had been told that I couldn't know how my injuries would surface in ten years; it was possible I wouldn't be able to work. So I'll need some money put away in case. I can see it's prudent, and since I haven't received any compensation or insurance claims,

I haven't got any to put away.' All he'd ever got was his not very grand pay-cheque for the months until he resigned. 'Christian gave me figures for a personal injury claim, a civil claim, in France, and it didn't sound as though it would even have covered my legal bills.' Trevor had permitted the complaint to be filed for him 'for the simple reason that I needed and wanted compensation'.

The other disturbing unknown, for the lawyers, was, of course, Fayed. As he became progressively maddened by an investigation and a bodyguard he could not control, his actions were no more predictable than Trevor's long-term health. At least this complaint gave their vulnerable client a small stone in his slingshot. But still nothing compared to Fayed's bottomless arsenal of money, lawyers, and passion for retribution and war.

The complaint created a sensation with the media, who immediately labelled it a 'lawsuit' against Fayed's Paris empire. It was not. It asked the judge to charge the hotel and the limousine company with criminal responsibility for Trevor's injuries.

Georges Kiejman called Curtil. 'What's this complaint? What exactly have you filed?' he asked his young colleague. 'I'm so sorry that the personal relationship between Trevor and Fayed is deteriorating.' Christian doubted that he felt real regret, but, in spite of the building adversarial climate, Christian felt that he and Kiejman still liked each other. They planned to have lunch.

The complaint was approved, and assigned to Hervé

Stéphan. Very good. But would the judge extend the case out this far, this late in the investigation? For this case, the judge must, and would, do an extra-thorough job, Christian believed. But the implications of now charging the Ritz and Étoile were, indeed, *délicat* – politically, diplomatically, but especially professionally. For it would be to say to a powerful prosecutor, 'You were wrong in pursuing only the photographers' guilt.'

Trevor might have agonized less about filing the complaint if he'd seen the hour-long *48 Hours* and CNN's *The Death of a Princess* at the time they'd been aired in August to commemorate the anniversary. When he did finally see a video of *48 Hours* and read a transcript of the CNN programme in mid-October, allegations of his own guilt turned his previous 'disappointment' into outrage. In *The Death of a Princess* Fayed focused his attack specifically on Trevor: 'His . . . incompetence, his unintelligent approach – you know, he put the seat-belt on. He didn't ask them to put the seat-belt on. He has a bullet-proof car there in the hotel, which I use from time to time or the VIPs of the hotel. He has not used that bullet-proof car.'

But, said CNN's co-host Judd Rose, 'Al Fayed's main complaint: he says he paid Rees-Jones's medical expenses, only to see him quit after he recovered.'

Said Fayed: 'In the hospital for six months [*sic*] day and night with his family, because he was the only hope to tell me the truth, and I am confident that this boy has recovered now, and he knows exactly what happened.'

'Why wouldn't he just come forward and say?' Rose asked.

'Because he's been influenced by other persons.'

Moving the interview to conspiracy, Rose asked, 'Do you still believe your son and the Princess were assassinated?'

'Definitely, definitely,' said Fayed.

Rose pursued it further: 'We checked back with [Fayed], and . . . he says he's no longer 99.9 per cent sure it was an assassination. It's now over 100 per cent . . . Fayed isn't saying Rees-Jones took part in such a plan,' Rose qualified, 'he is saying that the guard's alleged incompetence would have helped it happen. Rees-Jones's lawyer gave us a statement denying the charges and noting that, until now, Fayed has had nothing but praise for his client' – the same response David had given after the *Time* attack.

'Until the truth comes out, I am not going to rest. That's my son and Diana. It's a duty for me, to find out if it is God's wish or somebody else's wish,' the Boss said.

Watching the video triggered an outburst that had been building since the early criticism by 'experts' Trevor's parents had read him in hospital a year earlier. 'What makes me annoyed – not angry, but really annoyed – is when I watch something like the CBS programme, hearing these two blokes who were former heads of security for Fayed and Harrods say, "Security was a shambles . . . The whole thing was a bloody mess from start to finish." If it was a shambles, it's bloody not from

my doing . . . We did as good a job, in that situation, as
anyone could've done.

'Attacks on my professionalism by other professionals
truly rile me,' says Trevor, fired to rare intensity. 'These
two – Bob Loftus and Brian Dodd – have got all the credentials. They've worked for Fayed, know what happens.
Yet they dare to rant on about "Where was the armoured
car, and the two-car convoy? Where were the eight bodyguards?" . . . I agree. Ideally, yes, eight bodyguards,
ideally two cars. *Ideally is not a driver who's drunk at the
wheel*. The ideal doesn't happen in the real world, and
they know it. It can't all have gone perfectly in their time.
I'm the only one alive who was in that car, and *I* don't
know what happened.' But he stood by his actions up to
the time he entered the car and pulled away from the
Ritz. After that, his memory was still a blank.

As Jill and Ernie avidly read the CNN transcripts in
October, they echoed Trevor's resentment of Fayed's
'main complaint': that Fayed had paid Trevor's medical
expenses 'in the hospital for six months, day and night
with his family, because he was the only hope to tell me
the truth . . .' Finally, he had admitted that it was Trevor's
memories, not his well-being, he was paying for.

'Yes, he put my parents up in Paris. Yes, he flew them
across there – and he was fantastic to us, to them. That's
not an argument. But Mum and Ernie signed a form
which claims from our National Health Service,' Trevor
pointed out.

'Fayed's being economical with the truth,' Ernie

confirmed, as he shot holes in Fayed's ceaseless claims
that he'd paid for all of Trevor's recovery. Six months in
hospital! It had been thirty-five days. Through one of
Christian's contacts in Paris, they'd learned that the
British health service had paid the entire hospital bill,
except for a nominal seventy francs a day – Fayed's bill
for the hospital was less than £320.

Faced with Fayed's astounding treatment of the facts,
and his shameless bravado in publicizing his own fantasies, Jill and Ernie prayed that Trevor's and their own
quiet truth would not get drowned in the clamour. Where
did it come from, this unrestrained freedom to say anything that served his purposes – did he truly not see the
lies, or just not care? It was frightening, either way. Dull
and grey they may be, but the honest facts were all Jill
and Ernie could ever speak.

A week later the main attack on Trevor's actions during
the blank last three minutes was routed. Ian Lucas
received a tremendous surprise from Christian in Paris.
He immediately called Trevor at the sports shop to give
him the news. The police report on the crashed
Mercedes, due to be released on 1 November, had been
leaked to the press, and had one extraordinary finding for
his client: Trevor had not, *not*, been wearing a seat-belt at
the time of the crash. The early report from the scene that
had launched attacks on his professionalism and suspicion that he'd been part of a conspiracy had been false.

Christian's delight could scarcely be suppressed as

he reported the findings: 'The seat-belt is in perfect shape and cannot have been fastened. There is a light scratch showing that Trevor may have tried to put it on when seeing the crash coming.' The firemen had wrongly thought it had released spontaneously in the crash. The seat-belt safety movement had lost its hero; the claim that the seat-belt had saved his life was wrong. Trevor had been vindicated as a bodyguard. He had deprived his critics of one of their principal weapons of attack.

Trevor took Ian's call at the shop. He kept his feelings contained there, but went over to Jill and Ernie's right after work. 'I always suspected that I may not have had a seat-belt on, because of the extent of the injuries. I thought it was a bit incredible, if I had, that I didn't have a broken collarbone. But I was still quite shocked when I found I didn't have it on – in fact, I was shocked that I'd survived at all. It took me a couple of minutes to get my head around it.' Then he exploded. It was the excitement he showed when the team won a rugby match. He waved his arms, and let out a great, loud whoop. 'I was glad because it stuck two fingers up to everyone who'd been slagging me off and giving me a hard time in the papers about wearing one. What's annoyed me since is how little that fact was reported compared to the false fact that I was wearing one.'

The airbag had saved him. The report on the airbags was released at the same time. They had worked per-fectly. 'They only inflated during the shock on the pillar, and not while hitting the Fiat Uno . . . Trevor survived because of them.' When Trevor thought of the mangled devastation of the crashed Mercedes, he now marvelled that even the airbag could have saved him. He had gained a new respect for his own survival.

This is amazing, thought Dr Chikhani, shaking his head in disbelief, when he heard the news about the seat-belt. How could it be? How could Trevor have only facial lesions, just one wrist broken? Where were the orthopaedic injuries he'd expect – the chest and trunk lesions? The legs should have been crushed. This was very important for him because he felt he had to try to explain how Trevor's accident had happened. Now he had to rethink some earlier conclusions. A passionate, self-confessed 'freak of cars' – he just loved them – Chikhani had gone to see the Mercedes, taken pictures. The front was terribly crushed. But the inside – the place where the heaters were, the dashboard – was almost completely intact. Very important, the doors still opened. This car was the most efficient, most safe car you could ever ride in, he observed. The airbag had worked perfectly.

Chikhani could see from the damage that the greatest shock of deceleration had been absorbed in the car's first impact with the pillar, while Trevor's vital organs and limbs were cushioned by the airbag. When the car first crashed into the pillar at top speed, and the airbag went off, he was protected. But what had saved him beyond that perplexed the surgeon deeply. The airbag could only be used once, and it would have been deflating as the car crashed against something else . . . and then the third, or fourth time . . . If he had not had his seat-belt on, no protection, Trevor should have gone through the windscreen.

Chikhani was not saying the inquiry was wrong. He readily admitted he was not a jurist, or an inquirer, nor had he even been in the car. The seat-belt was irrelevant compared to the larger fact: Trevor was living, and happy. But how? Trevor could thank the car – 'in any other, you would be dead', he mused silently.

With no access to the police file, Chikhani may have missed the fact that, rather than the series of subsequent, secondary impacts he envisioned before the car lurched to a halt, there had been only one – against the tunnel wall, where much of the momentum dissipated. It was there that Trevor's face had been smashed and flattened against the dashboard.

The stunning truth about the seat-belt was now an official part of the file, as, on 1 November, the police report of the investigation's findings was delivered to the judge, complete. But Christian found the report's other conclusions 'a bit disappointing'. 'The investigation has been very thorough,' he thought, 'but its conclusions were very poor.' They gave Christian reason to doubt that Trevor's complaint would be heard. For the report concluded that at least one cause of the crash may have been photographers' motorcycles blocking Henri Paul's exit from the tunnel. 'The simple phrase that one or two motorcycles may have blocked the car and its way out is enough for manslaughter charges. It is a good argument for the prosecution to say, "As we've always said, the photographers are guilty" – and to ignore Trevor's charges against the Ritz and Étoile. But there's no evidence. They can never sustain involuntary homicide,' Christian was sure. And Trevor's complaint had merit on its side.

Now the world must wait for the judge to digest the police report, do any final investigation before he declared it complete, and then send his own conclusions and recommendations on to the prosecutor. The prosecutor would decide who, if anyone, was to be charged.

On 12 December Fayed went before the judge with a plea to pursue his conspiracy theory more aggressively, demanding 'evidence' to bolster his belief that the British Secret Service was involved in shadowing the Princess on the night of the crash. He urged the judge to investigate two MI6 agents he claimed were in Paris, at the British Embassy, at the time of the crash, and nagged the judge over the coming weeks to confront the embassy with whether or not the British government had sent its assassins out to kill the Princess. Fayed's imagination had been inflamed by the efforts of a gadfly former MI6 agent, Richard Tomlinson, to kindle interest in the theory that the deaths had been caused by the same MI6 agents who, he claimed, had conspired in a 1992 British plot to kill Serbia's president Slobodan Milosevic. With innuendo but not a shred of evidence, Tomlinson also stirred the two bodyguards into the conspiracy pot, as he told the judge that, since the two were former SAS members (a

404   THE BODYGUARD'S STORY

special forces unit in which Trevor and Kez had never served), ties to MI6 were strong and loyalty to the SAS lifelong.

Fayed went on to say that he intended to obtain access to a 1,056-page CIA file on the private life of Diana. Convinced it would break the investigation into the crash wide open, he hoped to liberate the file from America, and have it included as evidence. Though he would soon succeed in having an American court grant him access to Diana's file, Judge Stéphan would refuse to include it in the case, tossing this entire line of investigation on to the trash heap. America's CIA and National Security Agency, and the British Embassy in Paris, would dismiss Fayed's cloak-and-dagger efforts as mere chasing after shadows. In a strong letter to the judge, the embassy's Second Secretary of Foreign Affairs, Paul Johnston, rejected the Milosevic plot and MI6's 'involvement' in killing Diana as 'particularly offensive to the royal family, the family of the Princess, the British Embassy, and our government'. And when Kez heard that 'the English bodyguards' had been even vaguely suggested as part of the plot, he shot off, 'It's bollocks!'

Prince Philip! MI6! The wildest of attacks, without any proof – it alarmed the lawyers, as well as Jill and Ernie. Nothing – no one – was sacred. Nor should they be, if guilty. But Fayed shot from the hip with no credible evidence. With his attacks backed by deep pockets, he was capable of doing terrible damage without ever being called to account – what Jill and Ernie saw as moral

irresponsibility, and something they found truly terrify-
ing. Where would he stop?

By 15 January the judge had taken little action to pursue
Christian's complaint. He had only interviewed three of
the people on his list. But their statements were gold to
Christian, and devastating to Fayed. With these new rev-
elations, Fayed would need every diversion he could
create.

Driver Olivier Lafaye had told the judge in his second
interview on 21 December about a story from another
driver, François Fievet. Apparently Fievet told Lafaye
that on the night of 31 August he had been woken up at
4 A.M. by a telephone call from Étoile director Jean-
François Musa. Lafaye said that Musa told Fievet to pick
up Salah Al Fayed and Frank Klein at Le Bourget. Musa
then told Fievet about the deaths of Dodi and Diana,
saying that Trevor had been seriously injured, and that
Henri Paul was also dead. Fievet also reported to Lafaye
that Musa had added that Henri Paul had driven the car,
and that he had been drunk.

Christian had immediately asked the judge to interview Fievet, to have him confirm the story. When Fievet
appeared a few weeks later, he confirmed that he'd
received the call from Musa, but could not verify that it
was during the call that he found out about Henri Paul's
blood-alcohol level. 'He is of course being a bit careful,'
Christian saw, 'but he is not saying it is not true.'

Musa, in his interview, had also agreed that he had

called Fievet that night and asked him to drive. He was
very defensive about the decision that Henri Paul should
drive, and maintained that he had had nothing to do with
the decision; that it had been forced on him by the Ritz.
Trevor, he said, had delivered the message to him, but it
had been organized by Dodi. He then turned Klein's earlier claim that Musa had said there were no extra drivers
available on its head. Musa himself had offered to drive,
he stated, but was refused. And he had two other licensed
drivers he could have put behind the wheel of the
Mercedes – Philippe Dourneau and the 'car-jockey'
Frédéric Lucard.

Reading the file, Christian was pleased. 'Musa's
accusing the Ritz.' The Ritz and Étoile were turning on
each other. Christian knew that Trevor, as a *partie*, had
forced out a story that would not have been told. He had
led the evidence back from the lies told *after* the crash to
the decisions that had *caused* the crash. Christian could
never know how many half-truths, or lies, had been told
in the climate of fear that pressed in on these men. But
with this final round of questioning they had, at last, a
picture of the actions – or lack of them – in and around
the Ritz hotel in the decisive hour before the crash. They
were actions that, individually, might have had no effect,
but which, cumulatively, forged the chain of events that
led to catastrophe.

Whether the court eventually named or charged
anyone, Christian felt sure that grounds for criminal
charges lay in the cumulative evidence. But when

Christian noted that these last interviews, too, had been conducted by Mme Dévidal – a sign that the prosecution considered them secondary – he was not optimistic about the result.

On 29 January 1999, at 2 P.M., the complete report and the conclusions of the police investigation were hand-delivered by courier to the prosecutor and to the lawyers for each of the *parties civiles*. The investigation was over. Judge Stéphan issued an unprecedented press release, and then went on a week's holiday. It was now up to the prosecution to decide whether anyone was to be charged.

Christian had twenty days to respond to the findings, and to argue the charges in Trevor's complaint. In a six-page 'note' sent to the prosecutor on 12 February, he argued with the kind of persuasive courtroom style he'd learned at New York University's law school. Trevor might not get a trial against the Ritz and Étoile. But this note would stand as Christian's – and Trevor's – closing argument to history's jury.

He let the interview transcripts speak, building his case. He let Frank Klein himself confirm that Étoile had never before delivered a car without a chauffeur, even if they were asked for one, proving that sending up the Mercedes without a licensed driver was not an oversight or a mistake. He used Musa's word that the decision to entrust the car to Henri Paul – when Musa had offered to drive and had two other drivers available – had been imposed on him by the Ritz. Claiming he had acted under pressure from night manager Roulet, Musa had, according to Christian, 'knowingly agreed to break the rules, where he had previously been able to resist'. The Ritz security officer, Tendil, says he tried to talk Paul out of driving, but did not have 'sufficient authority' to do so.

To successfully advance Trevor's criminal charge of 'endangering a person', Christian believed he had only to show that 'a breach of the rules was capable of producing a serious accident'. As if any more 'breaches' were needed, he reminded the judge in his 'note' that Henri Paul was drunk and unqualified to drive this 'large automatic car'. Christian concluded that 'the fact of entrusting this heavy car to an inexperienced driver, who did not have the appropriate licence, and who had been drinking alcohol, constituted a risk of death or serious injury'.

He believed his six-page 'note' would have won over a jury. The wait began.

It was just before Christmas 1998 when the explosion Jill had feared since summer came. Trevor was feeling 'so fed up' – no, Jill would not use the word 'depressed' – that he hit out at a good friend in a pub, and was asked to leave. 'I'd noticed that I was going out, getting pissed more often, and into a worse state. And I was getting annoyed at things that wouldn't have annoyed me before. When that happened in the pub, I realized I had to do something.' He finally called Jill, saying, 'Mum, I think I need help.' Jill sent him to a general practitioner, who made him feel a bit of a fool when he started asking heavy questions about his state of his mind, like, 'Do you ever feel like crying?' Trevor thought, 'Get a fucking life!' and left with a prescription for anti-depressants. He took himself off the pills in a day or two. 'I admit I was down, but just admitting to Mum that I was fed up with things made me feel better.' For the first time in his life, he did not apologize for showing weakness to his mother. 'He knew he needed help and was prepared to ask for it. He didn't feel embarrassed by it. That's a step in recovery, isn't it?'

Trevor had given his mother flowers before, usually when he'd got in a scrape and wanted to win back her favour. But this Mother's Day, Trevor gave Jill a card with a loving, appreciative note written inside. She broke down when she opened it. 'He *does* have finer feelings,' as she had always known. 'I don't think he'll ever be a hugger. I don't think he'll ever be somebody who will lay bare his emotions any more than very many English men do. In the American culture, looking on from the outside, it appears people are more willing to bare their souls. But it's not in our culture to be emotionally open,' she recognized. And yet Trevor had emerged from all this as 'far more considerate than he ever was . . . And he's found that Ernie is a friend.' By May 1999, Jill could say, 'We're almost back to the situation of any mother and son – whether they've had an accident or not. You're concerned about them because you love them, and you hope they're going to make the right decisions in life . . . I feel no different about Trevor now than I did before, or any different than I feel about Chris and Gareth and John.'

Jill and Ernie felt that the family, and their marriage, were stronger than ever. 'I think when you lose a child, or have a child disabled or injured severely in a crash, those are the sorts of life events when you've got to be very strong to survive them. We are a very strong couple. It didn't destroy us, but it damn nearly did,' Jill reflected. 'Most people don't have one good marriage. I've been so lucky. I've had two. And Trevor is still Trevor. He's not turned into somebody else.'

Trevor's priorities – and humour – were back on track. When he went to the orthopaedic hospital for another wrist operation, he was more concerned about missing the semi-final of an important Cup match than about another round of discomfort, and began to fuss when he found he was fourth in line for surgery. Just as he was saying, 'God, I'm going to be here for ages,' one of the surgeons walked by, a Welshman and keen rugby player, and asked Trevor why he was so agitated. 'It's a Cup match, and I'm desperate to get out and see it.' The surgeon put him first on the list, and, as he was being wheeled into the theatre, one of the nurses asked, 'Good God, you're not *playing* today, are you?' He was barely out of anaesthetic before Jill and Ernie were driving him down to the club.

But he would not, and could never, be as he was before.

In the spring of 1999, Trevor had been drunk a few times with the lads in the local pubs, the Saturday night ritual after the game. Ian Lucas had got a tip-off from the

local press that stories were going round – Trevor was out
of line, partying too hard with the lads. Ian had learned in
his political campaign the tyranny of being in the public
eye. 'I always had to shave. I was always on display. But
I took it on voluntarily. Trevor didn't.' Ian called Trevor in
for a talk, dreading it. He must deliver a life sentence to
a bloke who didn't deserve it.

'Trevor, you have to accept that you're a public person.
Whatever you do, you must be prepared that it will get
back to your family, and reflect on them.' For eighteen
months, Trevor had worked to get his life back to normal.
He'd fanatically avoided the press. Ian could see that
'Trevor was taken aback'.

He was, in fact, 'pissed off. I remember Ian saying
that a photographer had seen me in town, luckily without
his camera, pissed up, and chatting up and all over a girl.
My reaction, inside, was "Fuck them, sod them, I'm not
going to change." I was just doing what every bloke of my
age does on a Saturday night and it really pissed me off
that I couldn't be left to get on with it.'

'I'll never be anonymous again. Is that what you're
saying?' he snapped back at Ian, his anger flaring. 'Then
he began to take it on board,' Ian saw. He would always
be pointed at, looked at. The bodyguard who survived the
crash. The images of him on the videos and photos from
the last hours in Paris were indelible, global. He and the
Princess shared the same final frames of film – he was
there in every new book and film on her, in his orange
shirt, in his blue blazer. If people weren't sure, the scars

would always give him away. How could you have a quiet date, or a beer with your friends? Most importantly, how could you do close protection, where it helped to be anonymous?

In May, when Kez came for a visit, Kez told his mate about a well-paid job abroad doing security work. Trevor was eager to go. 'I'd be happy to go away and never hear about this again as long as I live, to be honest.' He still clung to the hope that the end of the investigation would put it all to rest, let him get on with life, the way it had been.

But first he had a job to do. Clearly, he couldn't leave until the case was over, and as he had gradually tried to sort the whole thing out in his own mind, he began to reconsider an idea of Ian's he'd turned down flat the previous summer. 'When Ian first mentioned the option of telling my story in a book, way back, I said no, straight away. I really didn't want to do anything.' Then in October, he saw all these criticisms he thought were such crap. 'The way I came around to the idea of a book was that doing nothing was not an option after all – people will then write what they want. I began to think that a book would give me the most control, and that when it was all over I'd be able to say to anyone who wanted to know about what happened, "Read the book."

'Christian had met a few literary agents on one of his media trips to New York and I decided I'd meet a couple. A bit later I thought I'd explore the options with one of them.'

By April he had a publisher and a deadline. The book took up more and more of his time as he struggled with both a memory that was full of holes and his need to tell it as it was. His truth. Six months into it, he thought ruefully of the day he'd turned down $1 million from the *National Enquirer*. That might have taken only half a day of his time!

'But this is the only way of making sure it's *my* story. It should make it impossible for anyone ever to write an article again attributing stuff to me I've never done, said, or thought. Then I can let it go and never say another word.

'As the writing gets on, it often feels a bit funny. I'm still a bit reluctant, but I hope that my final decision to do this is right. I have to say that I still wouldn't have done it if Mum and Ernie hadn't said they would help out.'

For Jill, it had not been an easy decision. They'd fought so hard to rebuild their lives in their own way and now the book would take some of that away. She dreaded having to relive the memories; pain and tears were still so close to the surface. But Jill had encouraged Trevor to tell the story because she believed – she desperately hoped – that good would come of it for him. Perhaps, with it all down on paper, he'd see how well he'd done. How strong he was. He'd see how extraordinary it was that with none of the peace his mind and body needed to mend, he had survived and recovered. He'd healed under a spotlight and with pressures most people could never, in their lives, imagine. And, as Dr Chikhani told them, he'd healed himself. She hoped the book would let him see that, if he could stand up to the full determined force of one of the most powerful men in England and stay true to himself, then there was no pressure he could not withstand. For the rest of his life.

When Ernie had said, trying to buck up her spirits as they left Paris, 'We're the A-Team,' in truth, maybe they were. The whole family had undergone a profound trauma, Jill now saw, and healed itself. But what a terrible way to discover your strength. Her deeper hope – for Trevor, for them all – was that the book would, at last, let them close this chapter and move on.

On 17 August 1999, six months after the report had been handed to her, the prosecutor, Mme Coujard, released her decision: that all criminal charges against the photographers and the motorcyclist be dropped and dismissed. After two years and 10,000 pages, she had found insufficient evidence to support the suspicions that had driven and shaped the investigation.

[The] direct cause of the accident is the presence, at the wheel of the Mercedes S280, of a driver who had consumed a considerable amount of alcohol, combined with . . . medication, driving at a speed . . . faster than the maximum speed limit in built-up areas . . . Therefore the loss of control of the vehicle by the driver in the Alma tunnel constitutes the main cause of the accident.

The accident was 'involuntary', a wounding blow to conspiracy theories. The report was printed in its entirety in the *Sunday Times* on 29 August. Fayed later posted it, complete, on his website, the new global weapon in his arsenal.

Mme Coujard had dismissed Trevor's complaint. The two arguments against it seemed facile – even absurd. First, Trevor's charge of the crime of 'endangering the life of another person' was disqualified because he himself had suffered grievous injury. Sorry, the report said, only those who are *uninjured* have a claim, an argument embedded in the code that if you are already injured, the *risk* of injury is gone. Next, the chauffeur's licence Henri Paul should legally have had was irrelevant, it said, since anyone could capably drive the Mercedes – and, in the safe, controlled speeds of the streets of Paris, a professionally licensed driver would have had no effect on safety. Why, then, do we have the law, Christian marvelled. The court was trying very hard not to have a trial, he reckoned.

For, in the next breath, the report reversed itself, pointing directly at the 'special licence' it had just dismissed as irrelevant and admitting it *was* relevant after all:

If the appointment of Henri Paul as the driver poses a problem about the awareness of his state on the evening in question and his intemperance, it should also lead to an examination of the conditions in which it had been

decided to resort to a vehicle from the company Étoile
Limousine, whose fleet was made up of high-powered
cars, necessitating to drive them the possession of a
special licence, which Mr Henri Paul did not possess.

Christian was not surprised; the result was much as he'd
feared. 'They didn't want to look foolish. If they now
change to prosecuting the Ritz and Étoile, they are
admitting the error of wanting to prosecute the photographers for two years . . . They didn't want to accept a
charge that modifies completely their strategy from the
beginning.'

But overall, Christian was very proud. Mme Coujard
had named some of the interrelated factors Christian
believed had contributed to the crash; she had clearly
heard Trevor's complaint, and his and Kez's testimony
about Dodi's responsibility for the plan. The report identified 'divergence' in the stories told by Ritz management
and Étoile boss Jean-François Musa regarding pre-crash
decisions. Christian avidly read a paragraph which
revealed an incestuous relationship between the two
companies that made Musa and the Étoile drivers *de
facto* employees of the Ritz, subject to orders from its
bosses – a link that gave Dodi, it said, 'as a last resort,
the power to decide all matters'.

In the light of the chain of command that lay exposed,
Fayed's statement to the judge on 11 December was now
ludicrous. He had said then that on the day of the accident Trevor was the only one in charge of security, and

that he had all the powers he needed to take whatever security measures he saw fit.

Christian Curtil waited for the other shoe to drop. In a week or so, the judge would give his response to the decision. Judge Stéphan had the power, still, to over-rule the prosecutor and charge anyone he wished – photographers, the Ritz, Étoile Limousine. Curtil guessed that, after all this work, he would be reluctant to let his two-year investigation vanish in this limp and unsatisfying way. 'It is now for the examining judge to decide what to do, and he is not bound by the prosecu-tion's advice. He told me he would give his decision the first week of September,' Christian told Trevor in a 29 August letter.

He also warned Trevor that the judge's decision 'is unfortunately not the end of it'. The Spencers might do nothing. They had been completely passive so far. 'But one thing is sure: Fayed and the Pauls will appeal against any decision which does not charge at least six or seven photographers with manslaughter . . . The risk is that Fayed tries to charge you during that trial. Please be sure I am perfectly aware of your desire to bring this to an end at last, and not to appear too aggressive against this man . . . But if I were you, I would appeal this decision, at least to protect myself.'

If the judge did not charge any of the photographers, or anyone else, this whole page of history would be filed away with no one called to account – unless Trevor chal-lenged the decision and tried again to shine a spotlight on the chain of events which took the Princess to her death and had torn his life apart. Giving up the appeal meant losing the chance to bring the truth into the open, in a French courtroom. 'I do want the truth to come out. Basically, it's my right – my obligation, a lot of people think – to reply to Fayed's allegations of my being a contributing factor to the accident.' But Trevor did not have to appeal to do that. His reply to Fayed, he hoped, would be in the pages of this book. 'I hope the book, not a court case, will be the end of it for me.

'Also, the need for compensation was no longer there. Now I'm doing this book project there'll be some money, and there's no need to be greedy. First I'll be able to pay my legal fees.' The signed agreement to pay Trevor's lawyers up to the time he resigned had proved to be more trouble than it was worth. And all three lawyers had done a staggering amount of work for Trevor since he had left Fayed. He owed them. 'Also, I should be able to put a bit of money away in case my health doesn't hold out, so I know I'll have been sensible.'

While they awaited the judge's response, the second anniversary, though less dramatic than the first, revealed the strength of Diana's legacy.

A made-for-television melodrama 'based on the true story' built the myth of a sad, love-seeking humanitarian driven to her death, distraught and blinded, by swarming paparazzi – and called Trevor 'Tim'. It mentioned not a word about Fayed's agendas, about Henri Paul's drunkenness, Dodi's decisions, or the lapses that allowed an unlicensed driver to take the wheel of the Mercedes.

Diana was canonized by some: a global audience was reminded, again, that the previous year's Nobel peace prize for the fight against landmines was a direct tribute to her humanitarian role. In Britain a TV documentary, produced by Richard Belfield, in which Fayed's hand was suspected, glorified the romance and a well-known QC challenged the dismissal of the photographers.

Diana was criticized by others. An American book leaped on to the bestseller lists by exposing a Princess so disturbed she was scarcely recognizable as a functioning adult.

On 31 August 1999, the family did not go to Sweeney Hall to mark the anniversary, or play cricket, as Jill had thought they might. Life had moved on. Sweeney Hall, it turned out, was already booked up for the day. And it was hard to co-ordinate family schedules. Yet they felt the need to get everybody together, as they did every summer. So they met a week early, thirteen of them, and had lunch at The Walls, the old stone school Ernie and the boys had attended, which was now a handsome restaurant. Maybe it was best they'd done something different. The family would not turn this day into a funereal ritual.

On 3 September, the other shoe dropped. But not quite as Christian had predicted. On that day – the day Stéphan completed his job as examining judge – he, too,

dismissed all charges against the photographers, uphold-
ing the prosecution's decision. The judge blamed the
crash on the drunken driving of Henri Paul, caused by
Dodi's decision to put him at the wheel. The report, a
near duplicate of the prosecution's, was front-page news
across Europe and North America. But the photographers
were not blameless. The judges pointed the finger at
behaviour which 'raised moral and ethical questions' and
claimed the photographers' 'continuous and insistent
presence' had led Dodi Fayed 'to make decisions that,
however imprudent, were a response to being hounded'.

Trevor's complaint was dismissed; there would be no
criminal trial against the Ritz and Étoile. Stéphan and
Dévidal's thirty-two-page report affirmed the prosecution
down the line. Trevor heard the news in Oswestry. 'When
Christian called and told me about the judge's report, I'd
already heard something on the news on TV, and I have to
admit I was pretty relieved. I knew it wouldn't be the end
of it because Fayed would appeal, but I must admit I
had no desire by now to enter into another court battle. If
the judge had upheld my complaint it would have been
appealed and fought over, and I'd never see the back of
this crash. I think if I'm honest with myself, I never really
wanted to submit the complaint in the first place.'

Trevor was at work at the sporting goods store when
the judge's decision was given, and he was under siege.
He physically ejected one photographer from the shop,
and saw, with Sky News and the *Mirror* at his door, that
he would not be able to work that day. He escaped home,

barricaded himself in and stayed by the phone, talking only to Christian and to his parents.

It was, finally, all about pressure, Christian saw. In his decision, Stéphan had allowed Dodi off the hook because of the pressure he was under from the press. 'The photographers created the pressure, it's true,' said Christian, 'but you don't have to *react* to the pressure. You don't have to accelerate, as Henri Paul did.' Pressure didn't have to destroy your common sense, as it had Dodi's. The French justice system had reacted and changed under the global media pressure of this crash. Stéphan had now issued two unheard-of press releases. The investigative process would never be quite as closed and secretive again in France. The leaks and the wild speculation it led to had not served the public well.

On the whole Christian felt the results completely justified his strategy. The judges had avoided a trial for strategic reasons, Christian believed, 'but they say we were right'.

Under media siege in Paris, fielding fifty phone calls that day – and with Ian Lucas and David Crawford both on holiday – Christian was quoted by an AP wire-service bulletin. 'A lawyer for Rees-Jones, who has filed a suit against the Ritz hotel and its car service, Étoile Limousine, for "endangering the lives of others", praised the decision. Christian Curtil said he was pleased the judge had "emphasized the responsibility of the Ritz . . . and Étoile".'

Trevor felt little elation. He didn't agree with the

judge's blanket dismissal of the photographers. 'No photographers, no crash,' he believed. And a lot of contributing causes were left out. 'But I accept the decision.'

'This decision does not end the crash. It could lead to charges against the Ritz hotel,' NBC nightly news reported, 'opening the door for the bodyguard Trevor Rees-Jones and Diana's family to sue for damages . . .'

Fayed's spokesmen – Kiejman in Paris and Laurie Mayer in London, who had replaced Michael Cole – immediately declared that Fayed would appeal. The *Observer*'s headline read: 'FAYED RISKS HUGE LAWSUIT WITH APPEAL AGAINST DIANA VERDICT'.

It was a moment of humiliation for Fayed. Despite two years of his own global investigation, his conspiracy theory had been dismissed as the 'rubbish' Trevor and the lads had always believed it to be, and with his wild diatribes his public reputation had sunk to that of a joke. Fayed had seen his own son blamed for putting Paul behind the wheel. The 'crash' lawsuits expected to embroil Fayed grew more complicated in November, as the magazine *Eurobusiness* reported that Fayed and the Ritz's Frank Klein – not some third party, as previously reported – were joint owners of Étoile Limousine. If the report was true, now, if the Ritz was sued, Fayed could not, in turn, sue Étoile, as everyone had expected.

Trevor 'reserves the right to appeal once he has read the judge's report', said Curtil in his press release. An appeal had to be filed within ten days – 13 September.

Privately, he was urgently trying to persuade Trevor to ignore his qualms and protect himself by filing. Christian's most reliable press contacts had confided to him that Fayed planned not only to charge Trevor with criminal liability during the trial before the Court of Appeal, but 'to sue him in a civil court for negligence once the criminal case is over'.

They would never get Trevor to share their anxiety about Fayed, the three lawyers knew. Yet the danger was real, and growing. If the triumph of winning a department store, albeit a British icon, had led Fayed to gloat, 'I piss on the British. I bought Harrods so I can sit up here and piss on them,' it was hard to imagine what monumental Establishment 'pissing' an alliance between Dodi and Diana would have inspired – with Fayed step-grandfather to the heir to the throne. With that brief fantasy gone, Trevor, the only living link with that tragedy, could find himself with Fayed's epic frustration focused fully upon him. Fayed had held back, so far, from naming Trevor as part of the conspiracy, but his paranoid mind could be heading in that direction – there was a need to punish Trevor, too, for stripping him of the ultimate put-down of the Establishment; in a stroke, he could absolve Henri Paul of guilt and make Trevor the scapegoat, the surrogate, of Prince Philip and the rest of the royal family and government that had so callously rejected and humiliated him.

As the lawyers saw it, if you stood back and took the larger view of Fayed, attacks on Trevor could be driven by far more than anger at his resignation and thwarting of the conspiracy theory. Trevor's resignation could be seen as the culminating outrage of decades of 'taking it' from the British whose approval and passport he so desperately wanted. He'd endured vicious resistance to his buying Harrods, government investigations of his finances that had left a cloud, and persistent denial of a British passport. Currently, the problems continued to cascade.

Just when a passport seemed within grasp from a more sympathetic Labour government, it was again denied. Then came the ultimate slap in the face from the Queen: early in 1998 his sponsorship of the Windsor Horse Show was summarily cancelled. And Prince Philip and Prince Charles had never sent him a note of thanks for his note to them, another knife in the heart. Living in his 'Alice in Wonderland' world, he had such a different take on reality that, when he revealed that he had bribed several MPs to promote his interests in the House of Commons, he painted himself – the confessed briber! – as a crusading reformer sweeping government clean of corruption. He has stood accused, been sued, investigated and embarrassed by the press for all manner of scandal – break-in, sexual harassment, and, of course, creating a false story about his origins and background. He continues to blame his reverses on anti-Arab racism and snobbery, but never on himself.

And was there one final factor that might drive any attack against Trevor to new levels of intensity? Might

Fayed sense that his fictions and conspiracies were falling apart? 'As he hurtles towards inevitable self-destruction, Fayed might reflect where it all went wrong,' writes Tom Bower in his 1998 unauthorized biography, *Fayed*. 'Like so many autocrats, Fayed has become his own worst enemy.' Wounded lions can be the most dangerous of all.

Trevor's family agreed that he should appeal. 'Trevor, it's not right that your life, your health, has been torn apart and you'll not get a penny of compensation,' Jill and, especially, Ernie argued to him. 'In any other country in the world, you'd get at least some compensation for what's been done to you.' His lawyers, too, had to let him know that if he did not appeal he was giving up his right to claim damages within the French court system – one of the reasons he had become a *partie civile*. And time would run out swiftly on the chance to sue in a civil court.

Pressure to decide built as volleys against Trevor began. Laurie Mayer gave a press statement. 'In a taste of the courtroom drama to come, Mayer yesterday questioned Rees-Jones's reliability,' the *Observer*'s John Arlidge would write on 5 September. 'Mayer dismissed Trevor's account of the crash as "nonsense" and hinted that Rees-Jones himself was partly to blame: "Trevor Rees-Jones has conveniently remembered now that it is all somebody else's fault."'

'I'm not looking for anyone to be accountable. I'm not

looking for any massive compensation. All I want is to be able to get back to a job, and get back to living. And I don't get bitter, you know. If I did, I'd scare myself.' He felt contempt and pity, perhaps, for the Boss. 'But I'm not bitter at Mr Fayed. I don't believe I've done anything against him or that organization where I shouldn't be made welcome, even now. I hope that I could go down there next week, to the little kitchen area by the Ops Room and have a cup of tea and a chat with the lads. It might be more difficult for them if orders have come from upstairs about whether I'm allowed in or not. But it wouldn't bother me. The lads are the lads.'

On 7 September 1999 Fayed filed his heralded appeal. Henri Paul's family filed the same day. Both left their appeals wide open, freeing them to charge anyone, any entity, with criminal liability. As soon as the judge announced a hearing date, they would be required to set out their appeal and name their charges. The lawyers believed that Trevor would likely be named. Despite himself he might still be pulled into a legal war, forced into another media circus, but he had no desire to strike back.

'I didn't want to drag it out. I saw an appeal on the TV by the Spencer family just to let it rest, and that they respected the judge's decision, which I did, to be honest. I didn't want to be seen as the only person other than Fayed to be dragging the thing on,' says Trevor.

Holed up alone in his back-alley house, he was not unhappy. In the last six months, he'd come to 'be quite happy to be on my own. I enjoy my own company now more than I ever have. Sometimes it's nice to come back and sit down here, put on the answer machine, and just be on my own . . . It's only about now that I've been able to be a little selfish. Do things *I* want to do rather than things other people want me to do.'

He was over Sue. 'And I'm really enjoying being a single man again.' He had a phone chat every week or two with Lara, the good friend who'd brightened some of the bleakest days in Paris. He'd seen her a few times in Ireland, and she'd come over for a mutual friend's wedding at Sweeney Hall in November. 'I'll have to admit that occasionally, at home on my own, I get down in the dumps, thinking, "Is there no end to this?" But I've had to realize that my life will never be as it was. It still gets to me every now and then.'

He'd gone through a period of grief and sorrow. 'But you've got to pick yourself up and get on with it because sympathy runs out very quickly; it's got a short shelf-life, you know. If you wallow, people are going to get fed up and say, "Oh, for God's sake, here comes that bloke again."'

Respect here in Oswestry meant a great deal to him. 'It took me a long time to see that if I had continued with Fayed, I'd be seen as just his mouthpiece, his stooge. I like to think I've got the respect of people round here and a lot of friends, and I don't believe there would be that level of respect if I'd stayed.' He wanted to maintain that level of respect in the decision he now had to make. He had no doubts about what he'd do. Trevor had taken his own counsel in deciding to leave Fayed. He took his own counsel now. He would not appeal. He would not sue for damages in a civil court. Trevor was clear and firm about his decision.

'He's not capable of vindictiveness,' his mother fondly observed. 'I'm very proud of him. He's doing it his way. And I think he's right.'

Ian understood. He knew Trevor well. He saw him as 'more settled now as a person, more mature'. They'd all suffered, watching him struggle to make the big decisions. If his decision now was not to appeal or sue, it was not from fear of Fayed. He'd broken free. He'd taken this decision as his own man.

'Personally, I think Fayed's made himself look stupid with these attacks and the extraordinary claims he's made,' Trevor reflected. 'If I was with the Boss now, I'd say, "Sod you. I'm not going to do anything I don't want to do." Looking back on it, I don't owe Fayed or that organization *anything*.

'But I'd be ashamed if I didn't feel some sort of moral responsibility. You wouldn't be human if you didn't. I'm the only person that survived. But it's not the so-called survivor guilt. It's the fact that I was paid to look after Dodi and his guest, and they died on my shift. I've got this hanging over me for the rest of my life, you know, and I've taken that responsibility by helping the judge as much as I can to find out what went on.'

He'd taken his sense of moral responsibility too far in refusing to attack Fayed, some of those around him would always believe. If anything, the lawyers saw Fayed's energy for war with perceived enemies and betrayers building. The Neil Hamilton libel trial and his 'alfayed.com' website provided perfect outlets for his tirades and allegations. As Christmas and the new millennium approached, Trevor's lawyers spotted an ominous announcement on Fayed's website: a 'Bodyguards' page was 'under construction'. Was Fayed planning to launch it to coincide with his appeal moving into high gear – with Trevor as the principal target? Christian waited for the first hearing to be scheduled. It couldn't be long now, surely.

Trevor continues to ignore the surface events. He has thought too seriously about it. 'I know they died on my shift. What I don't accept is that my actions caused the crash, or my lack of actions caused it. I've now definitely got a Swiss-cheese memory about things. But I stand by the things I remembered and said to the judge early on, when I regained consciousness in hospital.

'I don't need another investigation to feel positive about myself. I have to look at myself in the mirror and I've bloody questioned myself many times if I could've done anything extra, and it wasn't there to do. We did as good a job, in that situation, as anyone would've done.

'I tell you now, if it could have been me that died and those three that survived, I would've done it. I really would. But you can't turn back the clock. You can't say if only, if only, if only.'

'It's important for Trevor to draw a line beneath it and get on with his life,' Jill felt very strongly. 'It's important for everyone associated.' He'd been offered a job in close protection with a Shropshire-based firm, and said yes. 'Be careful that they're not just hiring you for your name, Trevor,' Ian Lucas cautioned him, while delighted to see him moving on. He quit his job in the sports shop in September, and planned to be back in close protection by Christmas, the circle complete.

Trevor still thought about the Princes. 'William and Harry's grief is the same as if their mother had been selling newspapers in a corner shop. Feelings don't change; it's only the feelings of everyone else that are different because of who she was. I'm sure Prince William and Prince Harry have been put through the mill more because of who their mother was. They were cracking lads, and I'd like to think they enjoyed themselves on that first trip in July. But I know they're not going to remember my name with fondness. For them, I'll always be associated with the death of their mother. This is pretty sad to take, really. I'd like to see the two Princes again. If I met them, I'd say, "I'm bloody sorry. There's nothing more I could have done."' He kept the letter the Princes and their mother had signed, nicely framed, in a safe at the solicitors' offices.

Trevor wished he could put his thoughts and memories away as neatly. He still wanted only to close that door and get on with his life. 'I honestly want the same as I always did, and nearly had once: a nice wife, kids, a home, and a steady job. I can't believe that the last two years make that impossible.'

The scars would always be there, Trevor knew. The little girl came to mind who'd come up to him at the rugby club his first time back and said, 'Why have you got lines all over your face?' His answer, 'because I've had lots of operations', was too simple, looking back. But how would you tell a child all that had happened?